OUT OF EGYPT

Ahmed Osman was born in Cairo in 1934. He studied law at Cairo university and in the early 1960s worked there as a journalist. In the wake of continuing border disputes between Egypt and Israel, he decided in 1964 to leave Egypt for London in order to discover the historical roots behind the political conflict between the two countries. Since then he has been researching and writing in a sustained attempt to reconcile the stories of the Bible with the historical evidence uncovered by archaeologists in the last hundred years.

His three previous books all set out to demonstrate that the roots of Western religious beliefs lie not in the land of Judaea, but in Egypt, and provide the background to this book: *Stranger in the Valley of the Kings* (1987); *Moses: Pharaoh of Egypt* (1990) and *The House of the Messiah* (1992).

The author has been invited to lecture on his work by many educational institutions as well as cultural organisations in the UK, Germany, the US and Egypt.

Out of Egypt

'Out of Egypt I called my son'
Hosea 11:1

OUT OF EGYPT

The Roots of Christianity
Revealed

Ahmed Osman

ARROW

This edition published by Arrow Books Limited 1999

1 3 5 7 9 10 8 6 4 2

Copyright © Ahmed Osman 1998

Ahmed Osman has asserted his right under the Copyright, Designs and
Patents Act, 1988 to be identified as the author of this work.

First published in the United Kingdom in 1998 by Century

Arrow Books Limited
Random House UK Limited
20 Vauxhall Bridge Road, London SW1V 2SA

Random House Australia (Pty) Limited
20 Alfred Street, Milsons Point, Sydney,
New South Wales 2061, Australia

Random House New Zealand Limited
18 Poland Road, Glenfield
Auckland 10, New Zealand

Random House South Africa (Pty) Limited
Endulini, 5a Jubilee Road, Parktown 2193, South Africa

Random House UK Limited Reg. No. 954009

A CIP catalogue record for this book is available from the British Library

Papers used by Random House UK Limited are natural, recyclable products
made from wood grown in sustainable forests. The manufacturing
processes conform to the environmental regulations of the country of origin

ISBN 0 09 92 77965 4

Typeset by SX Composing DTP, Rayleigh, Essex
Printed and bound inGermany
Elsnerdruck, Berlin

To the Coptic Church of Alexandria.

Contents

Acknowledgements

I wish to thank Dr Helmut Koester, Professor of the History of Ancient Christianity at Harvard University, for discussing with me the significance of the Nag Hammadi Library for our understanding of early Christian history; Professor John Strugnell, chief editor of *The Dead Sea Scrolls* until December 1990, for his explanation of the nature of the Qumran community; Dr Peter Nägel, Professor of Christian and Coptic Studies at Bonn University, for his help in my attempt to establish a date for early Coptic manuscripts; and Andrew Best, my agent, for the great help and his many valuable suggestions.

I also wish to place on record my gratitude to the late J. Enoch Powell, MBE, for his kind help in discussing with me the Greek texts of the Book of Acts.

Ahmed Osman, 1998.

Prologue

One day in AD 391, the Roman-appointed Bishop Theophilus marched from his headquarters in the Brucheion Royal quarter of Alexandria, at the head of a large howling mob, heading west for the Serapeum in the heart of the Egyptian quarter of Rhakotis. The Serapeum, which had been the centre of Egyptian worship for seven centuries, was adorned with extensive columned halls, almost breathing statues, and a great number of other works of art, as well as being the house of the Great Alexandrian library. The frenzied people rushed through the streets along the Canopic way, turning into the short street that led to the temple-area of Serapis, meeting other crowds there, before climbing up the great flight of marble steps, led by Bishop Theophilus. They jumped across the stone platform and into the temple, where the events of the final tragedy took place.

In their agitated mood, the angry mob took little heed of the gold and silver ornaments, the precious jewels, the priceless bronze and marble statues, the rare murals and tapestries, the carved and painted pillars of granite and many marbles, the ebony and scented woods, the ivory and exotic furniture – all were smashed to pieces with cries of pleasure. But that was not all. Those shouting men, full of demoniac delight, then turned to the library, where hundreds of thousands of papyrus rolls and parchments, inscribed with ancient wisdom and knowledge, were taken off their shelves, torn to pieces and thrown on to bonfires.

A few years later the last of the Alexandrian scholars was

torn to pieces by a gang of Christian monks. On a Lenten day in March of the year AD 415 they stopped the carriage of Hypatia, who had succeeded her father as Professor of Philosophy in Alexandria, stripped her naked, dragged her into a nearby church, killed her, cut most of her flesh from her body with sharp oyster shells, and burned what remained of her in the street. The charge against Hypatia, who had taught the philosophy of Plato, was heresy.

As a result of this barbaric killing of Alexandrian scholars and destruction of its library, which contained texts in Greek of all aspects of ancient wisdom and knowledge, the true Egyptian roots of Christianity and of Western civilization have been obscured for nearly 16 centuries. The aim of this book is to rediscover these roots, with the help of new historical and archaeological evidence.

We are going to show that the stories of both the Old and the New Testaments are firmly established on models of Ancient Egyptian historical facts. Not only that, but we will also show that the essential doctrines that Judaism and Christianity are credited with, in fact came out of Egypt. We are even going further to an area which will not be easy for the ordinary reader to accept, but which will become more convincing as the evidence of this book accumulates. All the central characters of both the Old Testament and the New Testament were actually real historical Egyptian figures, who lived in a different period than we have believed up till now.

Western scholars, whether Christian, Jewish or Atheist, tend to ignore Egyptian views when interpreting the accounts of ancient history. Even Manetho, the great Egyptian scholar responsible for the arrangement of the Alexandrian library, has been dismissed as unqualified to write about scientific matters to the Greeks. Commenting on an account that Manetho wrote in *Epitome of Physical Doctrines*, W. G. Waddell wrote:

That an Egyptian priest should seek to instruct the Greek-speaking world of his time in the history of Egypt and the religious beliefs of the Egyptians . . . is not at all surprising, but it seems strange that Manetho should feel called upon, in the third century BC, to compose an Epitome of Physical Doctrines with the apparent object of familiarizing the Greeks with Egyptian science

[*Manetho*, London, 1940, p. xxvii]

In addition, Islamic documents are completely disregarded as a source of ancient tradition, when arguing the history of biblical stories. This cannot be justified, for the stories in the Koran come from the same source as the books of the Bible. Moreover, the Koran accounts agree with those of the Bible in the majority of cases, which makes it more important to examine the reason for various points of divergence.

The time has come for Egypt's voice to be heard again. Because of my Islamic background, I feel confident that I am qualified to offer a balanced picture, which does not exclude any source from examination.

Until the destruction of its library in AD 391, Alexandria had remained the most important cultural centre of the ancient world, and the focal point of the mutual influence exercised in the conjunction of Christianity and Hellenism, in spite of four centuries of Rome's political supremacy. Founded by Alexander the Great in 331 BC, it was the first real cosmopolitan city in history, where Macedonians and Greeks lived together with Egyptians and Jews, and scholars flocked from all over the world to do their research. They came from Italy and Greece, from Anatolia and the Levant, from north Africa, Arabia, and even from Persia and India. Not only did they share a common habitation in Alexandria, they all had the same longing for knowledge and the same interest in philosophy and ancient wisdom, as represented in the teaching of Hermes Trismegistus* and the worship of Serapis. The city was also the centre of Hellenistic Judaism. It was in Alexandria that Philo Judaeus, the first Jewish philosopher, wrote his 38 books in the 1st century AD. The city had, in addition, the only library containing almost all the books of ancient civilizations, including the Greek text of the Old Testament. Hence it is not astonishing that Alexandria rapidly became the main Christian intellectual centre.

The rich collection of ancient written knowledge in the Serapeum† proved irresistible for Diodorus Siculus, a Sicilian scholar, when he set out in the first century BC, in the time of Julius Caesar, to research his ambitious *Bibliotheca Historica* – the 'bookshelf of history'. Diodorus, who was an enthusiast of the teachings of Hermes Trismegistus (which have survived until today in the teachings of Islamic Sufis, Jewish Qabbalah and Christian Rosicrucians and Free-masons), became convinced of Egypt's importance as a source of knowledge. The Greek and Roman gods, he believed, had been born there, life had originated there, and there the first observations of the stars had been made. The last famous scholar associated with the Serapeum before its destruction was Theon, a celebrated mathematician whose recension of Euclid's *Element* was the only text of this work until the last century, and whose daughter Hypatia was to meet a terrible death at the hands of Theophilus's nephew Bishop Cyril.

Up to the end of the fourth century AD, the time when the

* Thoth, ancient Egyptian god of writing, became identified with the Greek god Hermes. Hermes Trismegistus means 'Hermes the Thrice-greatest'.
† The historian Ammanius Marcellinus (*c.* AD 330–391), who himself visited Alexandria, wrote about this temple: '. . . the Serapeum, which, although no description can do it justice, yet is so adorned with extensive columned halls, with almost breathing statues, and a great number of other works of art, that next to the Capitolium, with which revered Rome elevates herself to eternity, the whole world beholds nothing more magnificent. In this were invaluable libraries . . .' (22: 16, 12–13). The cult of Serapis will be examined in detail at the relevant stage of my argument, later in this book.

Alexandrian library was destroyed, Egypt was regarded as the holy land of the ancient world, the source of wisdom and knowledge where the gods became known for the first time. Pilgrims then, including Roman emperors, came from all over the world to worship in the temples of Isis and Serapis, as well as at the foot of Mount Sinai.

This situation came to an end, however, in the latter years of the reign of the emperor Theodosius I, who was zealous in his suppression of both paganism – the belief in the many gods of pre-Christianity – and heresy – any opinion contrary to orthodox doctrine. Emperor of the East (AD 379–392), and then sole emperor of East *and* West (AD 392–395), he enforced the Creed of the Council of Nicaea (AD 325) as a universal norm for Christian orthodoxy and directed the convening of the second general council at Constantinople in AD 381 to clarify the formula.

'It is our wish and pleasure that none of our subjects, whether magistrates or private citizens, however exalted or however humble may be their rank or condition, shall presume in any city or in any place to worship an inanimate idol . . .' declared Theodosius in his last edict. Fanatical mobs of the Church then roamed the lands, razing old temples to the ground and plundering their wealth. Ancient tombs were desecrated, walls of monuments scraped clean of names and depictions of deities, statues toppled over and smashed. In Alexandria, Bishop Theophilus was as ambitious as the emperor, Theodosius I, who had appointed him. It was one of his zealous actions that led to the burning of an estimated half a million books stored in the Alexandrian library, described above,

Theophilus of Alexandria (AD 385–412) was one of the orthodox leaders who represented the imperial government dispatched from Rome to impose official orthodoxy on the Alexandrian Church. He led a campaign against paganism and heresy in Egypt that included destruction of the Serapeum (the temple of Serapis – originally an ancient Egyptian god of the underworld, subsequently reintroduced as the official deity for Alexandria and Egypt by Ptolemy I

[305–284 BC]) where the Alexandrian library was placed. The Serapeum, at the same time as being the centre of worship for the ancient Egyptian trinity of Osiris, Isis and Horus, became a focal point for the emerging Christian Gnostic sects – those Christians who sought to gain spiritual knowledge through mysteries and the attempt to know oneself, interpreting the Scriptures allegorically.

The first Christian emperor, Constantine I (AD 324–337), had made Christianity the official religion of the Empire. He also granted political power to the Church. Bishops were not only recognized as councillors of state but obtained juridical rights: their solutions to civil suits were legally enforced. The bishops used their newly acquired power to spread the word of God and stamp out His enemies, who in this case were not only the pagans but the heretics – and Rome regarded Egyptian Christians as heretics. According to tradition, the Church of Alexandria was founded neither by St Peter nor by St Paul but by St Mark the Evangelist, even before what is said to have been the first Apostolic Council of Jerusalem in *c.* AD 50 (mentioned in the Book of Acts, 15:28). The first theological school to be established in the world also flourished in Alexandria before the end of the 2nd century AD, and became an influential centre of Christian scholarship. Among its directors were the famous Clement of Alexandria and Origen. Christian monasticism as an institution was initiated principally in Egypt by St Antony the Copt (*c.* AD 251–356), who fled to the solitude of the western desert from his native village of Coma, not far from Tell al-Amarna, in Middle Egypt. Others followed his example and a monastic colony arose around his cave in the Red Sea mountains.

Although Alexandria made an important contribution in developing the first systematic Christian theology, the Alexandrian theologians were strongly influenced by the Neo-Platonists' philosophy.* Biblical exegesis at Alexandria

---

* Neo-Platonists were Alexandrian philosophers who followed the same philosophy as the Athenian Plato; Plotinus of the 3rd century AD is the most celebrated.

was allegorical and mystical, following the same method as Philo Judaeus, who tried to harmonize philosophy and the Bible. From the start, Alexandrian exegesis did not attach to the literal sense of the Bible. Their primary interest was concentrated on the mystery of divine revelation revealed in the historical and literary details of the Old Testament. It was therefore a question of discovering Christ in the older revelation.

The Alexandrian authors sought out in the Old Testament symbols of the New. For early Egyptian Christians, accepting one God was an evolutionary process in which the old system was assimilated into the new, and old deities became angelic beings and mediators between man and the unseen Lord (this will be examined in detail later). Idols, for them, did not represent the deities themselves, but were merely a physical form in which the spiritual beings could dwell during prayer. The Gnostic teachers found their followers at Alexandria, and much of the ecclesiastical history of this city was concerned with the heresies that appeared there.

The Serapeum, originally established by the Ptolemies (the Macedonian kings who ruled Egypt after the death of Alexander the Great), later became also a centre for Gnostic communities, both Hermetic (i.e. adhering to the teachings of Hermes Trismegistus) and Christian. Some Gnostic Christian sects grew from within the cult of Serapis, who made no distinction between Christ and Serapis – this, too, will be explained as this book unfolds. The general library at the Serapeum gradually became a focal point for scholars and intellectuals, from all over the Roman Empire, whose views contradicted the teachings of the Church. For this reason it became regarded as heretical and had to be destroyed.

With the destruction of the Serapeum, not only Egyptian knowledge was lost; Mesopotamian, Syrian, Phoenician, Jewish and Greek learning also vanished. The whole scientific achievement of the old civilizations, regarded as heresy by Bishop Theophilus, disappeared in a single day –

books on astronomy, anatomy, medicine, geometry, geography, history, philosophy, theology and literature, as well as copies of the early Gnostic gospels of Christ. The result was the beginning of the dark ages, which lasted for more than ten centuries after that. All branches of science, as well as heretical writings which did not adhere to the teaching of the orthodox Church, were forbidden by the state. This left the canonic books of the Scripture as the main source of Western knowledge until the Renaissance in the 15th century.

While the discovery of some remaining copies of old forbidden manuscripts, especially the Hermetic and Neo-Platonic philosophies, produced the age of the Western renaissance from the 15th century in art, science and technology, history had to wait for modern archaeologists to dig out old remains and inscribed papyrus rolls before we could regain our memory. In his book *Archives In The Ancient World*, Ernst Posner, the American historian, has said of the achievements of archaeologists during this period that they are 'momentous – comparable in a way to the discovery of America . . . a new dimension of almost two millennia has been added to the history of mankind as it was known in 1850 . . . Now we can view with profound respect the cultural achievements of the countries surrounding the eastern Mediterranean, and we can begin to assess their inter-relations with, and their possible influence on, the cultures of Greece and Rome.'

I shall show how Egypt emerges as the birthplace of our spiritual teachers – from Imhotep, the first pyramid builder of the 27th century BC, to Moses and Akhenaten, who first recognized one God, to the followers of Osiris (Egyptian god of the underworld and judge of the dead), Hermes Trismegistus and of Jesus Christ who looked for spiritual salvation and eternal life. Thanks to modern archaeologists, a new age now appears on the horizon, with Egypt restored to its original place.

It looks like a fulfilment of an old prophecy which predicted that woes will come upon Egypt, but also promised that order would finally be restored again. This prophecy is found in the Hermetic text of Asclepius, discovered among the Nag Hammadi library (detailed in Appendix 1 at the back of this book). Asclepius is a dialogue between the mystagogue Hermes Trismegistus and an initiate, Asclepius. In an apocalyptic section with significant Egyptian and Israelite parallels, the speaker predicts the fall, then rise again, of Egypt:

> . . . are you ignorant, O Asclepius, that Egypt is (the) image of heaven? Moreover, it is the dwelling place of heaven and all the forces that are in heaven. If it is proper for us to speak the truth, our land is (the) temple of the world. And it is proper for you not to be ignorant that a time will come in it (our land) (when) Egyptians will seem to have served the divinity in vain, and all their activity in their religion will be despised. For all divinity will leave Egypt and will flee upward to heaven. And Egypt will be widowed; it will be abandoned by the gods. For foreigners will come into Egypt, and they will rule it . . . And in that day the country that was more pious than all countries will become impious. No longer will it be full of temples, but it will be full of tombs . . . Egypt, lover of God, and the dwelling place of the gods, school of religion, will become an example of impiousness . . . [Then Egypt will be restored again] And the lords of the earth . . . will establish themselves in a city that is in a corner of Egypt that will be built toward the setting of the sun.

Isaiah, the Old Testament prophet of the 6th century BC, confirms this prophecy and foretells the appearance of a saviour in Egypt:

> The burden of Egypt. Behold, the Lord rideth upon a

swift cloud, and shall come into Egypt: and the idols of Egypt shall be moved at his presence, and the heart of Egypt shall melt in the midst of it. And I will set the Egyptians against the Egyptians: and they shall fight every one against his brother, and every one against his neighbour . . . And the spirit of Egypt shall fail in the midst thereof . . . In that day shall there be an altar to the Lord in the midst of the land of Egypt, and a pillar at the border thereof to the Lord. And it shall be for a sign and for a witness unto the Lord of hosts in the land of Egypt . . . and he shall send them a saviour, and a great one, and he shall deliver them.

[Isaiah 19:1–3; 19–20]

The Gospel of Matthew, in his account of the birth of Christ, confirmed that the saviour foretold by Isaiah to appear in Egypt was the same character as Jesus. Matthew introduced the story of the holy family's flight into Egypt and, using the words of the prophet Hosea (11:1), announced the fulfilment of Isaiah's prophecy in him: '. . . that it might be fulfilled which was spoken of the Lord by the prophet, saying, *Out of Egypt have I called my son*' (Matthew 2:15).

Helmut Koester, Professor of the History of Ancient Christianity at Harvard University, who was responsible for translating the Nag Hammadi Gospel of Thomas (which includes many previously unknown sayings of Christ) into English, spoke about the need for 'a thorough and extensive revaluation of early Christian history'. He went on to say: 'The task is not limited to fresh reading of the known sources and a close scrutiny of the new texts in order to redefine their appropriate place within the conventional picture of the early Christian history. Rather it is the conventional picture itself that is called into question.'

That is what I shall address in this book.

Introduction

Until the 18th century – the Age of Enlightenment, which sought to apply critical and rational thought to assumptions previously taken for granted – the principal sources of Western knowledge about the history of the world and mankind were the Old and New Testaments. The Book of Genesis, the first in the Old Testament, told how God created the universe in six days and rested on the seventh. At the centre of this universe was planet Earth. It was perceived for many centuries as a flat entity around which revolved the sun, moon, stars and other planets. At the same time as he created the universe God was said to have created the first two human beings, Adam and Eve. As theology was the main source of our understanding of the world, scholars were so confident about the authenticity of this Book of Genesis account that they even provided a precise time and date for the appearance of Adam – 9 a.m. on 26 October 4004 BC.

Modern science has made it clear that various elements of this story and mankind's early assumptions about the nature of the universe are not to be taken seriously. The Earth is round, not flat; it has, according to scientists, existed for billions of years, and man himself has lived on it for at least 200,000 years.

The critical approach of biblical scholars, especially in Germany (the home of early biblical scholarship), at the time of the 'enlightenment' focused in particular upon the time-scale of the Old Testament itself. Until then it had been regarded as the inspired word of God, handed down to Moses on Mount Sinai in the 14th century BC. However, study of

the way the Old Testament has come down to us made it clear
that it was written in its present form in Babylon between the
6th and 2nd centuries BC. By then at least 800 years had
elapsed since the death of Moses and the Israelite Exodus
from Egypt. During the intervening centuries, biblical stories
had been transmitted orally from generation to generation,
with the inevitable distortion of, and uncertainty about, facts
that occurs when information passes by word of mouth. It
therefore seemed that many Old Testament accounts might
not be accurate. This suspicion has been confirmed in the
intervening two centuries by means of exploration, archaeological discoveries and a deeper knowledge and understanding of history. It has become clear, for example, that the
account in the Book of Joshua of the conquest of the
Promised Land in the 15th century BC as a result of a swift
military campaign is a total invention, as I shall show in due
course.

The conventional starting point for anyone seeking the
identity of the historical Jesus is the four canonical gospels of
Matthew, Mark, Luke and John. However, these gospels
should not be regarded as either biographies or histories in
the modern sense of the word, but as theological works
whose primary aim is to proclaim faith in Jesus as the Son of
God, Lord and Messiah, crucified and raised from the dead,
who will return in glory at some time in the future to judge
the world.

In the 2nd century AD the Roman fathers of the early
Church, combating what they regarded as heresy, began to
place this theology in a historical setting, providing locations
and dates for the life of Jesus. These doctrines were enforced
by the authorities from the second half of the 4th century,
when Rome adopted Christianity, causing it to spread
throughout the world. It was when Rome, then the centre of
civilization, adopted Christianity that old books were burned
to destroy the memory of the past, and history was rewritten
in order to 'confirm' new interpretations of past events.

Discovery of two sets of ancient documents in the years

immediately after the Second World War has served to reinforce the belief that Jesus lived, suffered and died many centuries before the accepted start of the Christian era. The better-known documents are *The Dead Sea Scrolls*, found in caves of Khirbet Qumran over a period, starting in 1947. These Hebrew and Aramaic manuscripts aroused great excitement because they were dated from 200 BC and AD 50, thus covering the years before and after Jesus's life in Palestine, according to the orthodox account. The name Qumran, of the location where the Essenes were dwelling, can itself indicate an Ancient Egyptian-Israelite origin for this community, for this word is also known as Imran, which would connect it directly to both the Amarna dynasty and Imran the father of Moses and Miriam. In my view, this name of the Essene location indicates that some descendants of Akhenaten and Moses were among the early leaders of this community. I can only identify the Essenes as members of the movement which produced prophets such as Isaiah and Jeremiah, up to the time of the Babylonian exile. After the return from exile, the priests of the Jerusalem temple never allowed prophecy again. The fact that the Essene community settled in Qumran during the 2nd century does *not* mean that this was the date when it came into existence. (The evidence for this, which will be no doubt revelatory to many readers, is presented in subsequent chapters.)

However, the writers of the scrolls make no mention of the life and mission of Jesus in Judaea and Galilee. Instead, they identify the Saviour as their Teacher of Righteousness, killed by a Wicked Priest, and they await his return to join them at their annual Messianic Banquet, similar in many respects to the Christian Last Supper. Although half a century has passed since the first of the scrolls came to light, it is still not clear whether all of their contents has been published. This has fuelled suspicion of ecclesiastical censorship, because they contradict the gospel accounts of the life of Jesus.

The scrolls also deflected attention from another important collection of ancient documents found at Nag Hammadi in

Upper Egypt two years earlier. These proved to be part of a library of the Gnostics (a sect condemned as heretical and persecuted in the early years of the Christian Church) and included previously unknown gospels and Christian writings about the character of Jesus. Remarkably, in them we find no mention of the places or characters familiar from the gospel stories – Bethlehem, Nazareth, Jerusalem, King Herod and John the Baptist, for example.

If the startling implication of the two finds is that the historical Jesus did not live when orthodox gospels claim, then when *did* he live? I shall show that the Old Testament itself offers evidence that Jesus lived *many centuries earlier*. He is identified as the same person as Joshua, who succeeded Moses as the leader of the Israelites. This was, indeed, once part of the teaching of the fathers of the early Christian Church. An attempt has been made to explain away this identification by saying that Joshua should be looked upon as a pre-existent Christ. However, St Paul's account of events on the Damascus road indicates that the person who succeeded Moses as the leader of the Israelites was the *real* Jesus, and those who believed later had *spiritual* encounters with the spiritual Christ, for Paul says of their meeting: 'I conferred not with flesh and blood' (Galatians 1:16).

The purpose of this book is to try, by an objective approach based on verifiable data, to establish the course of historical events that lie behind the stories we read in the Old and New Testaments, and to come to conclusions about how they shaped our understanding today. This is not a theological work: its purpose is to provide biblical stories with greater historical authenticity than they have enjoyed until now.

Part I
The Chosen People

AND God said unto Abraham,
as for Sarai thy wife, thou
shalt not call her name Sarai,
but Sarah shall her name be,
And I will bless her and give
thee a son also of her . . . and
she shall be a mother of
nations: kings of people shall
be of her.

Genesis 17:15,16

Chapter One

Abraham, Sarah and Pharaoh

More than 50 centuries ago, from their very early history, Egyptians believed that a human being consisted of spiritual as well as physical elements. They regarded death as the departure of the spiritual element from the body, but also believed, provided the physical being could be kept safe and protected, that the spirit would return to the body at some point in the future and the deceased would then lead a second life. That is why they devoted such care to preserving a dead body by mummification and building a secure tomb to keep it safe. They also believed in the divinity of their anointed kings. An Egyptian pharaoh was regarded as the personification of the god Horus, his father being Ra, the sun god. The Egyptians were the first nation to build temples for their many gods, and to establish an organized priesthood which performed daily rites and supervised the annual festivals. The great pyramids still stand, after 47 centuries, as witness to the divine power of the kings and are a lasting symbol of man's attempts to reach the universal cosmos. Astronomy was an important branch of Egyptian knowledge from the early part of their history and it can no longer be denied that the Great Pyramid was constructed in a way intended to help with the observation of the stars and provide a reading for their movements. Ancient Egyptians believed that the movements and position of the stars at a given moment would have particular effects on a man's behaviour and his destiny.

The Hebrew tribe made its first appearance in history in the 15th century BC, the time of Abraham, who has been

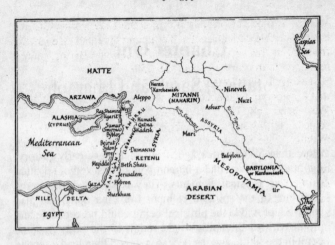

Western Asia at the time of Abraham

regarded by Jews and Christians alike as the founding father of the 12 tribes of Israel. In this chapter I shall argue that Abraham's patriarchy is by no means actual: rather it is of symbolic importance to the Israelites and to their descendants, and, indeed, to Christians.

Abram and his wife Sarai (to give them their original names) began their journey into history, according to the Bible, at Ur (modern Tell Muqayyar) in southern Mesopotamia, an important city 200 miles to the south-east of modern Baghdad, the capital of Iraq. The party, led by Terah, the father of Abram, also included Lot, Terah's grandson and Abram's nephew. The Book of Genesis gives no explanation of the reasons which prompted Terah and his family to set out on the great trade route that followed the valley of the Euphrates north-west through Babylon, sweeping west through Canaan to link with the ports of the eastern Mediterranean. Nor, as is usual in the Bible, is there any indication of the date when this migratory journey began. Because descendants of Abram and Sarai – Joseph and

Moses – can be identified as living in the 14th century BC, it is a reasonable deduction that Terah and his family departed from Ur at the very end of the 16th century BC or, more probably, in the early years of the 15th.

It is more than 700 miles from Ur to Canaan, which at that time occupied much the same area as modern Israel, the West Bank and Gaza. The family made the journey in two stages, settling for an unspecified time at Haran in the middle of the valley of the Euphrates, where Terah died. We are then offered the first intimation of a special relationship between Abram's family and God. The Lord is said to have told Abram: 'Get thee out of thy country . . . unto a land that I will shew thee . . . And I will make of thee a great nation . . .' (Genesis 12:1–2).

In response to this promise, they continued their journey to Canaan, the ancient land of Palestine, a country where the sudden appearance of strangers was a common occurrence. Traders used its coastal plain for their commercial journeys south to, and north from, Arabia and Egypt. It also afforded passage to armies during the recurrent imperialist rivalries between Egypt on the one hand and the Mesopotamian kingdoms of Mitanni, Assyria and Babylon on the other. In addition, at times of semi-drought the country suffered recurrent mini-invasions by tribesmen from the neighbouring Arabian desert, as attested by the Amarna letters.*

For anyone trying to make a living from the soil, the hills of Canaan posed an intimidating challenge. The climate was hostile. In summer the country was scorched by the sun and the hot, sand-laden sirocco wind. The late autumn rains, which made it possible to plough the baked soil, were followed by wet, and often bitterly cold, winters. Then, as the sun grew in strength, the gentler rains of March and April

---

* The Amarna letters, written in Akkadian by the rulers of Canaan to the Pharaoh of Egypt during the 14th century BC, speak of different invasion attempts on their cities, by tribal groups.

provided a little fresh pasture for sheep, goats and cattle before the onset of another dry season.

Grain could be grown only on the coastal plain and in the valleys, and the staple agricultural products of the country, all that the inhospitable stony hills would support, were the olive and the vine. Times of famine were common* – and it was at a time of famine that Abram and Sarai are said to have set out on their travels again from Haran, making their way south, a journey that was to forge the first links between this Semitic tribe and the royal house of Egypt, and ensured for Abram's family an enduring place in world history.

Compared with Canaan, Egypt was a rich and sophisticated country. While the greater part of it was desert, the land on either side of the Nile (watered by an intricate system of irrigation canals and dykes) and the land of the river's delta (flooded each year by the inundation that followed heavy rains and melting snows in the Ethiopian highlands) were exceptionally fertile. The inundation, attributed to a teardrop from the goddess Isis, was a particularly important feature of Egyptian life. Religious festivals were held in her honour, and even today, when the Nile begins to flood, 17 June is known as 'the night of the drop'.

Major Egyptian crops included wheat (for bread), barley (for beer), vegetables, fruit (including grapes for wine) and flax (for linseed oil and linen thread). The soil was so rich that two crops could often be harvested in the same growing season. The Egyptians also kept pigs, goats, sheep, geese and ducks, and could supplement their diet with fish from the Nile, wild fowl from the marshes and game from the desert. Although Abram and Sarai are said by the Bible to have set out for Egypt at a time of famine, it may have been some other motive – trade, perhaps – that

---

* The Book of Genesis talks twice about famine: the first took place during the time of Abraham and the second when Joseph was in Egypt, and archaeological evidence of migration during ancient times, as well as the nature of the climate, indicates the occurrence of such famines.

caused them to make the journey. Certainly they did not stay in the Eastern Delta of the Nile – which one might have expected had they simply been seeking food – but made their way to wherever the Pharaoh of the time (whom I believe to be Tuthmosis III, as will be demonstrated later) was holding court.

At this period, this could have been any one of three places – Memphis, Heliopolis or Thebes. Memphis, 12 miles south of modern Cairo, was an important trade centre, graced by the Great Temple of Ptah, patron of craftsmen and artisans. Heliopolis – known in the Bible as On, from the Greek – was the original Egyptian holy city, situated a short distance to the north of modern Cairo and chief centre of worship of the sun-god Ra. Both of these northern cities were used by the court to escape the worst of the blistering heat of an Egyptian summer. During the 18th Dynasty (1575–1335 BC), however, Heliopolis declined in importance as Thebes – modern Luxor, some 300 miles to the south, on the east bank of the Nile opposite the Valley of the Kings, and the main centre of worship of the state god Amun-Ra – developed as the main capital of The Two Lands of Egypt.*

Wherever Abram and Sarai went, and for whatever purpose, we are simply told that Sarai was 'a fair woman to look upon' and, as they approached Egypt, Abram, fearing that he might be killed if it were known that Sarai was his wife and Pharaoh took a fancy to her, said: 'Say, I pray thee, thou art my sister . . . and my soul shall live because of thee' (12:13). This, according to the Book of Genesis, proved a wise precaution. Courtiers advised Pharaoh of the 'fair woman' who had appeared in their midst and he 'took her into Pharaoh's house' and married her. Abram was well rewarded for the hand in marriage of his 'sister', with

---

* Egypt was called The Two Lands as a result of the union between the red desert and the black valley of the Nile.

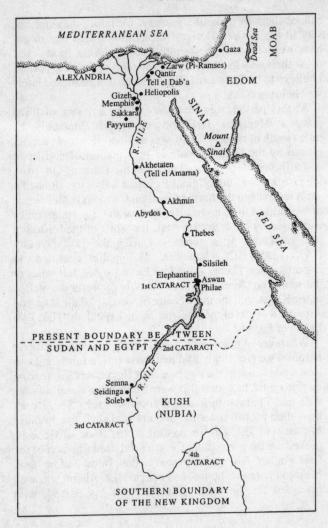

Egypt during the reign of the 18th dynasty

sheep, oxen, donkeys and servants.* The idyll did not last, however. The Bible tells us that 'great plagues' descended on the House of Pharaoh because he had married another man's wife, and Pharaoh sent for Abram and asked him: 'What is this that thou hast done unto me? Why didst thou not tell me that she was thy wife? Why saidst thou, She is my sister . . . now therefore behold thy wife, take her, and go thy way' (12:18–19).

Abram and Sarai were sent back to Canaan with generous gifts. Pharaoh also provided Sarai with an Egyptian maid, Hagar, and, once they had returned safely to Canaan, Sarai gave birth to a son, Isaac. The essence of the biblical account of the journey to Egypt is that Sarai, the wife of Abram, also became the wife of the ruling Pharaoh. This, in the custom of the time, would not only have involved the paying of the bride-price to Abram for the hand of his 'sister', but sexual intercourse on the same night as the actual marriage ceremony. The question therefore arises: Who was the real father of Isaac?

The available evidence – the marriage; Abram's pose as Sarai's brother; Sarai being seen by the princes of Pharaoh who commended her beauty to their king; her being taken into the royal palace; the king's marriage to her and his generous treatment of Abram (presents of sheep, oxen, etc.); the gift to Sarai of the maid Hagar; the elaborate efforts (as I shall show below) of the biblical narrator to put as many years as possible between the couple's return to Canaan and Isaac's birth; textual references in the Talmud (the most

---

* In passing, it is worth noting that Abram may not have been lying when he introduced Sarai in Egypt as his sister. The wife-sister relationship was very rare outside Egypt in ancient times, but the Nuzi documents show that in the Hurrian society, of which both Nuzi and Haran in the middle of the Euphrates valley were part, a wife-sister judicial relationship existed whereby a woman, in addition to becoming a man's wife, was adopted by him as a sister and, as a result, merited higher social status and greater privileges than those enjoyed by an ordinary wife.

important work of religious law in post-biblical Judaism), regarded as next in authority to the Old Testament in its account of the early history of the Israelites, and in the Koran, sacred book of Islam; the history of Isaac's immediate descendants – points to the Pharaoh, *not* Abram, as Isaac's father.

(The efforts of the biblical narrator to disguise the truth about Isaac's parenthood have, I believe, historical roots that go beyond the fact that he was the son of a second, 'sinful' marriage. In the course of the years that followed, the Israelites were to return to Egypt, where they remained for four generations until the Exodus when, burdened by harsh treatment and persecution by their Egyptian taskmasters, they were led out of the country by Moses on the first stage of their journey to the Promised Land. Many more centuries passed before an account of these events was put down in writing (the Egyptians did not chronicle this in any way), by which time Egypt and its Pharaoh had become a symbol of hatred for the Israelites. The biblical narrator was therefore at pains to conceal any family connections between Israel and Egypt. But to return to the immediate story . . .)

After the couple's return to Canaan, we read in the Book of Genesis of a series of prophecies in which, initially, Abram is given greater prominence than Sarai. The Lord is said to have appeared to Abram in a vision and told him: 'Know of a surety that thy seed [descendants] shall be a stranger in a land that is not theirs, and shall serve them . . . But in the fourth generation they shall come hither again . . .' (Genesis 15:13,16). God also made a covenant with Abram, saying: '. . . Unto thy seed have I given this land, from the river of Egypt to the great river, the river Euphrates' (15:18).

At this point the biblical narrator is at pains to make the point that Sarai was unable to have children: 'And Sarai . . . took Hagar her maid, the Egyptian, after Abram had dwelt ten years in the land of Canaan, and gave her to her husband Abram to be his wife' (16:3). Shortly afterwards (we learn) Hagar conceived, and an angel of the Lord appeared to her with the news that she would bear a son and 'call his name Ishmael' (16:11).

Abram, we are told, was 86 when Ishmael was born.* Another 13 years are allowed to pass before the account of another visitation – again to Abram – which resulted in his name and Sarai's being changed: 'Neither shall thy name any more be called Abram, but thy name shall be Abraham; for a father of many nations have I made thee . . . and kings shall come out of thee' (17:5,6). The Lord also said: '. . . Every man child among you shall be circumcised' (17:10). This command, which Abraham carried out, forged another link between the Hebrew tribes and Egypt, for until that time only Egypt among the eastern nations had adopted the custom of circumcision (the practice had appeared early in Egyptian history, as can be seen from surviving mummies). At the same time God said to Abraham: 'As for Sarai thy wife . . . thou shalt not call her name Sarai, but Sarah shall her name be. And I will bless her and give thee a son also of her . . . kings of people shall be of her' (17:15–16). On the matter of the change of names, *sar* in Hebrew means 'prince' and *Sarah* is the feminine form, which can even be interpreted to mean 'the queen'.

On hearing the news that Sarah, as she was now called, was at last to bear a child Abraham 'fell upon his face, and laughed, and said in his heart, Shall a child be born unto him that is an hundred years old? and shall Sarah, that is ninety years old, bear?' (17:17). God reassured him with the words: '. . . Sarah thy wife shall bear thee a son indeed; and thou shalt call his name Isaac . . .' (17:19).

Even then the biblical narrator did not feel it prudent to introduce the birth of Isaac. He interpolated two more stories to dispel any possible doubt about the identity of the

---

* Such ages are not at all reliable. According to bone remains belonging to this period, the average life-span at the time was around 30. Very few people lived to the age of 80 or 90, and even if they did, would not be able to father children at that age.

15

father of Isaac by placing a long gap – i.e. more than nine months – between Sarah's departure from Egypt and the birth of Isaac. Firstly, he described how Abraham sought to free his nephew Lot, who had been captured by some enemies. Then, on a visit to Gerar in southern Canaan (where, we are told, Abraham again took the precaution of claiming that Sarah was his sister), the king fell in love with her, despite her great age, and was about to marry her when the Lord appeared to him in a dream and warned him not to marry a woman who was already someone else's wife. It is only now, after the passage of many years since the return from Egypt, that we are finally allowed to learn of the birth of Isaac, a year after the Lord's promise to Abraham.

The chronology presented by the biblical narrator means that Ishmael must have been 14 years older than Isaac. One aspect of its unreliability becomes clear, however, with the account of how, after the birth of her son, Sarah banished Hagar and Ishmael after she saw him 'mocking' Isaac. The narrative that follows indicates that Ishmael was not old enough to be able to walk, let alone mock anyone:

And Abraham rose up early in the morning, and took bread, and a bottle of water, and gave it unto Hagar, putting it on her shoulder, and the child, and sent her away . . . she . . . wandered in the wilderness of Beersheba. And the water was spent in the bottle, and she cast the child under one of the shrubs. And she went, and sat her down over against him a good way off, as it were a bowshot: for she said, Let me not see the death of the child. And she . . . lifted up her voice and wept.

And God heard the voice of the lad; and the angel of God called to Hagar out of Heaven, and said unto her, What aileth thee, Hagar? fear not; for God hath heard the voice of the lad . . . And God opened her eyes and she saw a well of water; and she went and filled the bottle with water, and gave the lad drink.

[Genesis 21:14–19]

Although this story is not mentioned in the Koran, Islamic tradition* agrees with the Bible, representing Ishmael as a mere baby, carried by his mother and unable to move from the spot where she placed him, but a fountain of water appeared suddenly beneath his feet.

In all of the accounts of visitations before the birth of Isaac, with the exception of the change of Sarah's name and the promise that 'kings of people shall be of her', Abraham is presented as the principal figure. Once Isaac appears on the scene, there is a change of emphasis. The account of another appearance of the Lord to Abraham reads: '. . . in all that Sarah has said unto thee, hearken unto her, for in Isaac shall thy seed be called' (21:12). The literal sense of the Hebrew text in this verse does not necessarily mean that Isaac was Abraham's physical son, but that he was the adoptive father. It is also significant that, from this time, and even to the present day, a child cannot be regarded as a Jew, no matter who the father may have been, unless the mother is herself Jewish. This appearance of the Lord is followed by an account (Genesis 22:9–12) of how Abraham took Isaac to the top of a mountain where he proposed to sacrifice him as a burnt offering, a curious decision if Isaac had been his own son. However, Abraham sacrificed a sheep instead of Isaac after an angel of the Lord warned him: 'Lay not thine hand upon the lad, neither do thou any thing unto him . . .'

Identification of Isaac as a prince of Egypt does not depend solely on this analysis of the Book of Genesis account. Non-biblical sources point to the fact that, in the case of Isaac, Abraham – who had seven other sons (Ishmael by Hagar and six by another wife, Keturah) – was to be regarded as the *adoptive* father. The Talmud preserves a tradition that nobody who knew Abraham believed that Isaac was his son:

---

*The sources of Islamic tradition are mainly biblical, Talmudic and other Jewish literature. They are reliable in showing how old Jewish accounts were different from biblical ones in some cases, but they cannot be regarded as historical.

'On the day that Abraham weaned his son Isaac, he made a great banquet, and all the peoples of the world derided him, saying: "Have you seen that old man and woman who brought a foundling from the street, and now claim him as their son . . .?".' (*The Babylonian Talmud*, Isidore Epstein, London 1952.) A verse in the Koran (The Prophets, Chapter [Sura] 21:72) says of Abraham:

> . . . We bestowed on him Isaac
> and, as an additional gift,
> (A grandson), Jacob . . .

The verse indicates that Isaac and Jacob, the grandson who had not been born when Abraham died, were not his originally. Another chapter of the Koran, having mentioned three of the prophets – Moses, Aaron and Ishmael – speaks of them in Mary, Chapter 19:58 as being:

> The posterity of Abraham
> And Israel (Jacob) . . .*

The only possible explanation of this verse is that some of these prophets – Moses, Aaron and Ishmael – were descendants of Jacob, but *not* of Abraham. To elaborate on this point, we have two named ancestors (Abraham and Jacob) and three named descendants (Moses, Aaron and Ishmael). It is obvious that, had Jacob been a descendant of Abraham, he would have been named in the list of descendants rather than, together with Abraham, as an ancestor.

Who was the Pharaoh who contracted a bigamous marriage with Sarai and fathered Isaac? The evidence, and, in

---

* Jacob's name had been changed by the Lord, who is said to have told him: 'Thy name shall be called no more Jacob, but Israel: for as a prince hast thou power with God and with men . . . (32:28).

particular, the chronology of Sarah's descendants (Isaac, Jacob, Joseph and Moses – i.e. four generations separating Sarah and Moses), points to Tuthmosis III (*c.* 1490–1436 BC), fifth Pharaoh of the 18th Dynasty, the greatest warrior of the ancient world (and four generations before Akhenaten)* – and, as we shall see in the next chapter, the same person as the royal ancestor David from whose House, both the Old and New Testaments assure us, the promised Messiah (Christ the Redeemer) would come.

---

* Furthermore, he was the first Pharaoh to establish an empire between the Nile and the Euphrates, which the Bible promised as an inheritance for his descendants.

Chapter Two

The House of David

The task of identifying the historical David is complicated from the outset by the fact that the Old Testament provides us with two contrasting Davidic characters who cannot have been the same person. One is a warrior king who lived *c.* 1500 BC: the second is a tribal chief generally agreed by biblical scholars to have lived from 1000 to 960 BC, ruled over the traditional Promised Land – from Dan in the north to Beersheba in the south of the Israel-Judaean upland – and spent most of his life in conflict with the Philistines, the 'Peoples of the Sea', who had invaded the coastal area of Canaan in the middle of the 12th century BC and were trying to expand their territory.

Scholars have largely chosen, despite the lack of any genealogical link between him and the start of the Christian era, to identify this tribal chief as King David, who is presented to us in a number of guises – shepherd; rival to Saul and later Ishbosheth, one of Saul's surviving sons, for the Israelite leadership; an accomplished harpist; 'a man of war'; the slayer of Goliath in an epic duel; and a coward who fled from the wrath of his son, Absalom. However, he is *also* said to have been a warrior king who established an empire that stretched from the Nile to the Euphrates. The Book of II Samuel tells us: 'David smote also Hadadezer . . . as he went to recover his border at the river Euphrates . . . And David gat him a name [erected a stele] when he returned from smiting of the Syrians in the valley of salt . . .' (8:3 and 8:13). This account is repeated in I Chronicles: 'And David smote Hadadezer . . . as he went to

20

establish his dominion by the river Euphrates' (18:3).

The story of the founding of an entire empire by David the mere tribal chief has posed some problems for scholars. It does not equate with the fact that he is said to have had an army of just a few hundred men. Nor is there evidence of any kind to support the view that an empire stretching from the Nile and the Euphrates was founded in the early years of the 10th century BC. Indeed, *no* such empire can be said to have been created between the reign of Tuthmosis III in the 15th century BC and the second half of the 6th century BC, when Cyrus of Persia conquered both Mesopotamia and Egypt. Scholars have therefore had to explain – or, rather, explain away – the empire story of David by saying that the biblical narrator simply invented it as an act of aggrandizement towards an important biblical figure.

However, amalgamating the stories of two Davids – one a warrior king who lived in the 15th century BC, the other a tribal chief who lived five centuries later – should be seen as another facet of the attempt by Old Testament editors (Jewish scribes living in Babylon between the 6th and 3rd centuries BC) to conceal the fact that Tuthmosis III, not Abraham, was the father of Isaac, and therefore also the founding father of the 12 tribes of Israel. The first part of the Pharaoh's name, 'Tuth' (or Thoth), becomes 'Dwd' in Hebrew, the word used for 'David' in the Bible.

The story of the epic duel between David and Goliath, inserted to enhance tribal David's reputation as a 'man of war', is an adaptation of a much-admired Egyptian literary work, *The Autobiography of Sinuhe*, describing events that took place 1,000 years earlier, and it would certainly have been familiar to the Israelites from the earlier period of their Sojourn, the four generations they spent in Egypt during the 15th and 14th centuries BC.

Sinuhe was a courtier in the service of Nefru, daughter of Amenemhat I, the founder of the 12th Egyptian Dynasty in the 20th century BC. The form in which his autobiography is cast – the story of his sudden flight from Egypt, his wanderings, his battle with 'a mighty Canaanite man' like Goliath, and his eventual return to be buried in the land of his birth – makes it clear that it was inscribed originally in his actual tomb. Many copies of the story, which is recognized as being based on fact (see below), were found subsequently, dating from the 20th century BC (when the events actually occurred) until as late as the 21st Dynasty in the 11th century BC. It was a popular tale in ancient Egypt, taught as a literary example to students, and there can be no doubt that all educated persons in Egypt, no matter what their ethnic background, would have been familiar with its contents.

The similarities between the two accounts have been noted by many scholars. For example, William Kelly Simpson, the British Egyptologist, makes the point in his book *The Literature of Ancient Egypt* that the 'account of the fight with the champion of Retenu has frequently been compared to the David and Goliath duel, for which it may have served as a literary prototype.' Elsewhere* I have given a summary of the evidence indicating that this is the correct conclusion – that *The Autobiography of Sinuhe* survived in the memories of the Israelites when Moses led their Exodus to the Promised Land in the 14th century BC to escape from the harsh oppression of their Egyptian masters. Later, in the 6th century BC, the Hebrew scribes, writing the Book of Samuel during the Israelite 70-year exile in Babylonia – which had invaded Judaea and destroyed the Jerusalem Temple – and anxious to enhance the image of the tribal David in order to make it possible for readers to accept that it was he who established the great empire stretching from the Nile to the Euphrates, included Sinuhe's encounter with a 'mighty Canaanite man'.

However, as we shall see in the next chapter, the most significant fact of all in establishing the identity of David is that the biblical account of his campaigns matches in precise detail the accounts of the battles fought by Tuthmosis III,

* *The House of the Messiah.*

whose details are to be found inscribed in the Annals, a 223-line document at the granite holy of holies the king built after his Year 40 (1439 BC) at Karnak (modern Luxor) in Upper Egypt, on the east bank of the Nile opposite the Valley of the Kings.

Tuthmosis III, the son of a concubine (Plate 2), came to the throne of Egypt under strange circumstances in 1490 BC. The 18th Dynasty had been founded nearly 100 years earlier when, after just over a century of rule over the Eastern Delta of Egypt by the invading Hyksos (Asiatic shepherds, with some Semitic and other elements among them, who subdued the territory around 1630 BC and set up their capital at a fortified city on the eastern borders of Egypt, which they named Avaris), the princes of Thebes united in the 16th century BC in a successful attempt to drive them out of the country. This victory resulted in the crowning of Ahmosis I (*c*. 1575–1550 BC), as the first ruler of the 18th Dynasty, which started what is known as the New Kingdom. In all, he spent 15 years battling to ensure that no part of Egypt remained under foreign control, including pursuit of the remnants of the Hyksos into the Gaza region.

Ahmosis I was followed by his son, Amenhotep I (*c*. 1550–1528 BC), who pushed further into Palestine and Syria in continuing campaigns against the Hyksos. He, in turn, was followed on the throne by Tuthmosis I (*c*. 1528–1510 BC), one of his generals, after the king had arranged for him to be married to the royal heiress and appointed him as his co-regent. Despite his relatively short reign, Tuthmosis I was the original founder of the Egyptian Empire. He marched into western Asia at the head of his army and reached the River Euphrates in the area between northern Syria and Mesopotamia, south of Anatolia. There they succeeded in crossing the river into the territory of Mitanni (the ancient kingdom of northern Mesopotamia) where Tuthmosis I erected a stele (which has not been found) commemorating his victory. At this time, however, the Egyptians were satisfied simply to crush their enemies and never tried to establish control over the vanquished territories.

After these events we enter a mysterious period in Egyptian history. The next ruler was the king's son, Tuthmosis II (*c*. 1510–1490 BC), born of a minor wife and not the Great Royal Wife (Queen Ahmose). In order to inherit the throne he married – as was the custom – his half-sister, Hatshepsut, the heiress daughter of his father and Queen Ahmose. In *his* turn, Tuthmosis II chose his son, Tuthmosis III (*c*. 1490–1436 BC), by a concubine named Isis, to be his successor.

To ensure his son's right to the throne Tuthmosis II took the precaution of having him 'adopted' by the state god Amun-Ra. The story of the god's choice of Tuthmosis III to be king is found in an inscription at Karnak, written long after he had come to the throne. It describes how the selection ceremony took place in the Temple of Amun at Thebes as the Ark of the state god was carried in procession: '. . . On recognizing me, lo, he [the god] halted . . . [I threw myself on] the pavement, I prostrated myself in his presence . . . Then they (the priests) [revealed] before the people the secrets in the hearts of the gods . . .' At this point, the story describes how the young prince was whisked off to Heaven to be appointed king by Ra, the king of the gods: 'Ra himself established me. I was dignified with the diadems which were upon his head, his serpent diadem, rested upon [my forehead] . . . I was sated with the counsels of the gods, like Horus . . . at the house of my father, Amun-Ra.'

Tuthmosis III, who had been given the throne name (i.e. that given at his coronation, different from the one given at birth; in fact, the king usually had *four* names) Menkheper-Ra ('established in the form of Ra'), was still a young boy, aged about five, when his father died. His 'adoption' by Amun-Ra as king would in the normal course of events have been confirmed by marriage to *his* half-sister, Neferure, a daughter born to Queen Hatshepsut shortly before the death of Tuthmosis II. This marriage did not take place – we do not know why. We do know, however, that her mother, Queen Hatshepsut, prevented the young king from ruling. Instead, she (his aunt-stepmother) appointed herself as his guardian, allowing him only to appear behind her in reliefs of the period.

Soon, as early as Tuthmosis III's Year 2 (1489 BC), she even took the step of sharing the kingship, posing and being dressed as a man. For as long as she lived she kept Tuthmosis III in the background and regarded her daughter, Neferure, as the real heiress *and* heir, 'Lady of the Two Lands, mistress of Upper and Lower Egypt' (a title found on inscriptions of Hatshepsut). Her plans were frustrated, however, when Neferure died in Year 16 of the co-regency, and from this point onward Tuthmosis III gained increasing importance. He seems to have joined the Egyptian army as a young man, and there is evidence to suggest that he fought in the area of Gaza towards the end of the co-regency.

The chance for Tuthmosis III to rule Egypt on his own came in the middle of Year 22 (1469 BC) of the co-regency when Hatshepsut died. It seems that the first task he undertook was to deface many of the monuments erected to his aunt-stepmother: her reliefs were hacked out, her inscriptions erased, her cartouches (the oval rings containing names and titles of Egyptian rulers) obliterated, her obelisks walled up. So now, technically speaking, as he was neither the son of the Egyptian queen, nor had he married the heiress to inherit the throne, he ruled only by virtue of having been appointed by the state god Amun-Ra. Nor was Tuthmosis III the legal descendant of the earlier Ahmosside dynasty. From this time until the end of Amarna rule in Egypt – the rule of Akhenaten, Semenkhkare, Tutankhamun and Aye in the 14th century BC – it was the dynasty legitimized by the state god Amun-Ra and founded by Tuthmosis III that sat on the throne of Egypt.

The sarcophagus in the tomb of Tuthmosis III (No. 34 in the Valley of the Kings) was found to be empty when it was discovered. His mummy eventually came to light, together with 32 other royal mummies, hidden in a chamber, 3 metres wide and nearly 300 metres long, at the bottom of a narrow shaft dug in the slopes of the necropolis of western Thebes. They had lain there for more than 2,000 years, having been hidden by Egyptian priests who feared for their safety after many incidents of tomb-robbing.

Yet robbers did find their new hiding place. The mummy of Tuthmosis III had been torn from its coffin, and suffered considerable damage as it was stripped of its jewels. The head, which had broken free from the body, showed that the king was almost completely bald at the time of his death apart from a few short white hairs behind the left ear. All four limbs had also become detached from the torso, the feet had become detached from the legs and both arms had been broken in two at the elbow:

> *. . . before re-burial some renovation of the wrapping was necessary, and, as portions of the body became loose, the restorers, in order to give the mummy the necessary firmness, compressed it between four oar-shaped slips of wood . . . Happily, the face, which had been plastered over with pitch at the time of embalming, did not suffer at all from this rough treatment, and appeared intact when the protecting mask was removed.*

The author of these words, Gaston Maspero, director-general of the Cairo Museum at the time (1896), went on to say: 'His statues, although not representing him as a type of manly beauty, yet give him refined, intelligent features, but a comparison with the mummy shows that the artists have idealised their model.' More recently (1959), another view of the king's appearance has been provided by the American scholar William C. Hayes:

> *Incontestably the greatest pharaoh ever to occupy the throne of Egypt, Tuthmosis III appears to have excelled*

not only as a warrior, a statesman and an administrator, but also as one of the most accomplished horsemen, archers and all-round athletes of his time ... (Yet) physically he cannot have been very prepossessing. His mummy shows him to have been a stocky little man, under five feet four inches in height, and his portraits are almost unanimous in endowing him with the ... most beaked of all the Tuthmosside noses.

His lack of stature and the physical appearance, which Hayes found not 'very prepossessing', did not have a damaging effect on the domestic life of Tuthmosis III. His chief wife and the mother of his successor, Amenhotep II (*c.* 1436–1413 BC), was his half-sister, Meryt-Ra. Nothing much is known about her, but she was certainly not the heiress. In addition, he had at least three Asiatic wives, whose shared tomb was found in western Thebes, and a large harem.

We find no evidence of the relationship with the visiting Sarah that resulted in the birth of Isaac. Perhaps Egyptian scribes regarded it as an unimportant episode or as a great sin whose memory should not be preserved in official records in the same way that Hebrew scribes, while admitting the marriage, tried to obscure the identity of the father of the child born to it.

By the time that Tuthmosis III became sole ruler of Egypt in his Year 22 after the death of Hatshepsut, four decades had passed without a major Egyptian military campaign in western Asia. Now the situation changed completely. The King of Qadesh (a strong fortified city on the River Orontes in northern Syria) led a Syrio-Canaanite confederacy in a general rebellion against Egypt. In response, Tuthmosis III marched into western Asia to regain the territories between the Nile and Euphrates that had been conquered 40 years earlier by his grandfather, Tuthmosis I. In the next 20 years he led a total of seventeen campaigns in western Asia, at the end of which Tuthmosis III (David) had earned himself the reputation of being the mightiest of all the kings of the ancient world – and had re-established the empire that was the subject of the Lord's promises to Sarah's descendants, which are examined later in this book.

Chapter Three

Armageddon

The account at Karnak of these various wars, copied from the daily records of the scribe who accompanied the army on its campaigns, serves to provide from Egyptian historical sources considerable additional light on the identity of the historical David, and to show how the events of his reign were adapted by Hebrew scribes to fit the reign of a tribal chief who lived five centuries later. They include: the significance of the battleground Armageddon; how Jerusalem came to be known as the city of 'royal' David; how David and 'all the house of Israel brought up the Ark [boat] of the Lord [to Jerusalem] with shouting, and with the sound of trumpets' (II Samuel 6:1); and the origins of the name Zion, which has not been found in any historical source and makes its first appearance in the Bible as soon as we learn of King David's entry into Jerusalem: 'David took the strong hold of Zion: the same is the city of David' (5:7). I shall now examine these important points in greater detail.

The Egyptian account begins with Tuthmosis III's departure at the head of his troops from the fortified border city of Zarw during the last days of his Year 22. Ten days later he arrived in Gaza, where he celebrated the start of his Year 23 (1468 BC) with festivals in honour of his 'father', Amun-Ra, whose image he carried inside an Ark (a representation of a boat with a statue of Amun sitting in it) at the head of the marching army. He stayed there for the night before pushing north towards central Canaan, where he paused in a town called Yehem to the south of a mountainous ridge he had to cross in order to reach Megiddo, the city where the Qadesh enemy had gathered. At Yehem he was faced with a choice of three routes, but the shortest, called the Aruna road, was narrow and dangerous, and he therefore summoned a Council of War.

His officers were opposed to choosing the Aruna route. They said: 'How can one go on this road which is so narrow? It is reported that the enemy stand outside and are numerous. Will not horse have to go behind horse, and soldiers and people likewise? Shall our own vanguard be fighting while the rear stands here in Aruna (the starting point of the narrow road) and does not fight?' However, in the light of fresh reports brought in by messengers Tuthmosis III decided that he would make his way to Megiddo by the unappealing – but, to his enemies, unexpected – narrow road, a choice to which his officers replied: 'Thy father Amun prosper thy counsel . . . The servant will follow his master.' Thus was set the scene for the first battle of Armageddon.

Jerusalem, the 'city of David', owes its prominence in the Bible, and as a place of devout pilgrimage today, to the role it played in the opening campaign of the long military career of Tuthmosis III – against Megiddo, which he always looked back upon as the most important battle he fought.

The *Encyclopaedia of Archaeological Excavations in the Holy Lands* makes the point that the military importance of Megiddo and its long history as an international battleground is 'aptly reflected in the Apocalypse of John (Revelation, 16:16ff) in which Armageddon (*Har Megiddon*, the Mount of Megiddo) is designated as the site where, at the end of days, all the kings of the world will fight the ultimate battle against the forces of God'. This underlines the belief up to the Christian era that the Messiah (Christ the Redeemer) born of the House of David will one day have to re-enact the battle of his great ancestor who conquered Megiddo, where the final confrontation between Good and Evil will take place.

The combined Syrian and Canaanite forces facing Tuthmosis III outside Megiddo – modern Tell Megiddo in Palestine – had been divided into two armies. The king

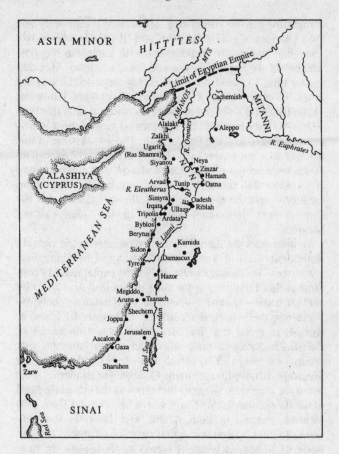

Tuthmosis III's campaigns in Western Asia

vanquished them in the ensuing battle, but the defeated enemy fled to the safety of the city, where, as the gates were shut, they were hauled to safety by citizens who let down 'garments to hoist them up'. The account of the battle

31

complains that the enemy had 'abandoned their horses and their chariots of gold and silver' and 'if only His Majesty's army had not given up their hearts to capturing the possessions of the enemy, they would [have captured] Megiddo at this time'. Instead, they had to lay siege to the city for seven months before it was eventually taken. However, Tuthmosis III did not remain with his troops during this time – 'His Majesty himself was in a fortress east of this town' – but returned to lead the final assault. The actual name of this fortress does not appear in the Egyptian version of events, no doubt because the official scribe stayed with the besieging army rather than accompanying the king, but their respective locations, and the evidence that follows, indicate that the fortress was Jerusalem, situated to the south-east of Megiddo.

Neither does the name 'Jerusalem' appear in the western Asiatic city-lists of Tuthmosis III or any of his immediate successors. This has not previously been explained. My own view is that Egyptians at the time recognized Jerusalem by another name – Qadesh,* a Semitic word meaning 'holy'.

Among the historical records of Tuthmosis III found at Karnak is a list that includes more than 100 names of Palestinian locations under Egyptian control after his first Asiatic campaign. Yet, at the top of this Palestinian (or Megiddo) list, we find the name Qadesh. The modern Arabic name for Jerusalem suggests that this was the city at the head of the Palestinian list: *al-Quds*, which becomes *ha-Qudesh* in Hebrew, means, in both Arabic and Hebrew, the holy (ground), and is used in the first verse of Chapter 11 of the Book of Nehemiah where it speaks of 'Jerusalem the holy city' (in Hebrew, *Yurushalayim ha Qudesh*).

Evidence of these peaceful relations with Egypt is also provided by the Tell el-Amarna letters, the foreign archives of the 18th Dynasty. Six communications, sent to the King of

* Not to be confused with the northern Qadesh on the River Orontes, not conquered until seven years after the conquest of Megiddo.

Egypt in the 14th century BC and written in Akkadian, the diplomatic language of the period,* have as their source not Qadesh but mat Urusalim, 'the land of Jerusalem'. They make it clear that Jerusalem had been under Egyptian control since the time of Tuthmosis III, with an Egyptian military garrison stationed locally.

Furthermore, the Akkadian name for Jerusalem found in the Tell el-Amarna letters can be divided into two elements, *Uru* and *Salim*. The first element, *Uru*, is derived from the verb *yarah*, meaning 'to found' or 'to establish'. The second element, however, has caused some misunderstanding. A number of scholars have argued that here we have a reference to a Western Semitic or Amorite god, Shulmanu or Shalim. Thus Urusalim would, in their view, mean 'Shalim has founded'. However, no textual or archaeological evidence has ever been found to indicate, either directly or indirectly, that the Amorite god Shalim was a deity worshipped at Jerusalem, which could not have been the case if the very founding of the city was related to him.

When we abandon this unsupported explanation of the second element in the word Urusalim we find that *Salim* – as was correctly understood by the early Jewish rabbis in the Haggadah, the legendary part of the Talmud, representing its non-legal element – means 'peace' (Hebrew *shalom* and Arabic *salam*). Thus the meaning of Urusalim would be 'foundation of peace' or 'establishing peace', an interpretation that is supported by the historical evidence: the lack of any mention of Urusalim in Egyptian sources outside the Tell el-Amarna letters; the fact that Qadesh, used in both the Bible and later Arabic texts as a synonym for Jerusalem, is mentioned in the lists of subdued Asiatic cities of most Egyptian kings of this period; and that the Qadesh in question

† Akkadian was a Semitic language that appeared in northern Mesopotamia in the 3rd millennium BC, and later became the general official language for all Mesopotamia and the Levant during the 2nd millennium, before being replaced by Aramaic from the 9th century BC.

cannot have been the city of that name on the River Orontes.

When Tuthmosis III went out to fight against the confederation of Canaanite and Syrian princes at Megiddo, Jerusalem did not take part in the rebellion. The king faced no need to take control of the fortress and, instead, was able to make his way straight from Gaza to Megiddo and, without need for military action, to seek safe sanctuary in Jerusalem during the long months that Megiddo was under siege. Thus identified, Jerusalem was the city of David.

The three principal victories in the long martial career of Tuthmosis III were the capture in his Year 23 (1469 BC) of Megiddo; the conquest in his Year 30 (1461 BC) of Qadesh on the River Orontes, the capital of his persistent enemy who had managed to escape from Megiddo; and the ultimate restoration of his empire in his Year 33 (1458 BC) when he crossed the River Euphrates, defeated the King of Mitanni and, in honour of his achievement, erected a stele alongside that of his grandfather, Tuthmosis I.

What did the biblical scribes make of these events? The Old Testament is notoriously suspect in matters of names and the chronological sequence of events, doubtless as a result of the many centuries when the stories it contains were passed down by word of mouth. However, although the order in which they occurred is muddled in places, the account we find in the Book of II Samuel is clearly dealing with the same events that are inscribed in the annals at Karnak.

II Samuel identifies Megiddo by the name Rabbah (meaning 'goddess') (11:1). We are told that the Ammonites (Semitic, non-Jewish people in east Jordan) 'hired the Syrians' (10:6), and it is quite clear that, in the subsequent battle against the army of David, the Ammonites and Syrians operated as separate units. This echoes the description of the divided forces Tuthmosis III found facing him when he arrived unexpectedly by the Aruna road before his assault upon Megiddo. The escape of the King of Qadesh and his troops to fight another day is reflected in the biblical account of the battle where it says: 'And when the children of Ammon saw that the Syrians were fled, then fled they also . . . and entered into the city . . .' (10:14). During the subsequent siege, matching the account of how Tuthmosis III left the field of battle for 'a fortress to the east', we are told that 'David tarried still at Jerusalem' (11:1).

Shortly after David's arrival, we have a description of how the Israelites 'brought in the Ark of the Lord, and set it in his place, in the midst of the tabernacle that David had pitched for it . . .' (6:17). If David is to be identified as Tuthmosis III, the Ark – an Egyptian idea introduced later to the Israelites – must have been the Ark of Amun-Ra, not the Ark of the Covenant, in which Moses is said to have placed the Ten Commandments, because Moses, as we shall see, was not to be born until a century *after* these events.

Although we have no supporting evidence, it is a logical assumption that the king would have been accompanied to Jerusalem by the Ark of his god, Amun-Ra, which had been carried at the head of his army as it advanced on Megiddo. We know that there were some rituals in Egyptian religion that only the king and high priests could perform before their deity. It is also a logical assumption that the resting place for the Ark would be Mount Moriah, the high holy ground to the north of the city, which had been looked upon as a holy place since the time of Abraham and is today the setting for two of the holiest shrines of Islam, the Dome of the Rock and al-Aqsa Mosque, as well as the Jewish Wailing Wall.

We find the details of this transaction – and further confirmation of the peaceful relations that existed between Egypt and Jerusalem – later in II Samuel where Araunah, the Jebusite king (the Jebusites were the Canaanite inhabitants of Jerusalem at the time), is said to have still been in control of Mount Moriah when David bought its threshing-floor 'for fifty shekels of silver' in order to build an altar. In the course of these negotiations Araunah said to David: '. . . behold, here be oxen for burnt sacrifice, and threshing instruments and other instruments of the oxen for wood. All these things did Araunah, *as a king* [my italics], give unto the king . . .' (24:22–23). The choice of a threshing-floor on Mount Moriah may seem a curious one for the site of an altar, but such elevated and exposed pieces of ground at the approaches to cities were often the site of cultic observance.

As did Tuthmosis III, David, according to II Samuel, rejoined his troops when it was clear that Rabbah (Megiddo) was about to fall, and he led them in the final successful assault. Then he took 'their king's crown from off his head . . . And he brought forth the spoil of the city in great abundance.' David also took a large number of prisoners of war to work for him, and, before finally returning to Jerusalem, subdued the rest of the Ammonite cities. Yet David was unable to control Syria until after he had defeated his implacable enemy, the King of Qadesh. This was a task he set out to complete seven years after the end of his successful campaign against Megiddo.

Although there has been some scholarly debate about the matter, the ultimately conquered city of Qadesh is conventionally identified as the biblical Zobah. The relevant references in II Samuel suggest that David smote 'Hadadezer . . . king of Zobah [Qadesh], as he went to recover his border at the river Euphrates' (8:3). The Book of II Samuel does not provide a date for this event, but we know from the Karnak inscriptions that another three years passed after the siege and capture of Qadesh before Tuthmosis III – as part of the continuing campaign to restore his empire – crossed the Euphrates in his Year 33 and defeated the King of Mitanni: 'My Majesty crossed to the farthest limits of Asia. I caused to be built many boats of cedar on the hills of the God's Land (Phoenicia) in the neighbourhood of the-mistress-of-Byblos.* They were placed on chariots (wheeled wagons), oxen dragging them, and they journeyed in front of My Majesty in order to cross that great river which flows

* I believe this refers to the Phoenician goddess Ashtaroth.

between this country and Nahrin (Mitanni) . . . Then My Majesty set up a stele on that mountain of Nahrin taken from the mountain on the west side of the Euphrates.'

Archaeological evidence leaves no doubt that the battles over the cities of Megiddo and Qadesh were fought by Tuthmosis III in the 15th century BC rather than by the tribal David five centuries later because, by that time, both Megiddo and Qadesh had already been destroyed. It has shown that Megiddo suffered 'sudden and total destruction' at the hands of the invading Philistines, the 'Peoples of the Sea', in the last third of the 12th century BC. While there is evidence that the site was used subsequently by the Philistines, archaeologists have concluded that this, too, suffered destruction in the second half of the 11th century BC, and that the 'city gate . . . did not apparently exist . . . Indeed, it seems that the city was entirely unfortified during this period.' This was the city – unfortified, not needing a siege to subdue it – in which the tribal chief identified as David is said to have lived in the first half of the 10th century BC.

Similarly, evidence of various wars, found by archaeologists excavating at Qadesh, makes it clear that the final destruction of this Syrian stronghold, like that of Megiddo, occurred in the 12th century BC at the hands of the Philistines.

The name 'Zion', as we saw at the start of this chapter, makes its first appearance in the Bible as soon as we learn of David's entry into Jerusalem and has not been found in any historical source. However, all the indications are that Zion (Sion in Hebrew) was used as an alternative name for the ancient holy ground of Mount Moriah, and its origins point to a link with Egypt. It is not an original Hebrew word, but consists of two elements, one Hebrew and Semitic in general, from which comes 'Sahara', the other Egyptian. The Hebrew first element, 'Si', means 'a land of drought, a barren place'. It is the Egyptian element whose meaning has hitherto escaped recognition.

'On' is the biblical name, from the Greek, of the ancient Egyptian holy city Heliopolis. From the time of its decline, when Thebes in Upper Egypt became the new capital city of the Empire as well as the holy city of the state god Amun-Ra, it became the custom to refer to Thebes as 'the southern On' and Heliopolis as 'the northern On', with the word 'On' being used in the sense of 'holy city'. Thus the very word 'Zion' – the holy city of the desert – used from the time King David entered the city to designate the holy ground to the north of Jerusalem in itself reveals its Egyptian origin.

The correct course of events is that Mount Moriah, until then holy to the inhabitants of Jerusalem, became holy for all the Asiatic kingdoms of the Egyptian Empire after Tuthmosis III made it his base during the siege of Megiddo and worshipped his god, Amun-Ra, there. Nevertheless, his descendants, through Sarah and Isaac, never really forgot their great ancestor and, after leaving Egypt and eventually settling in Canaan a century and a half later, they made his holy ground the most venerated and holy part of their new home, calling it Mount Sion.

Chapter Four

A Coat of Many Colours

While Tuthmosis III was creating the richest and most powerful empire the world had yet seen – and at the same time establishing his own enduring reputation as the greatest of all the Pharaohs – Sarah and her descendants were leading a nomadic life in Canaan. Tents provided simple homes and protection against the often harsh elements. Marriages were arranged, children born, the dead buried. The rhythm of their days was set by trying to coax a living from the unpromising soil and caring for their modest herds of sheep, goats and cattle. Nevertheless, the story of their lives at this time which we find in the Book of Genesis hints that memories of those distant links with the royal house of Egypt, although growing fainter with each passing year, still survived within Sarah's family.

When Isaac, the son of her bigamous marriage to Tuthmosis III (David), grew to manhood he is said (Genesis 25) to have taken a wife, Rebekah. Like Sarah before her, Rebekah is described as unfertile, but this may be simply an extravagant scriptural way of saying that, at a time when early marriage was the norm, a girl had been taken as a bride long before she reached child-bearing age.

Eventually, Rebekah gave birth to twin sons. The first to be born was named Esau, the second Jacob (*Y'qwb*, which means in Hebrew 'the one who follows'). The most intriguing aspect of their early life is Esau's sale of his birthright. The special blessing of the elder or eldest son is a theme that we find in many biblical stories, but this is the only case where a birthright is mentioned. To what exactly did this entitle its owner? The only logical explanation would be the inheritance of property or title. We know from the account in the Talmud that Jacob did not receive any of Isaac's property after his father's death:

> *When Isaac died, and Jacob and Esau wept together for their father's a mise. They carried his body to the cave of Machpelah, which is in Hebron, and all the kings of Canaan followed with the mourners in the funeral train of Isaac . . . Isaac bequeathed his cattle and his possessions to his two sons. Esau said then to Jacob, 'Behold, this which our father has left us must be divided into two portions, then I will select my share.' Jacob divided all his father's possessions into two portions in the presence of Esau and his sons, and then addressing his brother, said:*
>
> *'Take unto thyself both these portions which thou seest before thee. Behold, the God of Heaven and Earth spoke unto our ancestors, Abraham and Isaac, saying, "Unto thy seed will I give this land as an everlasting possession." Now, all that our father left is before thee; if thou desirest the promised possession, the land of Canaan, take it, and this other wealth shall be mine; or if thou desirest these two portions, be it as it is pleasing in thy eyes, and the land of Canaan shall be the share for me and mine.' . . . Esau . . . taking the personal substance, he gave Jacob for his portion the land of Canaan from the river of Egypt unto the great river, the River Euphrates.**

The only apparent alternative, therefore, is that the birthright that passed from Esau, the elder twin, to Jacob was the princely title that flowed from the identity of their grandfather, Tuthmosis III.

Such a sale or transfer of a birthright is possible only in a

---

**Selections From The Talmud*, H. Polano, pp. 83–84.

society where primogeniture (being the first-born) is not looked upon as the sole criterion for determining inheritance. Tablets found in the 1920s at Nuzi, the ancient city in north-east Iraq, make it clear that other criteria were sometimes used in biblical times. One concerns a man who transferred his birthright to his brother for three sheep.

The price Esau is said to have accepted for his birthright was 'a pottage of lentils' (the Hebrew original is *nazid adash*, literally, 'soup of lentils'). This is best interpreted as an indication that he did not value his birthright very highly. It cannot have been easy for him or for Jacob, living in tents and leading a simple nomadic life with their flocks, to believe the promise that one day their descendants would rule over a vast kingdom stretching from the Nile to the Euphrates. Yet, of the two, the Old Testament suggests that Jacob would have more faith in the fulfilment of such a promise at some time in the future. We are told in the Book of Genesis (15:18) that the twin brothers had vastly different characters. Esau was 'a skilful hunter, a man of the open country': in contrast, Jacob, like the son Joseph who would be born to him, seems to have been more of a dreamer, 'a quiet man, staying among the tents'.

The Talmud confirms that, when it came to dividing Isaac's estate, the cattle and all the rest of their father's possessions were inherited by Esau while Jacob chose the kingdom. After Isaac's possessions had been divided into two equal portions, Jacob is reported to have said to Esau: '. . . Behold, the God of Heaven and Earth spoke unto our ancestors, Abraham and Isaac, saying: "Unto thy seed will I give this land as an everlasting possession." Now all that our father left is before thee; if thou desirest the promised possession, the land . . . take it; or . . . the land . . . shall be the share for me and mine.' After seeking advice, Esau chose his father's possessions and left Jacob with the promised land 'from the river of Egypt to the great river, Euphrates . . .'

Later, Esau seems to have had second thoughts about his decision and, after a dispute about their father's blessing, threatened to kill Jacob, who fled on his mother's advice to the home of her brother in Haran. There he promptly fell in love with Rachel, the younger of his two cousins, but his uncle made him marry her elder sister, Leah, before he was allowed to marry Rachel. Rachel, too, proved to be unfertile, but in the course of the years Jacob is said to have fathered eleven children – six sons and a daughter by Leah, two sons by Rachel's maid, Bilhah, and two more sons by Leah's maid, Zilpah. At last Rachel, his first love, gave him an eleventh son. They named him Joseph.

Shortly afterwards, Jacob decided to return to his homeland, Canaan. It was on this journey that he is said to have had an encounter with the Lord which resulted in his name being changed, from Jacob to Israel. The significance of this event lies in the name Israel. The Hebrew term *el* is the short form of Elohim (God) and *Ysra* (or *sar*) indicates a prince or ruler.

The essential points are that Jacob had a number of children by different women; eventually he had a son, Joseph, by his first love, Rachel; and, in the story of his return to Canaan, the biblical scribes chose to emphasize again a special relationship between God and the Israelites.

Nor is there any means of knowing how much of the story of Joseph that follows this account of Jacob's early life is to be taken literally from the time of his birth until his appointment by an unnamed Pharaoh as his minister of state, the second most powerful man in Egypt. The biblical account (Genesis 37:3) goes on to make it clear that Jacob loved Joseph more than any of his other sons and gave him his celebrated coat of many colours.* Joseph's half-brothers hated Joseph because of this favouritism, and even more

---

* Here again we have a wrong English translation of a Hebrew phrase. In Hebrew it reads *ktener phessun*, which does not mean 'a coat of many colours' but literally reads 'robe (or tunic) ornaments'. The most recent translation renders it 'a richly ornamented robe' (*The NIV Interlinear Hebrew-English Old Testament*, John R. Kohlenberger, Michigan, 1987).

when he is said to have related a dream that came to him one night. 'We were binding sheaves of corn in the field when suddenly my sheaf rose and stood upright, while your sheaves gathered round mine and bowed low to it,' he told them.

'Do you think one day you will lord it over us?' the angry brothers asked.

Then Joseph had a second dream, which he related to his father as well as to his brothers: 'I had another dream, and this time the sun, the moon and eleven stars were bowing down to me.' This story served to fuel the jealousy of his brothers, and Jacob is reported to have rebuked him, saying: 'What is this dream of yours? Must your mother and I and your brothers come and bow down to the ground before you?' Yet he did not forget Joseph's words.

One day when his brothers were out grazing the sheep, Joseph's father said to him: 'Go and see if all is well with them and with the sheep, and bring word to me.' When they saw Joseph approaching in the distance, his brothers said to each other: 'Here comes that dreamer. Let's kill him and throw him into one of these pits and say that a wild animal devoured him. Then we'll see what comes of his dreams.'

Reuben, the eldest of the brothers, protested. 'Let's not take his life,' he said. 'Don't shed any blood.'

When Joseph finally arrived on the scene, his hostile brothers stripped him of his coat and dropped him into a pit while they sat down to a meal and considered what to do next. The matter was resolved when they saw a caravan of Ishmaelites approaching, their camels laden with spices, balm and myrrh, who were making their way down to Egypt on a trade mission. Judah, the fourth brother, said to the others: 'What shall we gain if we kill our brother and conceal his death? Why not sell him to the Ishmaelites and not lay our hands on him? After all, he is our brother.' They sold Joseph, then said to be 17 years of age, for 20 shekels and, to disguise their crime, slaughtered a goat, dipped Joseph's richly embroidered coat in the animal's blood and took the stained garment back to Jacob, who wailed: 'It is my son's robe. Some wild beast has devoured him. Joseph has surely been torn to pieces.'

Once in Egypt the Ishmaelite merchants sold Joseph on to Potiphar, the captain of Pharaoh's guard, who found him a faithful servant and entrusted to him everything he owned. However, Joseph was not only efficient but handsome, and after a while Potiphar's wife tried to seduce him. Joseph rejected her advances. 'Think of my master,' he told her. 'With me in charge he does not concern himself with anything in the house; everything he owns he has entrusted to my care. My master has withheld nothing from me except you, because you are his wife. How then could I do such a wicked thing and sin against God?'

Potiphar's wife was not prepared to give up easily. She continued to plead with Joseph and, when they were alone in the house one day, seized him by the cloak and said again: 'Come lie with me.' Joseph refused – and ran out of the house, leaving her clutching his cloak. Potiphar's wife told her other servants that Joseph had attacked her and run away when she screamed. This was the story she repeated to her husband when he arrived home: 'That Hebrew slave you brought us came to me to make a mockery of me, but as soon as I screamed for help he left his cloak in my hand and ran out of the house.'

Potiphar, who believed her account of these events and was understandably outraged, promptly incarcerated Joseph in the jail where the king's prisoners were kept. Joseph proved such a model prisoner that he soon became a trusty, running the affairs of the prison with the same efficiency he had shown in running Potiphar's home. It was thus that he met Pharaoh's chief cupbearer and chief baker, who had been locked up in the same prison after giving offence to the king.

When both of them had strange dreams, they asked Joseph to interpret their significance. Joseph predicted – accurately – that the cupbearer would be released and restored to his position but the baker would be hanged. Some two years later, according to the Book of Genesis (41:1), Pharaoh himself had two mysterious dreams that none of the wise men or magicians of Egypt could interpret for him. It was then that the cupbearer explained to Pharaoh how Joseph had interpreted his and the chief baker's dreams and events had turned out exactly as predicted. Pharaoh sent at once for Joseph and explained: 'I have heard it said that you can understand and interpret dreams.' Joseph replied, as he had done in the cases of the cupbearer and the chief baker: 'I cannot do it, but God will give Pharaoh the answer he desires.'

'In my dream I was standing on the bank of the Nile when out of the river came seven cows, fat and sleek, and they grazed among the reeds,' Pharaoh went on. 'After them appeared seven other cows – scrawny and very gaunt and lean. These lean, gaunt cows ate up the seven fat ones. But even after they ate them no one could tell that they had done so; they looked as gaunt as before. In my dreams I also saw seven ears of corn, full and good, growing on a single stalk. After them, seven other ears sprouted – withered and thin and blighted by the east wind. The thin ears swallowed up the seven good ears. I told this to the magicians, but none could explain it to me.'

'The dreams of Pharaoh are one and the same,' Joseph told the king. 'God has told Pharaoh what he is about to do. The seven good cows are seven years, and the seven good ears of corn are seven years. The seven lean, gaunt cows are seven years, and so are the worthless ears of corn blighted by the east wind. Seven years of plenty are coming throughout the land of Egypt, but seven years of famine will follow them . . .' Joseph suggested that 'a shrewd and wise man' should be appointed to deal with this emergency. Pharaoh replied that there was no one as shrewd and wise as Joseph: 'You shall be in charge of my household, and all my people are to submit to your orders. Only in respect of the throne shall I be greater than you.'

The Book of Genesis goes on to describe (41:42–45) how

Pharaoh took a signet ring from his own hand and placed it on Joseph's finger; put a gold chain around his neck and arranged for him to ride in a chariot as his second-in-command, and the people were ordered to cry before him: 'Bow the knee.' The king also gave him an Egyptian name, Zaph-nath-pa-a-neah, as well as an Egyptian wife, Asenath, daughter of Potipherah, the priest of On (Heliopolis), the centre in Lower Egypt of the sun-god Ra.

Joseph is thought to have been 30 years of age when he entered the service of Pharaoh. Two sons were born of his marriage, Manasseh (Anen in Egyptian) and Ephraim (Aye). Many countries were affected at the time of the famine he predicted, including Canaan, where Jacob said to his sons: 'I have heard that there is corn in Egypt; get you down thither, and buy for us from thence; that we may live, and not die' (42:1,2). On their arrival Joseph recognized his brothers but did not reveal his own identity. Later, as the famine continued to rage, the brothers made a second visit to Egypt. On this occasion, Joseph did reveal his identity. He found the occasion so moving that he 'wept aloud, and the Egyptians and the house of Pharaoh heard' (45:2). This, one of two references to the 'house of Pharaoh' in the Book of Genesis, has been misinterpreted because of the later biblical editors' lack of familiarity with Egyptian usage. Then, as now, the word 'house' was a synonym for 'wife' as well as being used to indicate a dwelling.*

This passage in the Book of Genesis should therefore be interpreted as signifying that the Queen was told of the

---

* It was not considered polite to speak directly about a person's wife or mention her name, and, even if she had no children, a wife would still be referred to as 'the house' of her husband. The memoirs in the tomb of Ahmose, son of Abana, a naval officer who fought in the battles that led to the ultimate defeat of the Hyksos conquerors of the Eastern Delta in the 16th century BC, makes this usage plain. Ahmose's account of his part in these campaigns contains the sentence: 'Now, when I had established a house' – that is, had married – 'I was taken upon the ship *Northern* because I was valiant.'

arrival of Joseph's brothers, and after her intercession with her husband on Joseph's behalf, he was able to say forgivingly to them:

> *I am your brother, whom ye sold into Egypt. Now therefore be not grieved, nor angry with yourselves that ye sold me hither: for God did send me before you to preserve life . . . and he hath made me a father to Pharaoh, and lord of all his house, and a ruler throughout all the land of Egypt. Haste ye, and go up to my father, and say unto him, Thus saith thy son Joseph, God hath made me lord of all Egypt: come down unto me: tarry not: And thou shalt dwell in the land of Goshen, and thou shalt be near unto me, thou, and thy children and thy children's children, and thy flocks and thy herds, and all that thou hast. And there will I nourish thee . . .*

(45:4–5,8–11)

The souls who accompanied Jacob into Egypt in response to this invitation are described as numbering 'three score and ten' (46:27). They include Joseph and his two sons, Anen and Aye, amounting to three, who were already there. The list in the Book of Genesis provides the names of another 66 immigrants who actually accompanied Jacob: the 70th name is missing because the later biblical editor would have attempted to conceal any blood connection between the Israelites and the Egyptians.

Joseph settled his family at Goshen in the extreme Eastern Delta – they were not allowed into Egypt proper because Asiatic shepherds had been 'anathema' to Egyptians since the century-long Hyksos occupation two centuries earlier - and introduced his father and five of his brothers to Pharaoh, who said: 'If you know of any capable men among them, make them chief herdsmen over my cattle.'

The Israelites had lived at Goshen for 17 years during the early part of the reign of Amenhotep III (*c.* 1405–1367 BC), the great-grandson of Tuthmosis III, when Jacob, who felt that the time of his death was approaching, sent for Joseph and said: 'Do not bury me in Egypt, but if I die carry me out of Egypt and bury me where my forefathers are buried.' 'I shall do as you ask,' Joseph promised. It was again the Queen whose intercession is said to have been sought when Jacob died and the time had come to fulfil the promise that he would be buried among his forefathers. The passage in question makes it clear that we are dealing with a person, not a building: '. . . Joseph spake unto the house of Pharaoh, saying, if now I have found grace in your eyes, speak, I pray you, in the ears of Pharaoh' (50:4). Joseph was granted his wish and with 'a very great company' of Egyptians and Israelites departed for Canaan where Jacob was buried in a cave.

The closing verses of the Book of Genesis are taken up with Joseph's own death. We have no indication of how much time had elapsed since his father's burial in Canaan. However, before dying Joseph said to the Israelites: 'God will surely visit you and bring you out of this land unto the land which he swore to Abraham, to Isaac and to Jacob. And Joseph took an oath of the children of Israel, saying, God will surely visit you, and you will carry up my bones from hence. So Joseph died . . . and they embalmed him, and he was put in a coffin in Egypt' (50:24–26).

This account of Joseph's experiences clearly contains some biblical embroidery. However, the details of his life after he is said to have interpreted successfully the dreams of Pharaoh are matched by only one person in Egyptian history – Yuya, the minister to Amenhotep III.

Chapter Five

Joseph the Patriarch

After studying the Bible and Egyptian history for a quarter of a century in the hope of establishing a link between a major biblical and historical figure, I shared the general view, which held that Yuya, a non-Egyptian, was not of any special importance.* It was only in what in retrospect seems a moment of inspiration that I changed my view. It happened one night when, unable to sleep, I made myself a pot of tea and sat down to read, as I often did, the Old Testament. The claim by Joseph the Patriarch in the Book of Genesis that he had been made 'a father to Pharaoh' seemed to leap off the page. It is a claim that nobody else in the Bible makes – and, although I was aware of it, Yuya is the only person we know of in Egyptian history to claim the same title, *it nṯr n nb tawi*, the holy father of the Lord of the Two Lands (Pharaoh's formal title). It occurs once on one of Yuya's *ushabti* (royal funeral statuette No. 51028 in the Cairo Museum catalogue) and more than twenty times on his funerary papyrus.

Could Joseph the Patriarch and Yuya be the same person? My quest for the evidence was to unlock many of the mysteries of biblical history. Among other things, it made it clear that the biblical story of Joseph the Patriarch must be dated to the 18th Dynasty (when we know Yuya lived). In the light of what can be established about the later Exodus – when Moses led the Israelites out of Egypt on the first stage of their journey to the Promised Land – it became clear that of two periods (four generations or four centuries) that the

* Some scholars believed he was a Marianu warrior.

49

Old Testament gives us for the Israelite Sojourn – the length of time they spent in Egypt – four generations is correct. This conclusion also demolishes the belief many scholars cling to, despite the evidence, that the Israelites' arrival coincided with the Hyksos conquest of the Eastern Delta, which began in 1683 BC and lasted for just over a century. Furthermore, the evidence points to the possible identity of the missing name in the list of the 70 Israelites said to have made their way down from Canaan initially to settle in Egypt.

Yuya is a particularly important figure because it was the marriage of his daughter Tiye to Amenhotep III, the Pharaoh served by Yuya, that restored the link between the Israelites and the royal house of Egypt, which had been severed nearly a century earlier when his great-grandfather, Tuthmosis III, sent the pregnant Sarah back to Canaan.

The tomb of Yuya and his wife, Tuya, was found in the Valley of the Kings in 1905. The site of their tomb was in itself considered to be a matter of some surprise. While both Yuya and Tuya were known from Egyptian historical sources, neither was considered to be of particular import-ance. Nor, as far as anyone was aware at the time, were they of royal blood, which one would expect to be the case if they were buried in the Valley of the Kings.

Yuya's tomb was the only one to be found almost intact in Egypt until the discovery of Tutankhamun's 17 years later. The two mummies lay in their coffins. Originally, Yuya's mummy (Plate 4) had been enclosed in three coffins and Tuya's in two (Plate 5), but earlier tomb robbers had evidently taken out the inner coffins and removed their lids. When Yuya's body was lifted, a necklace of large beads, made of gold and lapis lazuli and strung on a strong thread, was found behind his mummy's neck. The thread had apparently been broken in the robbers' quest for anything of value. Both mummies were so well preserved that it seemed to Arthur Weigall, one of the archaeologists involved in the dig, as if they might open their eyes and speak. Yet today, more than 90 years later, Yuya's mummy lies inside one of his inner coffins on the first floor of Cairo Museum, unseen by the millions of tourists who visit the museum each year.

Identification of Joseph the Patriarch as Yuya does not rest solely on the fact that each claimed the title 'a father to Pharaoh'. Here for reasons of space only some of the main points of evidence can be summarized (a more detailed account is to be found in my earlier book, *Stranger in the Valley of the Kings*).

Yuya Was a Foreigner. Joseph, too, was a foreigner. Many scholars have commented on the fact that unlike his wife Tuya, who had conventional Egyptian looks, Yuya was remarkably foreign in appearance. Arthur Weigall made the point in his book *The Life and Times of Akhenaten*, published in 1910:* 'He was a person of commanding presence, whose powerful character showed itself in his face. One must picture him now as a tall man, with a fine shock of white hair; a great hooked nose, like that of a Syrian; full, strong lips; and a prominent, determined jaw. He has the face of an ecclesiastic, and there is something about his mouth that reminds one of the late Pope, Leo III.'

Henri Naville, the Swiss Egyptologist, took the view that Yuya's 'very aquiline face might be Semitic'. Other scholars and experts in particular fields have voiced reservations about whether it is possible on the basis of appearance alone

---

* My own account of the life and times of Akhenaten, the son of Amenhotep III and Queen Tiye, Yuya's daughter, forms the basis of a later chapter.

to argue that Yuya was a foreigner. However, there are other indications – his name, for instance, which was not known in Egypt before his time and proved difficult to render into hieroglyphics – which point to this having been the case.

Yuya's Name. Eleven different versions of Yuya's name are to be found on his sarcophagus, the three coffins and other funerary furniture – *Ya-a, Ya, Yi-Ya, Yu-Ya, Ya-Yi, Yu, Yu-Yu, Ya-Ya, Yi-Ay, Yi-a, Yu-y.* Yet what was the name the craftsmen were trying to inscribe? Egyptian names usually indicated the name of the god under whose protection the person was placed – Ra-mos, Ptah-hotep, Tutankh-*amun* and so on. The evidence suggests that, despite the years he spent in Egypt and the high office he held, Joseph remained aloof from Egyptian religious worship. It seems therefore a reasonable assumption that, by the time Joseph died, Egyptians must have realized that he would not accept the protection of any Egyptian gods, only that of his own God, *Yhwh* (Jehovah) or *Yhwa* (the final *h* is read as an *a* in Hebrew), and what they were trying to write, following Egyptian tradition, was the name of his God.

Generally speaking, ancient Egyptian did not use vowels, although some consonants were used as long vowels. In the case of Yuya's name, long vowels were used because with foreign names no one could be expected to know the correct form of the reading.*

---

* The two parts of Yuya, 'Yu' and 'Ya', are both short. The letter 'J' in both Egyptian and Hebrew, and even German, is read 'Y' in English, so these parts are read 'Ju' or 'Jo' and 'Ja'. Which is a short form of the Israelite God 'Yahweh' or 'Jehoveh'. The biblical story tells us that Pharaoh gave Joseph an Egyptian name on his appointment as his minister, which starts with 'Zef' or 'Sef'. This was actually a real Egyptian name, and the Egyptian historian Manetho, who wrote an account of Egypt's history in Greek for Ptolemy II to be part of the Alexandrian library, confirms that Amenhotep III, who appointed Yuya as his minister, had a minister called 'Sef'. So we have both the two elements of Joseph's name, the Israelite 'Yu' and the Egyptian 'Sef', related to Yuya. The Hebrew and Arabic name for the Patriarch is 'Yosef' or 'Yusef'.

Yuya's Burial. The way Yuya was buried points to his not having been Egyptian. His ears, unlike those of most royal mummies of the 18th Dynasty, were not pierced, and the position of his hands, the palms facing his neck under the chin, is different from the usual Osiris form – Osiris was the Egyptian god of the underworld and judge of the dead – in which the dead man's hands are crossed over his chest. Yuya, as far as I am aware, is the only Egyptian mummy to be found with his hands in a different position.

Yuya's Insignia of Office. Yuya's tomb contained Pharaoh's ring and a gold chain. Pharaoh gave Joseph three objects as a sign of his office: 'And Pharaoh took off his ring from his hand, and put it on Joseph's hand, and arrayed him in vestures of fine linen, and put a gold chain about his neck' (Genesis 41:42). There were two attempts to steal small objects from Yuya's tomb, one in ancient times, just after the burial, and the other just after the tomb was opened in 1905. The ring might have disappeared because of either robbery, but we do have written evidence that one existed in the tomb. Yuya, like many other ministers, was 'bearer of the seal of the king of Lower Egypt' as well as 'bearer of the ring of the king of Lower Egypt'.

The honour bestowed on Joseph by the presentation of a gold chain was a custom mentioned in texts before the New Kingdom (the period from the 16th to the 11th centuries BC, the 18th and 19th Dynasties), but it is not until the reign of Tuthmosis IV (*c.* 1413–1405 BC), the father of Amenhotep III, that such a presentation was produced by the artist on the tomb walls. Receiving gold was looked upon as one of the highest distinctions of the time, and, as we saw earlier, Yuya had a gold necklace that had fallen inside his coffin and come to rest under his head when the thread was cut by robbers.

Chariots. Yuya's tomb contained a chariot. In the biblical account of Joseph's life we find three references to chariots. At the time of Joseph's appointment as minister we are told that

Pharaoh 'made him ride in the second chariot he had; and they cried before him, Bow the knee . . .' (Genesis 41:43). Again, when Jacob and his family arrived in Egypt, 'Joseph made ready his chariot and went up to meet Israel (Jacob) his father, to Goshen . . .' (Genesis 46:29). Finally, when Joseph set out after Jacob's death to bury his father in Canaan, 'there went up with him both chariots and horsemen . . .' (Genesis 50:9).

The first of these references suggests that Joseph had a responsibility for the chariotry. Alan Richard Schulman, the American Egyptologist, has made the point, in an article published in the *Journal of the American Research Centre in Egypt* in 1963, that '. . . in the later 18th Dynasty two ranks are attested which indicate that such a technical nuance' – chariotry as distinct from infantry – 'has come into being: Adjutant of the Chariotry, the earliest occurrence of which is known from the Amarna period (of Yuya, who was appointed as Adjutant (Deputy) of His Majesty in the Chariotry as well as Officer for the Horses) . . . which dates, most probably, to the early years of the reign of Amenhotep III'. Thus the first person in Egypt to be appointed to the position ascribed to Joseph in the Bible was Yuya, the minister to Amenhotep III.

The fact that a chariot was found in Yuya's tomb is another indication of his position. It was the custom in ancient Egypt to place in a tomb objects that had a special significance in the life of the dead person. This particular chariot is too small to have been Yuya's, yet too big to have been a model. It is possible that it belonged originally to Tuthmosis IV* when he was the young crown prince or to the

---

* Although we have no written evidence to confirm it – none of the titles found in the tomb of Yuya (Joseph) mentions Tuthmosis IV – strong indications exist that it was this king who first appointed him as his minister, and his son, Amenhotep III, confirmed Yuya in the post. While in the case of Joseph the Book of Genesis does not make this clear, the Talmud states that the Pharaoh who appointed Joseph died before him and Joseph continued in office during the reign of his successor: 'And it came to pass

young Amenhotep III, who was only about 12 when he came to the throne. This would explain why, although ornamented in gold, it was not inscribed.

'Bow the Knee'. Pharaoh ordered citizens to 'bow the knee' before Joseph (Genesis 41:43). The expression 'bow the knee' is an English translation of the Hebrew word *abrek*. It is an imperative, meaning 'do obeisance', that entered Egyptian vocabulary during the 18th Dynasty and was not known before that time.

Yuya's Wife. While it is easy to see how the name Joseph could have been transcribed into Yuya, the transformation of Asenath into Tuya, the wife of Yuya, can only be a matter of conjecture.† However, it is a fact that it was a common practice at the time for Egyptians to have several names, some of which were kept secret. Tutankhamun had three names in addition to the one we know him by. It was also the custom to use pet names as well as abbreviated forms for longer and more complex names. Some allowance must be made, too, for the fact that many centuries passed between the events described and the time they were set down in the Bible. To use a simple analogy, if the Tudor era of English history was far more remote than it is and, as in the case of Egypt, vast quantities of the relevant documents had been destroyed, it might prove difficult to establish that Queen Elizabeth I and Good Queen Bess were the same person.

The Cattle of Goshen. Two more of Yuya's titles provide a further link with the biblical story of Joseph. After the

---

... that Pharaoh the friend of Joseph died ... Before his death Pharaoh commended his son, who succeeded him, to obey Joseph in all things, and the same instructions he left in writing. This pleased the people of Egypt, for they loved Joseph and trusted implicitly in him.'

* The Egyptian origin of the name Asenath for Joseph's wife is 'Nes-net', which means 'belonging to the goddess Nut'. Nut was the sky-goddess.

Israelites had arrived in Egypt, Pharaoh is said to have told Joseph: '. . . in the best of the land of Egypt make thy father and brethren dwell; in the land of Goshen let them dwell; and if thou knowest any men of activity among them, then make them rulers over my cattle' (Genesis 47:6). One of the titles found in Yuya's tomb was Overseer of the Cattle of Min, Lord of Akhmin (a town on the east bank of the Nile, in Upper Egypt), and a second was Overseer of the Cattle of Amun.

Yuya's Lifespan. Of Joseph's burial in Egypt, the Book of Genesis says: 'So Joseph died, being an hundred and ten years old: and they embalmed him and put him in a coffin in Egypt' (50:26). From the medical report made by Sir Grafton Elliott Smith, the anatomist who examined Yuya's mummy after its discovery, we know that Yuya was probably not less than 60 at the time of his death. Smith was unable, judging by facial appearance alone, to decide the exact age, but Henri Naville, who translated Yuya's copy of *The Book of the Dead*, wrote in his subsequent commentary upon it in 1908: '. . . the artist wished to indicate that Iouiya (Yuya) was a very old man when he died: therefore he made him quite a white wig . . .'

As the average age to which people lived at the time was about 30, Ancient Egyptians considered old age to be a sign of wisdom, and those who attained long life were looked upon as holy figures. Both Joseph and Yuya were considered wise by Pharaoh. Of Joseph he said: '. . . there is none as discreet and wise as thou art' (Genesis 41:39). Yuya is also described on his funerary papyrus as 'the only wise, who loves his god'. The age Egyptians ascribed to those who lived to be wise was 110, irrespective of how old they actually were when they died. Amenhotep, son of Habu, an Egyptian magician in Yuya's time, was said to have lived 110 years although the last information we have about him puts his age at 80. Since 1865, when the British scholar Charles W. Goodwin suggested that the age the biblical narrator assigned to Joseph at the time of his death was a reflection of the Egyptian tradition, this idea has become more and more accepted by Egyptologists.

The Use of Money. In the Old Testament narration Joseph's brothers are said to have used money to pay for provisions but, before sending them on their way, Joseph restored 'every man's money into his sack' (Genesis 42:25). It used to be thought that money did not come into use in Egypt until around 950 BC and the authors of the Genesis story were reflecting the customs of their own era when they referred to money rather than payment in kind. However, recent studies have found evidence to support the idea that, at least from the reign of Amenhotep II (*c.* 1436–1413 BC), sixth ruler of the 18th Dynasty, pieces of metal – gold, silver and copper, of a fixed weight or value – were used as a means of exchange. Abd El-Mohsen Bakir, the Egyptian scholar, makes the point in his book *Slavery in Pharaonic Egypt* that a reference in a legal document of the 18th Dynasty indicates that 'two debens [about 90 grams] of silver' were paid as the price of a slave. The role that money played in the brothers' grain purchase again conforms with the situation in Egypt during the New Kingdom.

The Many-Gated City. According to the Koran, before their second visit to Egypt, accompanied by Benjamin (Joseph's younger brother), Jacob advised his sons not to enter the city by one gate:

> Further he said:
> 'O my sons! enter not
> All by one gate: enter ye
> By different gates . . .'
> [Chapter 12:67]

The same story is found in Jewish traditions: 'His brothers, fearing the evil eye, entered the city at ten different gates'

(Midrash Bereshith Rabbah 89).*

As this was to be the brothers' second visit, it is reasonable to assume that Jacob could not have known anything about the city except through hearing details of his sons' previous trip. Which city had they visited? The evidence suggests that their encounter with Joseph took place at Thebes, the capital of the 18th Dynasty kings on the Upper Nile. Thebes was known throughout the ancient world as 'the city with many gates' and the Greek poet Homer mentioned it around the 8th century BC as 'the hundred-gated city'. This does not refer to entrances through the city's walls, but to gates belonging to its temples and palaces.

Identification of Joseph as Yuya provides further support in the form of chronology for my earlier identification of Tuthmosis III (David) as the father of Isaac. Joseph is thought to have arrived in Egypt and been appointed to his first post as a minister during the brief reign of Tuthmosis IV (*c.* 1413–1405 BC). His father Amenhotep II ruled slightly longer (*c.* 1436–1413 BC). Even the combined total of their reigns, 31 years, does not provide sufficient time for Isaac to father the twins Esau and Jacob, Jacob to father Joseph, and Joseph to arrive in Egypt as either a teenager or grown man. The problem is resolved, however, once Tuthmosis III, who ruled for 54 years (*c.* 1490–1436 BC), is introduced into the equation.

Chapter Six

Pharaoh's Queen

The Book of Genesis makes no mention of Joseph having fathered a daughter as well as the two sons, Manasseh (Anen) and Ephraim (Aye), who were already with him in Egypt at the time the tribes of Israel made their Descent from Canaan to join him. This is not to say that he did not have a daughter. It has been suggested that she is the 70th name missing from the list of Israelite immigrants in the Book of Genesis.

Her absence from the list may be simply explained by the fact that it was the practice for biblical scribes to omit women's names unless they had played a significant role in the story being told, a practice that often suggests the Hebrews fathered only male descendants. A more plausible explanation, once the identification of Joseph as Yuya is accepted, argues that Joseph's daughter in her turn is to be identified as Yuya's daughter Tiye (Plate 10) who, despite being half-Israelite, became Queen of Egypt, and that, to mask the Israelite-Egyptian connection, when the Book of Genesis was set down in writing many centuries after the events it describes, her name was excised from the Old Testament as a result of bitter memories of the Exodus – bitterness that still survives in politics today.

If, as we saw earlier, it was Tuthmosis IV who appointed Yuya (Joseph) initially to the post of minister, this

---

* These traditions were transmitted orally before being written. The biblical narrator left some of it out either because he did not know it, or did not regard it as important or suitable.

sequence of events would make sense of what happened after the death of Amenhotep III's father in 1405 BC when Amenhotep III (Plate 9) was only about 12 years of age. In accordance with Egyptian custom he married his sister, Sitamun, in order to inherit the throne, but shortly afterwards married Tiye, the daughter of Yuya and Tuya, and made her rather than Sitamun his Great Royal Wife (queen). At the time of these marriages Sitamun is thought to have been about three years of age and Tiye eight.*

The childhood romance between Amenhotep III and Tiye can be explained by the posts held by both her parents, which meant that the two children grew up together. As a minister to both pharaohs, responsible for the chariots, a similar unit to the king's guard, Yuya would have been required to live in the royal residence. This was also true of his wife, Tuya, who was the king's 'ornament' (*khrt nsw*), a position which might be said to combine the duties of a modern butler and lady-in-waiting, and could also indicate that she had been the king's nanny. It has also been suggested that Tiye was acceptable as a bride for the young king because Tuya, her mother, was herself of royal blood. Arthur Weigall makes the point in his book *The Life and Times of Akhenaten* that she 'may have been . . . the grand-daughter of Tuthmosis III [David], to whom she bears some likeness of face' (Weigall here refers to Tuya's mummy). This view is supported by three titles found in her tomb – 'favoured of the good god (the king)', 'favoured of Horus in his house (the king in his palace)', 'favoured of Horus, Lord of this land' – and the fact that Tiye, the daughter of her marriage to Yuya, is often referred to as 'royal daughter'. This, Weigall argues, would also help to explain why she and Yuya were given such a fine tomb in the Valley of the Kings.

The fact that the marriage of Amenhotep III and Tiye took place early in his reign is established by two of five commemorative scarabs (sacred beetles – see Plate 6) issued by the king and discovered in the latter part of the last century. The first, reporting the marriage, reads in part: 'Live

. . . King Amenhotep [III], who is given life, [and] the Great King's-Wife Tiye, who liveth. The name of her father is Yuya, the name of her mother is Tuya. She is the wife of a mighty king whose southern boundary is as far as Karoy and northern as far as Naharin.' The mention of Karoy in the Sudan and Naharin in northern Iraq essentially establishes Amenhotep III's empire as stretching from the Nile to the Euphrates. No date is given here. That the marriage took place early in his reign is clear, however, from the second scarab, relating to a wild-cattle hunt that took place in the king's Year 2 (1404 BC). Here Tiye is described as 'the Great Royal Wife'.

After their wedding, Amenhotep III presented Tiye with the frontier fortress of Zarw (in the area of modern Quantara East of the Suez Canal) as a kind of summer palace so that she could be near her Israelite relatives, settled at Goshen (beyond Egypt proper, because shepherds were still 'an abomination'). Goshen was in those days linked with the fortress of Zarw by water. The last of the above scarabs describes the construction of a pleasure lake for Queen Tiye at Zarw in Year 11 (1395 BC) of Amenhotep III's reign. Six versions of the scarab have been found. Although there are some minor differences, they all agree on the main points of the text, which runs as follows:

> *Year 11, third month of Inundation (first season), day 1,*
> *under the majesty of Horus . . . mighty valour, who*
> *smites the Asiatics, King of Upper and Lower Egypt,*
> *Neb-maat-Ra, Son of Ra Amenhotep Ruler of Thebes,*

---

* Some scholars have argued – wrongly, I think – that Sitamun was the daughter of Amenhotep III and Tiye rather than the infant sister he married in order to inherit the throne. Without going into all the details, the latter view is reinforced by the inscription on a kohl (powder) tube, which probably came from Sitamun's palace at Thebes and is now in the Metropolitan Museum in New York. It reads in part, '. . . King's Great Wife (Sit-Amun)', suggesting she is challenging Tiye over a title Sitamun felt should rightly have belonged to her.

who is given life, and the Great Royal Wife Tiye, who
liveth. His Majesty commanded the making of a lake for
the Great King's Wife Tiye, who liveth, in her city of
Zarwkha (kha signifies city). Its length 3,700 cubits
(about 1,020 yards), its breadth 700 cubits (200
yards).* His Majesty celebrated the feast of the opening
of the lake in the third month of the first season, day 16,
when His Majesty sailed thereon in the royal barge
Aten Gleams.

The Egyptians had three seasons, Inundation, Winter and
Gathering, each of four months, with the year beginning in
mid-July. Thus the third month of the first season would be
October of the king's Year 11, 1395 BC.

These scarabs suggest that Queen Tiye enjoyed an idyllic
marriage to an immensely rich, powerful and indulgent
husband, happy to grant her every wish, even to presenting
her with a summer palace, so that she could be close to her
Israelite relatives in Goshen, together with a pleasure lake.
However, the man at her side on that October day, when they
were enjoying a kind of second honeymoon, could foresee –
because his wife was not the heiress and only half-Egyptian
– a serious crisis ahead over his line of succession if his
wife's expected child proved to be a boy, a crisis that would
not be easy to resolve, even for Amenhotep III. Today, 3,500
years later, he still enjoys the reputation of someone who was
infinitely wise.

Amenhotep III was Solomon.

Solomon is presented to us in the Old Testament in a number
of guises: King of Israel, who succeeded his father, David, in
the 10th century BC; the son of David and Bathsheba,
adulterous wife of Uriah the Hittite; commander of a vast
army of men and a host of chariots ('a thousand and four
hundred' and 'twelve thousand horsemen' according to I
Kings 10:26); overlord of a vast empire that underwent
decline during his reign; the husband of Pharaoh's daughter;

and the lover of 'many strange women, together with the daughter of Pharaoh' (I Kings 11:1).

Here we find ourselves facing a similar situation to that encountered earlier in this book where the Old Testament presented us with two contrasting characters for David – a mighty warrior who created an empire stretching from the Nile to the Euphrates (Tuthmosis III, *c.* 1490–1436 BC) and a modest tribal chief who lived in the 10th century BC – and events separated by five centuries which are lumped together as if they happened at the same time. Now we have to deal with two Solomons. To examine briefly some of the attributes ascribed to him in the Book of I Kings:

- Solomon cannot have succeeded his father David in the 10th century BC because David (Tuthmosis III), as we have seen, lived five centuries earlier and was, in fact, not his father but his great-grandfather;
- In the Old Testament one often comes across accounts where the oral memory of ancient events is retold in a fictionalized form with different characters and a different time-scale. I believe the David (Tuthmosis III)-Bathsheba-Uriah story found in the Book of II Samuel should be seen as another version of the David (Tuthmosis III)-Sarah-Abraham story, related in the earlier Book of Genesis, in which – to refresh memories in the matter – the king married Sarah and, on discovering that Sarah was Abraham's wife, sent the couple back to Canaan where the pregnant Sarah gave birth to Isaac, the king's son.

The David-Bathsheba-Uriah story is set in the fortress of Jerusalem while Tuthmosis III was staying there during the siege of Megiddo (Armageddon), the first military encounter of his campaign, shortly after Hatshepsut's death, to restore

* One of the scarabs, a copy of which is in the Vatican, gives the breadth as 600 cubits, and also mentions the names of the queen's parents, Yuya and Tuya, indicating that they were still alive at the time.

the Egyptian empire stretching from the Nile to the Euphrates. It is said that he made inquiries about the identity of Bathsheba after seeing her bathing. Despite being told that she was the wife of Uriah the Hittite, who was serving with the king's forces at Megiddo, David sent messengers to bring her to his house where 'he lay with her' (II Samuel 11:4).

As a result of this liaison, Bathsheba became pregnant. In the hope of disguising his guilt, David had Uriah brought to Jerusalem, but the warrior refused to sleep in the comfort of his own home while the king's army suffered the hardships of living in tents outside besieged Megiddo. David therefore sent him back to the front accompanied by the order: 'Set ye Uriah in the forefront of the hottest battle . . . that he may be smitten and die' (II Samuel 11:15). Once Uriah had met his death, David married Bathsheba, who bore him a son.

Up to this point, both stories are remarkably similar. Both Abraham and Uriah are foreigners, Abraham a Canaanite in Egypt, Uriah a Hittite in Jerusalem. In each case their wives are made pregnant by a king and give birth to a son. The fate of the two 'children of sin' is different, however. In the case of Abraham we have a hint of moral disapproval of the circumstances that led to the birth of Isaac: he is said to have been tempted by God initially to offer Isaac as 'a burnt offering' (Genesis 22:2), but after Abraham responded to the temptation Isaac's life was spared and Abraham took a ram 'and offered him up for a burnt offering in the stead of his son' (22:13).

In the case of David we find a more precise moral judgement. We are told that after David had caused the death of Uriah and married Bathsheba, who bore him a son, 'the thing that David had done displeased the Lord. And the Lord sent [unto David] Nathan [the prophet] who said to David, . . . Wherefore hast thou despised the commandment of the Lord, to do evil in his sight? thou hast killed Uriah with the sword, and has taken his wife to be thy wife . . . Now therefore the sword shall never depart from thine house . . . the child also that is born unto thee shall surely die' (II Samuel 11:27,

12:1,9–10,14).

These condemnations were followed by the promise that the awaited child, which proved to be very sick, would not survive. This un-named boy died on the seventh day and David 'comforted Bathsheba his wife, and went in unto her, and lay with her: and she bare a son: and he called his name Solomon . . .' (12:24).

Hermann Gunkel, the distinguished German biblical scholar, dismisses the whole story of Uriah and his wife as having no historical basis. This is not the case. The names used in these fictional accounts based on real events usually point to the identity of the original historical characters and, as a rule, provide evidence that we are dealing with fact disguised as fiction. This is clearly the case with the name Uriah. It is composed of two elements – Ur, a Mesopotamian word meaning 'city' or 'light', and Yah (iah), which is the short form of Jehovah, the Israelite God. The meaning of the name could therefore be 'Jehovah's light'. Yet he is described as being a Hittite. How can we accept that a Hittite, a traditional enemy of Egypt and the Israelites, could be a worshipper of the Israelite God and one of the heroes of David's army? Nor do we have any information to explain the sudden appearance of this foreigner and his wife in Jerusalem, where they seem to have had their home.

To look at the matter from another point of view, Ur, the first part of Uriah's name, relates him to the birthplace of Abraham. The first reference to this in the Bible describes how Abraham and Sarah 'went forth . . . from Ur of the Chaldees, to go into the land of Canaan' (Genesis 11:31). This could mean either 'a city of the Chaldees' or, if the word Ur was used as a proper noun, 'Ur of the Chaldees'. Whatever the situation regarding this early reference, later on Ur certainly became a proper noun indicating the birthplace of Abraham. Thus the name Ur-iah relates the invented character both to the God of Abraham and to the city of Abraham's origin.

We have a similar situation with the name Bathsheba. Here again we have two elements – Beth, meaning 'a girl' or 'a daughter', and Sheba, an area to the south of Canaan that takes its name from the local well, Beer-Sheba. The name Beth-Sheba can therefore be interpreted as 'a girl (or daughter) of Sheba', which was the area in which Sarah and Abraham settled after their return from Egypt.

The statement that Solomon commanded a vast army and was overlord of a huge empire that underwent decline during his reign finds no historical support in the 10th century BC, by which time the empire founded 500 years earlier by Tuthmosis III, the great-grandfather of Amenhotep III, had ceased to exist. The description of Solomon as the husband of Pharaoh's daughter also cannot be true. He would have had to be a member of the royal house of Egypt rather than King of Israel before he was able to marry an Egyptian princess.

We know from the Amarna letters – the foreign archives of the 18th Dynasty, a period of rule that lasted roughly from 1575 to 1335 BC – that it was not the custom of Egyptian kings to give their daughters in marriage to foreign rulers. The reference to marriage to Pharaoh's daughter reflects the fact that Amenhotep III married his infant sister, Sitamun, in order, as was the Egyptian custom, to inherit the throne.

The Old Testament also assures us that Solomon was both rich and extremely wise: 'So King Solomon exceeded all the kings of the earth for riches and for wisdom' (I Kings 10:23). The best-known story about the wisdom of Solomon is the dispute between two mothers over the parenthood of a child, to be found in I Kings 3:16–28. Each of the women, who lived in the same house, gave birth to a baby boy. One of the babies died, however, and both women claimed the surviving child as her own and eventually came before the king with their dispute. Thereupon Solomon ordered the child to be cut in half with a sword, and one half to be given to each woman. This immediately helped to identify the real mother, who tried to save the boy's life by asking for the child to be given to the other woman.

It is hardly to be believed that the king, who had professional judges and officials, would involve himself personally in such a dispute between two women, who are described in the Bible as harlots. In fact, I believe that we are dealing here with another story that is being told with a different cast: the real story concerns the circumstances surrounding the birth of Moses and Pharaoh's threat to kill him, which will be the subject of a subsequent chapter.

Solomon's reputation for wisdom, as well as the name by which he is known, does not rest on resolving a dispute over the motherhood of a child, but on the masterful way he – or, rather, Amenhotep III – ruled Egypt and the vast empire founded originally by his great-grandfather, Tuthmosis III (David), an empire that encompassed 'all the kingdoms from the river (Euphrates) unto the land of the Philistines, and unto the border of Egypt' (I Kings 4:21). An important element of his rule was his marriages to 'many strange women' – princesses from neighbouring states with whom, because of these marriages, Egypt enjoyed peaceful relations and avoided costly wars.

Chapter Seven

The Wisdom of Solomon

The task of identifying the historical Solomon is complicated not only by the biblical red herrings we have already looked at, but by the fact that we have no historical record of a king of that name. It is only when we match in detail the Old Testament account of his exploits with the reign of Amenhotep III that it becomes clear we are dealing with the same person.

The actual name Solomon derives from the Semitic word *salaam* and means 'safety' or 'peace'. Other than a minor military operation in northern Sudan during his Year 5 (1401 BC), Amenhotep III's reign was almost entirely peaceful. He was the first ruler of the Egyptian empire who did not launch any military campaigns in western Asia. Instead, he relied on alliances and exchanges of gifts and diplomatic letters between himself and other leaders of the then-known world to create a climate of international friendship. He also furthered the cause of peace by a series of judicious marriages to 'strange women' – two princesses from Syria, Mitanni and Babylonia, and one from Arzawa in south-western Asia Minor. The extravagance of the age is indicated by the fact that Gilukhepa, one of his Mitannian wives, is said to have arrived in Egypt with a caravan that included more than 300 ladies-in-waiting.

The passage about Solomon's marriage to 'strange women' is followed by a warning from the Lord that 'surely they will turn away your heart after their gods: Solomon clave unto these in love' (I Kings 11:2). Shortly afterwards we are told that 'it came to pass, when Solomon was old, that his wives turned away his heart after other gods: and his heart was not perfect with the Lord his God . . . For Solomon went after Ashtoreth* the goddess of the Zidonians,† and after Milcom the abomination of the Ammonites' (11:4–5). This sequence of events can hardly ask for greater confirmation than we find in the historical evidence relating to the reign of Amenhotep III. Although there are many indications that he became converted to the worship of Aten, who was to be introduced into Egypt a few decades later as a monotheistic God, he also worshipped other gods. Towards the end of his life he suffered severe dental problems, as shown by his mummy, where his teeth were found to be badly worn and his gums riddled with abscesses. This could be the reason why Tushratta of Mitanni, his brother-in-law, sent him an image of the Mitannian goddess Ishtar in Amenhotep III's Year 35 (1371 BC), hoping – in vain – that her magic would effect a cure.

The possession of a large and secure empire, and not having to fight any wars, are said to have enabled Solomon (Amenhotep III) to embark on a large number of projects and administrative reforms. According to Otto Eissfeldt, the German biblical scholar, there were five characteristic features of Solomon's reign:

1) Change in his kingdom's military organization and the introduction of chariotry as an essential arm of war;
2) The creation of new administrative districts;
3) Changes in the taxation system;
4) The refinement of court procedure and the maintenance of diplomatic relations with foreign courts; and
5) Building activity on a large scale, including the royal palace and its adjoining temple, and fortified barracks for his garrisons in the north.

All of these can be related to the life and times of Amenhotep III, as I shall show:

---

* Or Astarte, the great goddess (and Queen of Heaven) of ancient Phoenicia and the Near East.

† Or Sidonians, the people of the ancient port of Sidon, the oldest Phoenician city, built in the 3rd millennium BC.

Military Organization. Tuthmosis III, who founded the great Egyptian empire in the 15th century BC, did have a strong, well-trained, well-organized army equipped with the best chariots of his age, otherwise he would not have been able to establish his extended empire. However, the American Egyptologist Alan Richard Schulman has shown that the chariotry formed only a part of the army at this time. It was not until the early part of the reign of Amenhotep III that the chariotry became identified as a separate entity from the infantry, with Yuya (Joseph), as we saw earlier, the first minister we know to bear the title Deputy of His Majesty in the Chariotry. Thus it was Amenhotep III (Solomon) who organized the chariotry as a separate unit of warfare.

Administrative System. Structure of the administrative system up to the time of Solomon was, according to the Bible, tribal. Solomon did away with tribal divisions and united Israel, together with other parts of the empire, in one political entity: 'And Solomon had twelve officers over all Israel, which provided victuals for the king and his household: each man his month in a year made provision' (I Kings 4:7). Yet, if we examine the matter closely, we find that this administrative system does not belong to the Palestinian Israel, but to the Egyptian empire.

From as early as 3000 BC, the Egyptian administration controlled the activities of the Two Lands of Egypt. It organized the royal court as well as the economy in the name of the king, the official owner of all the land. Palace officials were responsible for each administrative region, where there was another high official with a local bureaucracy under his control. During the empire period – and particularly during the time of Tuthmosis III (David) – the administrative system was reorganized to suit the needs of the age, and later further developed by Amenhotep III. It was then that, for the purposes of taxation, the empire was arranged in 12 administrative sections, an arrangement that the biblical narrator drew on for his account of the king the world now knows as Solomon.

Almost all scholars agree* that the taxation system that the Bible says was introduced by Solomon matches precisely the system that was used in Egypt after Tuthmosis III had established the new Egyptian empire. Each of the 12 areas was the responsibility of a high official and was expected to contribute sufficient tax to cover the country's needs for one month of the year.

Administration. Coping with the administrative burdens of a vast empire needed a highly developed administration. The sudden appearance of such a supposed administration in Israelite tribal society during the 'United Monarchy of David and Solomon' in the 10th century BC, without any roots in the nation's previous history and followed by its sudden disappearance after Solomon's death, has been a source of puzzlement to scholars. The apparent contradiction is resolved, however, once identification of the historical David (Tuthmosis III) and Solomon (Amenhotep III) makes it clear that the sophisticated administration described in the Old Testament is the administration established by these two monarchs in the 15th and 14th centuries BC to deal with the day-to-day task of ruling Egypt and its empire.

The Names of Court Officials of Solomon. We find among the list of officials the priests, the scribes, the commander-in-chief of the army, the official in charge of the palace and another in charge of the tribute. All of these new offices are similar to appointments made by Amenhotep III. Even the forced labour pressed into service in Egypt for the king's building projects is said to have been imposed for the first time by Solomon (Amenhotep III) on native Israelites as well as foreigners: 'And king Solomon raised a levy out of all Israel; and the levy was thirty thousand men' (I Kings 5:13). The number of senior officials argues for a large number of

* For example, the German scholar Otto Eissfeldt, who wrote about this subject in *The Cambridge Ancient History*, 1975.

minor ones. I Kings 9:23 gives a figure of 550 simply to supervise labour.

Empire in Decline. According to the Bible, the empire inherited by Solomon became to some extent weakened during the course of his reign. He faced troubles in Edom (in southern Palestine). His influence in Syria was also weakened when Rezon is said to have seized Damascus and made himself king there.

These rebellions find their echo in the Amarna letters, the foreign archives of the 18th Dynasty, relating to the reign of Amenhotep III. Frederick J. Giles, the Canadian Egyptologist who made a study of them, came to the conclusion that 'most of the letters that deal with the alleged collapse of the Egyptian empire during the Amarna period' come from the period of his rule. Thus the biblical account of changes in King David's empire during the time of Solomon can be seen to agree with historical records relating to events during the reign of Amenhotep III.

Letters sent by Canaanite kings, especially Abdi-khiba of Jerusalem, speak of continuous trouble in the area of Edom and southern Palestine: 'All the king's land is rebellious.' These problems in southern Palestine were not so serious that they led to any weakening of the king's control in the area, but the situation in northern Syria was far more critical. Even before Amenhotep III came to the throne, the northern Mesopotamian kingdom of Mitanni, to the east of the Euphrates, defeated by Tuthmosis III, had begun to reassert its influence over city states in northern Syria. Amenhotep III responded to this threat by a peace treaty with the King of Mitanni and marriage to two Mitannian princesses. He also sent the King of Mitanni thirty units of gold each year in return for his protecting the north Syrian section of the empire.

However, Amenhotep III's problems in the region were not yet over. Towards the end of his reign, the king's authority over the northern part of the empire, including

Damascus, was endangered by the powerful Hittite* king, Suppiluliuma. He also posed a threat to Mitanni, Egypt's ally in the area. Akizzi, ruler of the northern Syrian city of Qatna, a few miles north of Qadesh, spoke of these dangers in letters to Amenhotep III: 'To King Annumuria (Amenhotep III), Son of the Sun, my Lord, thus [says] this thy servant Akizzi . . . I am afraid . . . men who are destroyers serve the king of the land of the Hittites: he sends them forth . . .'

In a following letter, Akizzi informed the king that the land of Ubi, west of Damascus, was under threat: 'Just as Damascus . . . is terror-stricken at the league of the enemy, and is lifting up its hands in supplication at the feet of the king, so likewise does the city of Qatna lift up its hands.'

The Amarna letters also throw some light on the biblical account which states: 'King Solomon gave to Hiram (the king of Tyre) twenty cities in the land of Galilee' (I Kings 9:11). The name of Tyre's king in these letters is not Hiram, but Abimilichi. From his letters we know that: 'The king, my Lord, hath appointed me the guardian of the city of Tyre . . .' In another letter, No. 99, in the Berlin Museum, Abimilichi asked the king to 'give the city of Huzu to his servant'. In yet another letter, No. 29, which is to be found in the British Museum, the King of Tyre indicated that another of the

---

* The Hittites were an Asiatic people who settled in Anatolia in the 3rd millennium BC, and who spoke an Indo-European language. Their capital was at Hattusas, at the site known as Boghazkoy. They invaded Syria and northern Mesopotamia during the 16th century BC, but were driven out by Tuthmosis III in his campaigns during the 15th century BC. From the time of the Amarna kings in Egypt (14th century BC) they conquered northern Syria and threatened Egyptian influence in western Asia. The most famous military confrontation with Egypt took place during the early reign of Ramses II of the 19th Dynasty, which culminated in the celebrated battle of Qadesh in 1274 BC. This was followed by a peace treaty between Ramses II and the Hittites, which allowed them to keep control of northern Syria. The Hittite kingdom completely disappeared in the 12th century BC, when it was invaded by the 'Sea People' who came from the Greek islands.

Egyptian cities had been placed under his control: 'And now the city Zarbitu is to be guarded by the city of Tyre for the king, my Lord.'

The Builder. Solomon is said to have been a master creator of spectacular buildings. He built 'the house of the Lord, and his own house, and Millo (the filling material used to enlarge the surface area of Jerusalem on the top of the mountain), and the wall of Jerusalem, and Hazor, and Megiddo, and Gezer' (I Kings 9:15), and 'Beth-horon the nether, And Baalath and Tadmor in the wilderness . . . And all the cities of store that Solomon had, and cities for his chariots, and cities for his horsemen, and that which Solomon desired to build in Jerusalem, and in Lebanon, and in all the land of his dominion' (I Kings 9:17–19). Further reference to this mass of building work, including 'store cities, which he built in Hamath', is to be found in II Chronicles 8:4–6. From these biblical accounts we can conclude that Solomon built: 1) garrisons and fortifications; 2) the Millo; 3) a royal palace; and 4) a temple.

We have archaeological evidence in the case of only three of the places listed – Hazor, Megiddo and Gezer. All were among the western Asiatic cities conquered by Tuthmosis III in the middle of the 15th century BC. This has been confirmed by archaeological digging, which has produced evidence of each city's destruction in the right strata for this period. In addition, in all three cases evidence has been found of large-scale reconstruction work half a century later during the reign of Amenhotep III. New royal palaces, temples, ordinary houses and fortifying walls were established. In each case a local ruler was appointed, paying tribute to Pharaoh and enjoying the support of an Egyptian garrison. Egyptian objects, including a cartouche of Amenhotep III, were found in the strata belonging to this period, as was also the case in other excavated cities of Canaan such as Beth-shean and Lachish. Evidence of the cities' wealth and trade was found. It was clearly in this period – during the 14th

The land of Solomon's empire

century BC – that these cities prospered.

The British archaeologist Kathleen Kenyon succeeded in uncovering the remains of the Millo, inserted to widen the upper surface of the rock on which the ancient fortress of Jerusalem was built by extending its limits towards the sloping ground to the east. She was also able to date the first construction of the Millo to the 14th century BC, the time of Amenhotep III.

One of the major building achievements attributed to Solomon was the new royal house, reputed to have taken 13 years to complete. This great palace is said to have been constructed to the north of the ancient city of Jerusalem and south of the temple area, yet no further biblical mention of it is made during the period that is said to have followed the supposed time of Solomon's death. Moreover, although Jerusalem has been extensively excavated, no remains of such a palace have been found. However, when we compare the biblical description of Solomon's royal palace with the great palace of Amenhotep III at Thebes, it becomes clear that this was the royal residence described by the biblical narrator.

From the account in I Kings 7:2–12 we can see that Solomon's palace consisted of five elements: 1) the king's palace; 2) the house of Pharaoh's daughter, 'whom he had taken to wife'; 3) the throne room; 4) a hall of columns; and 5) the house of the forest of Lebanon. The foundations were of costly stones while pillars of Lebanon cedarwood supported the roofs.

Up to the time of Amenhotep III, although Thebes was the religious and administrative capital of Egypt, the main royal residence was at Memphis, on the west bank of the Nile a few miles to the south of the Great Pyramid of Giza. With the vast wealth of his empire at his disposal and no wars to fight, Amenhotep III embarked on the construction of a great royal complex at Thebes. His own palace was ready by Year 8 (1398 BC) of his reign, but the whole complex was not completed until towards the end of his third decade (1375

BC). The area of the palace was excavated between 1910 and 1920 by the Egyptian Expedition of the Metropolitan Museum of Art of New York. From the result of these excavations we can see that, although they form part of a much larger complex, the five elements ascribed to Solomon's palace are to be found in Amenhotep III's palace at Thebes.

The King's Palace. This was the oldest and most important building, occupying the south-east quarter of the great complex and adjoined on the east by its kitchens, offices and store-rooms. It had also a section for the king's harem and was connected with a smaller palace, the residence of Queen Tiye, daughter of the king's high official, Yuya.

The House of Pharaoh's Daughter. As we saw before, Amenhotep III married his sister Sitamun, the daughter of Tuthmosis IV, in order to gain his right to the throne, which was the Egyptian custom. William C. Hayes, the American scholar, commented in an article in the *Journal of Near Eastern Studies* in 1951: '. . . the great North Palace . . . appears to have been the residence of an extremely important royal lady, quite possibly Queen Sitamun'.

The Throne Room. The reception quarters consist of a large squarish hall with many rows of columns in wood and a throne dais set along the axis of the entrance corridor, a second, smaller hypostyle (columned) hall with a throne dais near it, a throne room and a bedroom.

The Hall of Columns. Hayes describes this as 'the royal Audience Pavilion, its floor elevated above the surrounding terrain, its northern facade provided with a balcony-like projection jutting out into a deep, colonnaded courtyard'. ('And he made a porch of pillars . . . and the other pillars and the thick beam were before them' [I Kings 7:6].)

The House of the Forest of Lebanon. This was, according

to Hayes, a 'Festival Hall, prepared for the celebration of Amenhotep III's second *sed* [rejuvenation] festival', a big colonnaded building that extended at the very north of the palace complex. The complex also included houses for other members of the royal family as well as court officials and servants. Exactly as the Bible says, all the pillars were of cedarwood imported from Lebanon. Alexander Badawy, an Egyptian scholar, gives a detailed description of the hall in his book *A History of Egyptian Architecture*: 'Ceilings were of timber rafters, covered beneath with lath and plaster and painted with a series of protecting Nekhebet vultures* in the official halls and in the bedroom of Pharaoh, or with vines within a frame of rosettes and chequered pattern, spirals and bulls' heads, similar to Aegean ornament. Floors were decorated in the same technique to represent a pool with papyrus, lotus and fowl.'

Badawy's description of the floor of the smaller hypostyle hall with a throne dais near it suggests that an incident, described in the Koran, during a visit by the Queen of Sheba to Solomon can only have taken place in this room where 'the floor resembles a water basin filled with fish, aquatic plants, swimming ducks, geese and land birds, and bordered by papyrus and plants . . .' In describing the Queen of Sheba's visit, the Koran tells how:

> She was asked to enter
> That lofty Palace: but
> When she saw it, she
> Thought it was a lake
> Of water, and she (tucked up
> Her skirts), uncovering her legs.
> He said: 'This is
> But a palace paved

---

* Nekhebet was a vulture-goddess whose iconographic significance was firmly rooted in the dual nature of the Egyptian kingship. She and the cobra-goddess Wazyt represented dominion over the Two Lands of Egypt.

Smooth with slabs of glass.'
She said: 'O my Lord!
I have indeed wronged
My soul . . .'
[The Ants Chapter 44]

Amenhotep III is known to have built many temples, both in Egypt and in Canaan. He began his building programme in his Year 2. The sites of his temples for different deities, including himself, were at Hermopolis, opposite Amarna (the new capital that would be founded by his son, Akhenaten), two temples at Karnak to the north of Thebes, the great Luxor temple in Thebes itself, three temples in Nubia, his mortuary temple north of his palace complex in western Thebes, and temples in almost all the Canaanite cities that had Egyptian garrisons.

According to the Bible, much precious material was used in the construction of Solomon's temple. This is equally true of the mortuary temple that Amenhotep III built at western Thebes. The king himself has given a description of it on the other side of the stele known as the Israel Stele, which came from this temple and was used later by Merenptah, the fourth king of the 19th Dynasty, to give an account of the Libyan war in his Year 5. Amenhotep III describes the temple as:

. . . an everlasting fortress of sandstone, embellished with gold throughout, its floor shining with silver and all its doorways with electrum [alloy of silver and gold]. It is wide and very long, adorned for eternity, and made festive with this exceptionally large stele. It is extended with royal statues of granite, of quartzite and precious stones, fashioned to last for ever. They are higher than the rising of the heavens: their rays are in men's faces like the rising sun . . . Its workshops are filled with male and female slaves, the children of chieftains of all the countries which my majesty conquered. Its magazines have stored up uncountable

*riches. It is surrounded by villages of Syrians, peopled
with children of chieftains; its cattle are like the sands
of the shore, totalling millions.*

On the subject of the riches used by Amenhotep III in his
construction of temples, Donald B. Redford of Toronto
University says in his book *Akhenaten the Heretic King*:
'The recorded figures of metals and precious stones that went
into the Montu temple (one of the Karnak temples) is quite
staggering: 3.25 tons of electrum, 2.5 tons of gold, 924 tons
of copper, 1,250 pounds of lapis lazuli, 215 pounds of
turquoise, 1.5 tons of bronze and over 10 tons of beaten
copper. Such was the return on Egypt's investment in an
empire!'

To summarize, we have historical and archaeological
evidence of buildings during the reign of Amenhotep III that
matches the building attributed to Solomon, who ruled *four
centuries earlier* than the present composition of the Old
Testament would have us believe. Now we can see why,
despite diligent efforts by biblical scholars, historians and
archaeologists, no single piece of evidence has been found in
Palestine to support what has become known as the period in
the 10th century BC of the United Monarchy of David and
Solomon. The absence of such evidence does not mean that
they are not historical characters, but that scholars have been
confused by the nature of the biblical account and have been
seeking their evidence in the wrong century.

This was a golden age for Egypt. A combination of
diplomacy, judicious marriages and equally judicious use of
gold had secured a balance of power, at least temporarily,
between Egypt and the neighbouring Hurrian state of
Mitanni, the Hittites, the Assyrians and Babylonians.
Palestine and Syria, conquered by Tuthmosis III (David) in
the middle of the 15th century BC, posed no threat; the
southern frontier had been secured up to and beyond the
Nile's Fourth Cataract. Luxuries from the Levant and the

Aegean world poured into the country on a greater scale than ever before, more land was brought under cultivation, art flourished,* prosperous state officials and priests enjoyed the pleasures of new town houses and country villas with large estates. How the common people fared is less clear, but they must have benefited from the general prosperity and state projects that offered alternative employment during long summer droughts. Throughout the country, new temples were founded, old ones restored. It was into this peaceful, opulent world that Moses was born – to face the instant threat, we are told, of being murdered on his father's orders.

---

* The Amarna art renaissance, which started from the time of Amenhotep III, produced great works in both the naturalistic and romantic styles. The objects found in Tutankhamun's tomb, including his mask, are samples of this new art.

Chapter Eight

The Royal Birth of Moses

The account of the birth of Moses in the opening chapters of the Book of Exodus is a classic example of how the true course of events can become distorted when a story, as in this case, has been the subject of a long oral tradition before being set down in writing. The first chapter of the Book of Exodus introduces an immediate note of confusion. It suggests that the birth of Moses coincided with a number of events that we know from Egyptian historical sources did not occur until more than half a century later, and it makes a number of statements that are obviously contradictory.

We are told initially that the land was 'filled with' Israelites (1:7). This can hardly have been the case when all the evidence from other sources points to Moses having been born only a couple of decades after Jacob, his grandfather, led the group of 66 Israelites on their journey from Canaan to Egypt to join his son Yuya (Joseph). That we are dealing with events that postdate the birth of Moses by several decades is clear from the next verse where we have a reference to the appearance of a new king 'who knew not Joseph'. Until the time of Horemheb, the last ruler of the 18th Dynasty who came to the throne nearly half a century later, there is no king of whom it can strictly be said that he did not know Joseph, since all four of the kings who preceded Horemheb – Akhenaten, Semenhkhare, Tutankhamun and Aye – were, as we shall see, descendants of Yuya (Joseph). Next comes an account of the Oppression when the Egyptians set the Israelites to the task of building the treasure cities of Pithom and Raamses and made their lives 'bitter with hard bondage, in mortar, and in brick, in all manner of service in the field' (1:14). These events, again, can be dated to the reign of Horemheb.

The muddled nature of this chronology is made clear yet again when we are told that – just as Moses is about to be born – the ruling Pharaoh ordered that all male Israelite children are to be killed at birth. He instructed the midwives: 'When ye do the office of a midwife to the Hebrew woman . . . if it be a son then ye shall kill him.' At the time, however, the Israelites are said to have had only two midwives, 'of which the name of the one was Shiphrah, and the name of the other Puah' (1:15). This argues again that we are reading about events that happened *early* in the Israelite Sojourn in Egypt, when only two midwives were sufficient for the needs of the Israelite women. The fact that the Pharaoh was able to speak to the midwives in person also implies that when he gave this order he would have had to be living in the vicinity of Goshen, the location outside the frontiers of Egypt proper where the Israelites had been allowed to settle. The midwives failed to carry out Pharaoh's orders, explaining, when questioned, that 'Hebrew women . . . are lively, and are delivered ere the midwives come in unto them'. Pharaoh then issued a further edict: 'Every son that is born ye shall cast into the river . . .' (1:22).

Despite the muddled chronology it is clear that the target of Pharaoh's hostility, the child he wished dead, was Moses because, as his mother was not the heiress and only half-Egyptian, a male child posed a threat to the 18th Dynasty. The actual birth of Moses occupies the early verses of the second chapter of the Book of Exodus. His mother, we are told, was 'a daughter of Levi'. In face of the threat to all new-born male Israelite children, she kept him hidden for three months. Then, unable to conceal him herself any longer, she 'took for him an ark of bulrushes, and daubed it with slime and with pitch, and put the child therein; and she laid it in the flags (reeds) by the river's brink' (2:3). Pharaoh's daughter saw the basket when she went down to the river to bathe and 'sent her maid to fetch it' (2:4). When she opened the basket the baby was crying and she felt sorry for him. 'This is one of the Hebrews' children,' she said.

We learn at this point that Moses had a sister, Miriam, who, having watched this sequence of events from a distance, now approached the princess and asked: 'Shall I call to thee a nurse of the Hebrew women, that she may nurse the child for thee?' (2:7). When the princess agreed to this suggestion, Moses's sister fetched her mother. The princess told her: 'Take this child away, and nurse it for me, and I will give thee thy wages. And the woman took the child, and nursed it' (2:9). Later, after Moses had grown up, his mother is said to have returned him to Pharaoh's daughter 'and he became her son. And she called his name Moses: and she said, Because I drew him out of the water' (2:10).

This familiar account of the birth of Moses raises some intriguing questions. What possible threat can a Hebrew baby, born into a race of despised Asiatic shepherds, have posed to a mighty Pharaoh? Why would a mother, anxious to save the life of her three-month-old son, set him afloat in an ark of bulrushes close to Pharaoh's residence? Who was the princess who rescued him and returned him to his mother to nurse? Why was the life of the child, now returned to his mother, no longer under any apparent threat? Why, contrary to Egyptian custom, was an unmarried princess allowed later to adopt Moses and bring him up in the palace as her son?

We then have a gap in the story until Moses, by now 'grown up', is said to have killed an Egyptian who was attacking a Hebrew, then fled to Midian in southern Sinai where he married Zipporah, one of the seven daughters of a Midian priest named Reuel, and settled down to the task of looking after his father-in-law's sheep. His pastoral life continued until the Lord appeared to him in a burning bush and ordered him to return to Egypt and deliver the Israelites from the harsh Oppression which, according to the opening chapters of the Book of Exodus, had taken place several decades before Moses had even been born.

Some clues to the historical events behind a story that raises so many questions are to be found in other accounts of the life of Moses. The Talmud - the compilation of Hebrew laws and legends, dating from the early centuries AD (but derived from ancient oral traditions, believed to go back to the time of Moses himself) and regarded as second only to the Old Testament as an authoritative source on the early history of the Jews – provides some additional details about his life. One is that he was a king.

It is said that after the slaying of the Egyptian he fled to Ethiopia, not Midian, where he fought on the side of the king against Bi'lam, a wise Egyptian magician who had usurped the throne, and became such a favourite at court that, when the king later died, Moses himself was appointed the new King of Ethiopia, Moses reigned 'in justice and righteous-ness. But the Queen of Ethiopia, Adonith (Aten-it in Egyptian), who wished her own son to rule, said to the people: "Why should this stranger continue to rule over you?" The people, however, would not vex Moses, whom they loved . . . but Moses resigned voluntarily the power which they had given him and departed from their land.' Only then did he make his way to Midian.

While the Talmud suggests that the departure of Moses was peaceful, the account of these events in the Koran indicates that he fled because his life was in danger:

> And there came a man,
> Running, from the furthest end
> Of the City. He said:
> O Moses! the Chiefs
> Are taking counsel together
> About thee to slay thee:
> So get thee away, for I
> Do give thee sincere advice.
>
> [Sura 28:20].

The Talmud also makes it clear that Moses was to be murdered at the time of his birth because he posed a threat to the throne of Egypt. Pharaoh, it records, had a dream in which he was sitting on the throne when he saw an old man holding a large pair of scales. The old man placed the elders and princes of Egypt on one side of the scales and a lamb on the other. The lamb proved to be heavier. The king asked his adviser Bi'lam – who had made his escape from Ethiopia and returned to his native Egypt (and who does not occur in the Bible) – the significance of this strange dream. Bi'lam explained that a great evil would befall the country: 'A son will be born in Israel who will destroy Egypt.'

When Moses was about three years of age, the story goes on, in the course of a banquet at which his family and princes of the realm were present, Pharaoh took Moses on his lap, whereupon the child stretched out his hand, removed Pharaoh's crown from his head and placed it on his own. The king felt this action had some possibly sinister significance. 'How shall this Hebrew boy be punished?' he asked.

Bi'lam confirmed the king's suspicions. 'Think not, because the child is young, that he did this thing thoughtlessly,' he said. 'Remember, oh king, the dream this servant read for thee, the dream of the balances. The spirit of understanding is already implanted in this child, and to himself he takes thy kingdom.'

It is reasonable to assume that scribes who wrote their accounts of these happenings many centuries later did not invent the facts but based what they wrote on genuine historical events whose memory had been transmitted orally for generations, with the distortions and accretions that are inevitable when stories are passed on by word of mouth. The principal points of the Moses story from the above sources are that he:

1) was a Hebrew child, born in the early years of the Israelite Sojourn in Egypt;
2) posed a threat to the Egyptian throne;

3) was sent into hiding to save his life;
4) was later restored to his mother and lived in the royal palace;
5) became a king;
6) abdicated and fled to Midian when his life was again threatened;
7) and, of course, as we learn later, believed there was only one God.

In order to establish the historical identity of Moses we have to seek a personality of whom at least the majority of the above statements are true. There is only one such personality of whom they are actually *all* true – the Pharaoh Akhenaten (Plate 12).

The scribes who wrote the story of the birth of Moses faced a daunting task. They had to accommodate in their account, in addition to Moses himself, a ruling Pharaoh and his queen, two future Pharaohs and their queens, a daughter of Levi, a sister of Moses who was actually a half-sister, a brother of Moses who was not actually his blood brother, a wet-nurse and a 'house' that went for a swim in the Nile and came across an abandoned baby. This was a formidable amount of information to pack into the first ten verses of the second chapter of the Book of Exodus and, in the circumstances, it is perhaps understandable that the scribes did not name any of the principals in the story, particularly when many of them had two names, one biblical, the other Egyptian. Rectifying this omission will help to make a complex tale simpler:

Amenhotep III:	The father.
Queen Tiye:	The mother.
Akhenaten:	Moses.
Nefertiti:	Miriam, Amenhotep III's daughter by Sitamun, the infant heiress sister he married to inherit the throne.

87

The Daughter of Levi: Jochebed (Tiy in Egyptian). She was the sister-in-law of Queen Tiye through her marriage to Aye (Ephraim), the second son of Yuya (Joseph), who was Queen Tiye's brother and would later rule over Egypt himself. Tiy was also the wet-nurse to both Nefertiti and Akhenaten (Moses).

Aaron: Tiy's son, who is described in the Old Testament as the Levite brother of Moses. This was not, however, a blood relationship, but based on the fact that, then as now, a wet-nurse was given the honorary title of 'mother' and her own children were looked upon as brothers and sisters of the nursed child.

The Princess: Queen Tiye, the mother of Akhenaten (Moses). Two reasons explain why she appears in the biblical story as the princess who adopted Moses. Firstly, in the 6th century BC, when the Old Testament was given permanent form, the word for 'daughter' and the word for 'house' were written identically, *bt*, creating doubt in any context about which particular meaning was intended. It did not make any sense to the scribe to suggest that a house went down to bathe in the river, rescued Moses, later adopted him and brought him up in the palace. He therefore chose to use the word 'daughter', unaware that – as we saw in the earlier chapter about Joseph – the word 'house' is a polite Egyptian way of referring to someone's wife. Consequently, it was Pharaoh's 'house' – the Queen – who rescued Moses and the supposed adoption represents his safe return to his mother.

Akhenaten (Moses), who was given the birth name Amenhotep, was the second son of Amenhotep III and Queen Tiye. An elder son named Tuthmosis had disappeared in mysterious circumstances while being educated and trained with the sons of nobles at Memphis, the administrative capital 15 miles south of modern Cairo. His fate remains a mystery.

From what we know of his later life, it is a reasonable deduction that Akhenaten (Moses) was born in the latter part of 1395 BC, nine months after his parents went sailing on the pleasure lake at Zarw during a kind of second honeymoon. We have no historical evidence to support the stories that Amenhotep III ordered the two midwives to kill his wife's child if it proved to be a boy and, when this plan failed, arranged for all new-born sons of Israelites to be drowned. Indeed, it is difficult to credit that a mighty Pharaoh should have to resort to such an extravagant measure.*

We do have factual evidence about other aspects of the young prince's life. We know that from the time he was born – and throughout his life – he had influential enemies, particularly among the powerful priesthood of the state god

---

* As information about Akhenaten was not allowed to appear in official and temple records, oral transmission of the story of his life must have started from the beginning of the 13th century BC immediately after his death, both among Israelites and Egyptians. These stories were put down in writing many centuries later, after a long period of oral translation.

Amun-Ra at Thebes in Upper Egypt. Their hostility stemmed from his parenthood. In Egypt the king was regarded as the son of Amun-Ra, born as a result of the god's union with the heiress. As Queen Tiye was not the heiress, she could not be regarded as the consort of Amun-Ra, and a male child born to her could not be considered the son of Amun-Ra and therefore the legitimate heir. Furthermore, as Queen Tiye herself was of mixed Egyptian-Israelite blood, if one of her sons did come to the throne this would be regarded as forming a new dynasty of non-Egyptian, non-Amunite, part-Israelite kings over Egypt. We encountered a similar case earlier when his father arranged for Tuthmosis III, the son of a concubine, to undergo an adoption ritual where the image of Amun-Ra, carried by the priests, chose the prince as the god's son before he could be established as the legitimate heir.

We also know that Akhenaten (Moses) spent most of his childhood and early youth in hiding – we hear nothing of him until his sudden appearance in the royal palace at Thebes in his mid-teens – and that he was nursed by Tiy, who is described in the tomb she later shared with her husband, Aye, as 'the great nurse, nourisher of the god (king), adorner of the king (Akhenaten)'.

My interpretation of these events is that Queen Tiye, aware, as a result of the death of her first son, Tuthmosis, of the dangers facing the new-born Akhenaten (Moses), may have tried initially to smuggle him out of the Zarw palace, his birthplace, to the safe keeping of her sister-in-law, Tiy, and other Israelite relations at Goshen, the fertile land surrounding Zarw and linked to it by water. She then seems to have kept him at Zarw during his early childhood, not allowing him to travel to Memphis or Thebes.*

---

* I think that, as in the case of Abraham-Sarah-Pharaoh and David-Bathsheba-Uriah, the conspiracy between Tiye and Tiy to save Moses provides the inspiration for a repeated Old Testament story – the wisdom of Solomon when he had to decide between two women in a dispute over who was the mother of a child.

If Akhenaten (Moses) was given the birth name Amenhotep, which he later changed to Akhenaten, it seems odd that the world should remember him as Moses. His identity and the origin of his name eventually engaged the attention of Sigmund Freud, the father of psychoanalysis, who argued in *Moses and Monotheism*, a controversial book published shortly before the outbreak of the Second World War, that Moses was an Egyptian. He showed also that the story of the birth of Moses is a replica of other ancient myths about the birth of some of the great heroes of history. Freud pointed out, however, that the myth of Moses's birth and exposure stands apart from those of other heroes and varies from them on one essential point. In order to hide the fact that Moses was Egyptian, the myth of his birth has been reversed to make him born to humble parents and succoured by the high-status family: 'It is very different in the case of Moses. Here the first family, usually so distinguished, is modest enough. He is a child of Jewish Levites. But the second family – the humble one in which as a rule heroes are brought up – is replaced by the royal house of Egypt. This divergence from the usual type has struck many research workers as strange.'

Freud remarked on the oddity that the Israelite law-giver, if actually Egyptian, should later have passed on to his followers a monotheistic belief rather than the classical Ancient Egyptian belief in a plethora of gods and images. At the same time, he found great similarity between the new religion that Akhenaten tried to impose on his country and the religious teaching attributed to Moses. For example, he wrote: 'The Jewish creed says: "*Schema Yisrael Adonai Elohenu Adonai Echod*"'. As the Hebrew letter *d* is a transliteration of the Egyptian letter *t* and *e* becomes *o*, he went on to explain that this sentence from the Jewish creed could be translated: "Hear, O Israel, our God Aten is the only God".'

Freud came to the conclusion that Akhenaten had been murdered by his own followers because of the harsh nature of his monotheistic regime and suggested that subsequently one of his high officials, probably called Tuthmose, an adherent of the Aten religion, selected the Hebrew tribe, already living at Goshen in the Eastern Delta, to be his chosen people, took them out of Egypt at the time of the Exodus and passed on to them the tenets of Akhenaten's religion.

Of the name Moses he wrote: 'What first attracts our interest in Moses is his name, which is written *Moshe* in Hebrew. One may well ask: "Where does it come from? What does it mean?"'

It certainly does not come from, or mean, what the biblical narrator would like us to believe when he quotes Pharaoh's daughter as saying that she called the child she is supposed to have adopted Moses 'because I drew him out of the water'. As a verb, the Hebrew word *m sh a* can mean either 'to draw' or 'one who draws out'. Therefore, in order to agree with the explanation given by the biblical editor the name should not have been *Moshe* but *Moshui*, 'one who has been drawn out'.

Freud came to the conclusion that the origin of the name Moses was *mos*, the Ancient Egyptian word for 'child', which is found in many compound Egyptian names such as Ptah-mos and Tuth-mos. It is simple to trace the link semantically. In Ancient Egyptian the word for 'child' was written with the consonants *m* and *s* – neither Egyptian nor Hebrew wrote short vowels although they were pronounced – and, if we remove the vowels from Moshe, we are left with two consonants, *m* and *sh*. The Hebrew letter *sh* is the equivalent of the Egyptian *s*. It is therefore easy to see that the Hebrew word came from the Egyptian word *mos* (the final 's' of Moses derives from the Greek translation of the biblical name).

I am sure Freud is right about the word *mos*, but, in relation to Akhenaten, I think, as we shall see, that it has a broader significance dating from the latter years of his life when mere mention of his name was punishable by death.

Chapter Nine

The One God and His Prophet

Scholars generally accept* that Akhenaten (Moses) was in his teens when he made his first appearance at Thebes in 1378 BC. This dating agrees with his having been born at Zarw in 1394 BC. At the time he arrived in Thebes he was still known by the name he had been given at birth, Amenhotep.† We know very little of his early life. There is no evidence that during his childhood he spent any time at Memphis, where his father, Amenhotep III, had his main residence and where the heirs apparent were normally trained and educated with the sons of nobles. His behaviour and the kind of knowledge he had acquired suggests that, after his childhood at Zarw, he had been sent to be educated at Heliopolis (the biblical On), north-east of modern Cairo, which was the early religious centre in Egypt and the main centre for worship of the sun-god Ra, whose temple had been built there. The father-in-law of Yuya (Joseph) had been a priest at Heliopolis and was followed in a similar priestly role by Anen (Manasseh), Yuya's first son and Akhenaten's uncle.

Akhenaten arrived in Thebes with highly developed views about the deity Aten, which suggests that he must have been involved during his early years in an Aten cult at Zarw. We have various indications that such a cult began to appear in that area from the time of the young prince's grandfather, Tuthmosis IV (1413–1405 BC), who, as we have seen, is believed to have appointed Yuya (Joseph) as his minister. The very first shrine to Aten appears to have been in this city of Zarw. One of the titles of Neby, the mayor of Zarw during the reign of Tuthmosis IV, was 'Overseer of the Foremost Water in the *hnt* (lake or lake area) of the Temple of Aten'. Even before Akhenaten (Moses) was born, as we saw earlier, the vessel in which his father and mother sailed on the pleasure lake at Zarw was named *Aten Gleams*. The enduring nature of the cult in the Zarw lake area of the Eastern Delta – what the Bible calls 'the land of Goshen' – is indicated by the text on a wine jar placed in the tomb of Tutankhamun, who would succeed Akhenaten (Moses) on the throne: 'Year 5. Sweet wine of the House-of-Aten [from] Zarw. Chief vintner Pen-amun.'

In his Year 20 (1386 BC), eight years before the appearance of the young prince on the scene, Amenhotep III had chosen to change his main residence from Memphis to Thebes – modern Luxor – in Upper Egypt. Thebes, a huddle of modest villages in the 16th century BC, had grown in the intervening years to a giant metropolis. It was also the seat of the state god Amun-Ra. The city's prominence stemmed in part from the fact that it was the princes of Thebes who had united to conquer and drive the Hyksos invaders from the Eastern Delta at the start of the 16th century BC. Its religious importance had also grown because, from the reign of Amenhotep II (1436–1413 BC), the grandfather of Amenhotep III, there had been a gradual but growing fusion between the solar cult of Ra and the cult of Amun. This greatly increased the joint-god's status. While ancient cults of other gods continued to flourish locally, the cult of Amun-Ra had received, and continued to receive, royal treatment – generous endowments, munificent gifts of land, gold and slaves – so favourable that it had become virtually an arm of the state executive.

---

* For example, Professor Donald B. Redford of Toronto University.

† Amenhotep did not change his name to Akhenaten until the fifth year of the later co-regency with his father, but I refer to him from this point as Akhenaten (Moses).

Amun-Ra also dominated the architecture of Thebes. The Luxor temple had been founded by Amenhotep III primarily as a setting for the annual Festival of Opet when the cult statue of Amun was carried along an avenue of sphinxes that led from the temple of Amun at Karnak to Luxor. Karnak, two miles north of Thebes (Luxor), was a huge complex of religious buildings that covered more than a hundred hectares. The three major sacred precincts were dedicated to the deities Amun, Mut (vulture-goddess consort of Amun) and Montu (falcon-headed god of war).

On the opposite (west) bank of the Nile Amenhotep III built for himself a magnificent home – the Malkata palace complex. His own palace, as we saw, was ready by Year 8 (1398 BC) of his reign, but the whole complex, including four probable palaces as well as kitchens, storerooms, residential areas and the mortuary temple for service of the king's spirit after his death, was not completed until towards the end of his third decade (1375 BC). On his arrival at Thebes, Akhenaten (Moses) moved into the Malkata palace complex. His mother's was not the only familiar face from childhood that awaited him. Other residents in the palace included Sitamun, his father's sister/wife, who was the young prince's aunt, and her daughter Nefertiti, his half-sister. Yet, although he had been allowed to settle in Thebes without any threat to his life, Akhenaten (Moses) cannot be said to have been *persona grata*. The only mention of him before his accession to the throne as co-ruler with his father in 1378 BC was found in Malkata in the form of an undated wine jar seal with the inscription '. . . [of] the estate of the true King's Son, Amenhotep'. The use of the expression 'true king's son' indicates an early challenge – no doubt from the Amunite priests – to his right ultimately to inherit the throne.

By the time Akhenaten (Moses) arrived in Thebes, Queen Tiye, who is known to have been a woman with a powerful personality, had become an increasingly influential presence behind the throne as her husband's health declined with his advancing years. This increased influence is reflected in the fact that her name, unlike that of earlier queens, was placed regularly in a cartouche, a distinction previously limited to the ruling monarch, and was also included in royal titularies. Furthermore, she was represented as being of equivalent stature to the king.

In order to ensure her son's ultimate inheritance of the throne, she seems to have arranged for him to marry his half-sister, Nefertiti, the heiress. It was Tiye, too, who must have persuaded her husband to appoint Moses as his co-regent, with special emphasis on Nefertiti's role in order to placate the hostile priests and nobles.

Whether or not Akhenaten (Moses) was co-regent with his father has been the subject of interminable debate among scholars. Some say he wasn't: I say he was – for 12 years. Evidence adduced includes wine jar dockets, reliefs, cults, cartouches, temples, pylons, stelae, sarcophagi, statues, paintings, letters, nomen (birth name), praenomen (coronation name) and the length of kings' reigns. In my view, the evidence pointing to a co-regency of 12 years - from 1378 BC until 1367 BC, when Amenhotep III died – is overwhelming. In order not to burden the reader with a lengthy debate about these various viewpoints (which I have dealt with at some length elsewhere), it may suffice to summarize some of the main pieces of evidence.

Many objects bearing the name of Amenhotep III were found at Tell el-Amarna, the new capital city built by Akhenaten (Moses), roughly halfway between Thebes and modern Cairo, starting in his Year 4 (1375 BC). Amenhotep III, with Queen Tiye, is shown alive in many Amarna tombs of the nobles and small stelae found there – all representing him in the distinctive Amarna art style. This has been taken by a large number of Egyptologists as confirmation that Amenhotep III was alive at the time the new city was being built and may even have visited it.

For example, a stele found in the house of Panehesy, the Chief Servitor of the Aten temple at Amarna, shows

Amenhotep III with Queen Tiye seated before a pile of offerings. As the Aten is depicted in the scene shining over them in his later form, it cannot date from earlier than the second half of Year 8 of Akhenaten. The old king is shown here in the realistic Amarna style with thick neck and bent head, indicating his old age at the time. Neither in the scene itself nor in the accompanying text is there any indication that the king was already dead. He is not represented in the usual Osiris form of dead kings. On the contrary, the queen is shown sitting next to him, not facing him, and she was still alive, as there is separate evidence that she visited Amarna before Year 12 of her son's reign. Furthermore, the artistic nature of the Amarna style used here gives a realistic portrayal of the couple in Amarna, under the Aten's rays, not an abstract or idealized scene, drawn from memory, of a king who had died at Thebes a decade or so earlier.

Another combination of scene and inscription in the tomb of Huya (steward to Queen Tiye) at Amarna enforces the argument that Amenhotep III was still alive and visiting Amarna some time after the second half of Akhenaten's Year 8. The scene is drawn in two halves on the lintel of the doorway leading from the first hall of the tomb into the inner rooms.

The scene on the left shows Akhenaten with his wife and four of their daughters, that on the right Amenhotep III with his wife and his youngest princess Baketaten. For Howard Carter, the British archaeologist who discovered the tomb of Tutankhamun, this was strong evidence of a co-regency between Akhenaten and his father: 'This equipoise of the two households not only confirms the co-regency of the two kings, but gives reason to suppose that Amenhotep III continued to live for at least a year or so after the birth of Akhenaten's fourth daughter, Neferneferuaten Tasheri' (*The Tomb of Tutankhamun*, p. 5).

Two objects have also been found at Amarna bearing Amenhotep III's name, indicating not only that he was still alive but also that he was visiting the city of Amarna. The first is a fragment of a granite bowl with the late name of the Aten, the name of Amenhotep III and the phrase 'in Akhenaten' (Amarna). The second is a fragment of a statue of a kneeling person holding an offering slab. Between his outstretched hands is an inscription that includes the late name of Aten, followed by the name of Amenhotep III.

In an article that appeared in the *Journal of Egyptian Archaeology* in 1957, the Scottish Egyptologist Cyril Aldred argued that scenes in two Amarna tombs where the king was shown receiving gifts from foreign nations in his Year 12 (1367 BC) were part of the celebrations on his accession to sole rule. This seems likely. There was no war campaign at this time that would account for such tribute and, if it were simply the regular yearly tribute, it is difficult to imagine all the foreign nations depicted in these scenes having gathered in Amarna at the same time. Furthermore, this is the only time that such an event is to be found depicted in the Amarna tombs.

Howard Carter was persuaded by a graffito from the pyramid temple of Meidum in Middle Egypt, dating from the time of Amenhotep III, that the text indicates a co-regency between the king and his son. He wrote in his book *The Tomb of Tutankhamun*: 'The graffito reads: "Year 30, under the majesty of the King Neb-maat-Re, Son of Amun, resting in truth, Amenhotep [III], prince of Thebes, lord of might, prince of joy, who loves him that hates injustice of heart, placing the male offspring upon the seat of his father, and establishing his inheritance in the land." The "heir" referred to in this graffito has to be Amenhotep IV, who afterwards assumed the name Akhenaten . . .'

The most significant archaeological evidence pointing to a co-regency between Akhenaten (Moses) and his father, however, was unearthed as recently as 1989 with the discovery at Sakkara, ten miles south of Cairo, of the tomb, almost intact, of Aper-el, the hitherto unknown chief minister to Akhenaten. Funerary furniture in the tomb, found by the French archaeologist Alain-Pierre Zivie after ten years' work, included a box given to Aper-el by Amenhotep III and Queen Tiye. Amenhotep III's cartouche and praenomen, Neb-Maat-Ra, were found in two other cases in the tomb. In relation to a co-regency, the two main points are that Akhenaten would not have had a chief minister unless he were ruling, and his father's praenomen would not have been found in the tomb unless he was still alive *after* his son came to the throne.

The tomb also makes it clear that Aper-el served as a high priest to Aten before becoming a chief minister. Similar names to Aper-el are known to have existed in Egypt at this period of history, but never in the case of high officials. The 'Aper' corresponds to the Egyptian word for 'Hebrew', which meant to ancient Egyptians a nomad, working for the state at heavy manual labour, and the final 'el' is the short form of 'Elohim', one of the words used in the Bible as the name of the Lord. The tomb of Aper-el is the first evidence we have of a link between a Pharaoh and someone of Hebrew stock living in Egypt during his reign. Furthermore, Queen Tiye's association with her husband in donating a box to the funerary furniture of Aper-el indicates the possibility that the chief minister was a relation, most probably through her Israelite father, Yuya (Joseph).

Akhenaten's rejection of the beliefs and authority of the Theban priesthood, who had denied his right to the throne from the time of his birth, began shortly after he appeared in Thebes. On his accession to the throne as co-regent, he took the names Neferkheprure Waenre Amenhotep – that is, Amenhotep IV – and from his very first year provoked the priests by his aggressive attitude. He had barely assumed his new position when he used some of the wealth amassed by his father to build a large new Aten temple within the precincts of the existing Amun-Ra temple at Karnak. This was followed by a second Aten temple within the Luxor Amun-Ra temple, which had been built by his father. He snubbed the traditional priests by not allowing them to any of the festivities in the early part of his co-regency and, in his fourth year (1375 BC), when he celebrated his *sed* festival or jubilee – usually, but not necessarily, a rejuvenation celebration that marked Year 30 of a monarch's reign – he banned all gods but his own God from the occasion. Twelve months later he made a further break with tradition by changing his name from Amenhotep to Akhenaten in honour of his new deity.

Aten had not been worshipped as a deity before the middle of the 18th Dynasty and was then regarded as just one of Egypt's many deities. Akhenaten (Moses) was the first person to recognize Aten as the sole deity, a God not simply for Egypt but for the whole world. This monotheistic concept developed in stages as he grew up. Early representations of Aten showed the deity, like Ra-Harakhti, the sun-god, as of human shape with the head of a falcon, surmounted by a solar disc, in keeping with the conventional way gods were depicted in Egyptian art. Akhenaten (Moses) seems also to have drawn at this early stage on the traditional ritual of the solar god of Heliopolis. The name given by the king to his early Karnak temple, *ben-ben* (obelisk), was the same as that of the Heliopolitan temples where the *ben-ben* (a small pyramid on a square base) was a characteristic of the solar temples.

At the end of the second year, or early in the third, of the co-regency an important development took place in this representation. The human figure vanished. Only a golden disc appeared, whose rays descended over the king and queen as well as over the temple, altar and palace. This golden disc did not represent the sun but was the symbol of Aten, who had no physical image. The rays, in their turn, were not the endless rays of the sun. They ended in hands, and the hands held the *ankh* – the Egyptian cross, a symbol of life, not death – before the nostrils of the king and queen. To indicate the kingly statues of Aten, an uraeus (cobra) hung from the disc in the same way as an uraeus adorned the brow of the king. At the same time the name and epithet of the God was placed inside two cartouches, matching the manner in which the ruling king's name was written.

From inscriptions at both the Karnak Aten temple and rock tombs constructed at Amarna, the independent capital Akhenaten (Moses) was to set up as a rival to Thebes, we have a clear picture of how he regarded his God: 'The living Aten, there is none other than He' . . . 'Who Himself gave birth to Himself' . . . 'He who decrees life, the Lord of sunbeams' . . . 'The world came forth from Thy [Aten] hand' . . . 'Thou . . . creator of months and maker of days, and reckoner of hours'.

'Thou createst the earth when Thou wert afar, namely men, cattle, all flocks, and everything on earth which moves with legs, or which is up above flying with wings. The foreign countries of Syria (north) and Kush (south), and the land of Egypt, Thou placest every man in his place, and makest their food. Everyone has his food, and his lifetime is reckoned; and similarly their languages are wholly separate in form. For their colours are different, for Thou hast made foreign peoples different.'

We find echoes of these attributes in the God of Moses as he is described in the Old Testament. He was:

A Sole God:	Hear, O Israel, Adonai (Aten) our God is the only God. A translation, as Freud pointed out, of Deuteronomy 6:4, which is to be found in Jewish liturgy today.* Thou shalt have no other gods before me. (Exodus 20:3).

* The words *Schema Yisrael Adonai Elohenu Adonai Ohod* can also be translated, using the personal name, Jehovah, of the God of Israel. This form of the translation may be written and read by Jews, but when it is read aloud Adonai must be substituted for Jehovah. No convincing explanation has ever been put forward for this tradition, nor does anyone know precisely when it started, but I believe it dates from the time of Akhenaten (Moses).

Without a Cult Image: Thou shalt not make unto thee any graven image, or any likeness of any thing that is in heaven above, or that is in the earth beneath, or that is in the water under the earth (Exodus 20:4).

Creator of the World: In the beginning God created the heaven and the earth (Genesis 1:1).

Universal King: The Lord shall reign for ever and ever (Exodus 15:18).

The Father: And thou shalt say unto Pharaoh, Thus saith the Lord, Israel is my son, even my first born. (Exodus 4:22).

We also find reflections of Egyptian practices in Israelite practices. Moses is said to have introduced the Ark, the receptacle in the temple of Jerusalem in which the Pentateuch, the first five books of the Old Testament, were kept: 'And the Lord spake unto Moses, saying . . . make an ark . . . and in the ark thou shalt put the testimony that I shalt give thee' (Exodus 25:1,10,21). The Ark, regarded as the holiest part of Israelite temples after the Pentateuch itself, is a version of the Egyptian holy boat, usually kept in the temple and, as we have seen, serving to carry the deity during processions.

To the resentful Egyptian Establishment, Aten was seen as a challenger who would replace the powerful state god Amun-Ra and deny his domination. It was at this point, in a climate that was becoming increasingly hostile towards her son, that Queen Tiye arranged a compromise by persuading Akhenaten (Moses) to leave Thebes and establish his new capital at Tell el-Amarna on the east bank of the Nile, on land that had never been dedicated to any other deity. He named this new city, where he and his followers could be free to worship their monotheistic God, Akhetaten, the Horizon of Aten.

Chapter Ten

Tell el-Amarna

At Amarna the cliffs of the high desert recede from the river, leaving a great semi-circle about eight miles long and three miles broad. The bright yellow sand slopes gently down to the river. Huge boundary stelae, marking the limits of the city and recording the story of its foundation, were carved in the surrounding cliffs. One of them, stressing that Akhenaten (Moses) looked upon Aten as his father, read:

> . . . I shall make Akhetaten (Amarna) for Aten my father in this place . . . Akhetaten extends from the southern stele as far as the northern stele . . . likewise from the south-west stele to the north-west stele . . . the area between these four stelae is Akhetaten itself; it belongs to my father; mountains, deserts, meadows, islands, high ground and low ground, land, water, villages, men, beasts and all things which Aten my father shall bring into existence eternally for ever . . .

The city was on the east bank with a large area of agricultural land on the bank opposite, apparently with a view to making the new capital self-supporting if it ever came under siege. Building of Akhenaten's new city lasted from Akhenaten's Year 4 to Year 8, but he is thought to have taken up residence there in his Year 8 (1371 BC) together with Queen Nefertiti and their six daughters – Merytaten, Maketaten, Ankhsenpa-aten, Neferneferu-aten the younger, Neferneferure and Setepenre.

Akhetaten was a capital city possessed of both dignity and

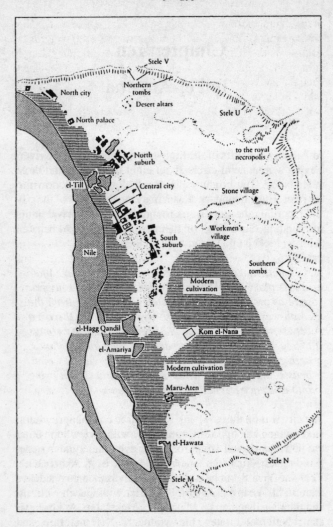

City of Amarna

architectural harmony. Its main streets ran parallel to the Nile with the most important of them, known even today as *Sikket es-Sultan*, the King's Way, connecting all the city's most prominent buildings, including The King's House where Pharaoh and his family lived their private family life. Its plan was similar to that of a high official's villa, but on a grander scale and surrounded by a spacious garden. To the south of the house was the king's private temple. The Great Temple of Aten, a huge building constructed on an east-west axis, lay less than a quarter of a mile to the north along the King's Way. It was entered through a pylon (temple gate) from the highway and a second entrance gave access to a hypostyle hall called The House of Rejoicing of Aten.

Six rectangular courts, known as Gem-Aten (*gem* means 'gleaming'), lay along a processional way and were filled with tables for offerings to Aten. At the eastern end of the enclosure there was a sanctuary equipped with a great altar and more offering tables. Abreast of the northern wall of the enclosure lay the pavilion where the great reception for foreign princes bearing tribute was held in Year 12 (1367 BC), thought probably to have been the high point of Akhenaten's reign. The house of the Chief Servitor of Aten, the priest Panehesy, lay outside the enclosure's south-east corner.

It was not just the form of worship that was new in Akhetaten. Queen Nefertiti (Plate 14), like her mother-in-law, Queen Tiye, enjoyed a prominence that had not existed for earlier queens. On one of his new city's boundary stelae her husband had her described as: 'Fair of Face, Joyous with the Double Plume, Mistress of Happiness, Endowed with Favour, at hearing whose voice one rejoices, Lady of Grace, Great of Love, whose disposition cheers the Lord of the Two Lands.' The king gave tombs, gouged out of the face of surrounding cliffs, to those nobles who had rallied to him. In the reliefs which the nobles had carved for themselves in these tombs, Queen Nefertiti is shown as equal in stature to the king.

Akhenaten Hymn to Aten	Psalm 104
When thou settest in the western horizon	Thou makest darkness and it is night
Of heaven,	Wherein all the beasts of the forest do creep
The world is in darkness like the dead.	Forth.
They sleep in their chambers,	The young lions roar after their prey;
Their heads are wrapt up,	They seek their meat from God.
Their nostrils stopped, and none seeth the other.	(Psalm 104:20–21)
Stolen are all their things, that are under their heads,	
While they know it not.	
Every lion cometh forth from his den,	
All serpents, they sting. Darkness reigns.	
The world is in silence.	
He that made them has gone to rest in his horizon.	
Bright is the earth,	The sun ariseth, they get them away,
When thou risest in the horizon,	And lay them down in their dens.
When thou shinest as Aten by day.	Man goeth forth unto his work,
The darkness is banished,	And to his labour until the evening.
When thou sendest forth thy rays,	(Psalm 104:22–23).
The Two Lands are in daily festivity,	
Awake and standing upon their feet,	
For thou hast raised them up.	
The barques sail up-stream and down-stream alike.	Yonder is the sea, great and wide,
Every highway is open because thou hast dawned.	Wherein are things creeping innumerable.
The fish in the river leap up before thee,	Both small and great beasts.
And thy rays are in the midst of the great sea.	There go the ships;
	There is leviathan, whom thou hast Formed to sport with him.
	(Psalm 104:25–26)

How manifold are all thy works!
They are hidden from before us.
O thou sole God, whose powers no other possesseth.
Thou didst create the earth according to thy desire.
While thou wast alone:
Men, all cattle large and small,
All that are upon the earth,
That go upon their feet;
All that are on high,
That fly with their wings.

O lord, how manifold are thy works!
In wisdom hast thou made them all;
The earth is full of thy creatures.
(Psalm 104:24).
(*A History of Egypt*, James Henry Breasted, pp. 371–374)

By the early years of this century, when the city of Amarna had been excavated and more was known about Akhenaten and his family, Egyptologists of the period saw him as a visionary humanitarian as well as the first monotheist. He was looked upon as a poet who wrote hymns to Aten, the longest of which has a striking resemblance to Psalm 104 of the Bible. He had instructed his artists to express freely what they felt and saw, resulting in a new and simple realistic art that was different in many respects from the traditional form of Egyptian artistic expression.

Some of Akhenaten's Writing

Thy dawning is beautiful in the horizon of heaven,
O living Aten, Beginning of life!
When thou risest in the eastern horizon of heaven,
Thou fillest every land with thy beauty;
For thou are beautiful, great, glittering, high over the earth;
Thy rays, they encompass the lands, even all thou hast made.
Though thou art afar, thy rays are on earth,
Though thou art on high, thy footprints are the day.

For the first time we were allowed to see the king as a human being with his wife and daughters, eating, drinking and making offerings to Aten. John Pendlebury, the British archaeologist who took part in much of the early excavations at Amarna, was enthusiastic about Amarna art and, especially, the hymns to Aten. In his book *Tell el-Amarna*, published in 1935, he wrote: '. . . the new spirit of realism is strikingly evident. The incidental groups of spectators are so alive, the princesses turn to one another with their bouquets so naturally.' Although kings and princes of western Asia tried hard to involve Akhenaten in recurrent wars, he had refused to become a party to their disputes. It is no wonder that the early Egyptologists of this century saw in him an expression of their own modern ideas.

'The most remarkable of all the Pharaohs and the first individual in human history' are the words that James Henry Breasted, the American scholar, chose to describe him in his book *A History of Egypt*. It is a theme he returned to and developed in a later book, *The Dawn of Conscience*: 'It is important to notice . . . that Akhenaten was a prophet . . . Like Jesus, who, on the one hand, drew his lessons from the lilies of the field, the fowls of the air or the clouds of the sky, and, on the other hand, from the human society about him in stories like the Prodigal Son, the Good Samaritan or the woman who lost her piece of money, so this revolutionary Egyptian prophet drew his teachings from a contemplation both of nature and of human life . . .'

The same theme finds an echo in the work of Arthur Weigall, the British Egyptologist, who wrote in his book *The Life and Times of Akhenaten*:

> . . . at the name of Akhenaten there emerges from the darkness a figure more clear than that of any other Pharaoh, and with it there comes the singing of the birds, the voices of the children and the scent of many flowers. For once we may look right into the mind of a King of Egypt and may see something of its workings, and all that is there observed is worthy of admiration. Akhenaten has been called 'the first individual in human history'; but if he is thus the first historical figure

whose personality is known to us, he is also the first of all human founders of religious doctrines. Akhenaten may be ranked in degree of time, and, in view of the new ground broken by him, perhaps in degree of genius, as the world's first idealist.

For the Reverend James Bakie, another British Egyptologist, he was '. . . an idealist dreamer, who actually believed that men were meant to live in truth and speak the truth'.

Not all scholars, however, took such an enthusiastic and flattering view of the first of the Amarna kings. Certain of them have shown themselves anxious to put as much distance as possible, in terms of time as well as belief, between Moses, the biblical Israelite, and Akhenaten, whom they have regarded as an Egyptian intruder on the scene. They have questioned whether Akhenaten actually introduced a monotheistic God into Egypt.

It has been suggested* that Aten cannot be looked upon as a God without an image because his symbol is depicted in paintings and sculptures as a circle sending rays that end in hands holding the Egyptian cross, *ankh*, the key of life, to the nostrils of the royal family. This is not a physical representation of the deity, however. Like the Christian cross or Jewish star, it is a symbol, indicating salvation (as in Christianity), not the literal deity. At the Aten temple there was no physical representation to be addressed in prayer any more than the physical Ark of the Covenant, placed in the holy of holies in the Temple at Jerusalem, can be looked upon as an image of God. Nor was Aten ever identified in the history of Egyptian worship with the sun-god Ra under any of the sun-god's three names – Khepri† at his rising in the

---

* This has been suggested by Professor Donald B. Redford of Toronto University, and by Ian Shaw and Paul Nicholson who composed *The Dictionary of Ancient Egypt* published by the British Museum in 1995, and others.

† Creator-god manifested in the form of the scarab or beetle. His name means 'he is coming into being'.

morning, Ra when full grown at midday and Atum when he set on the western horizon in the evening.

Towards the end of Year 9 (1370 BC) of Akhenaten (Moses) the name of Aten received a new form to rid it of any therio-anthropomorphic (worshipping a god presented in a form combining animal and human elements) or pantheistic (heathen worship of all gods) aspect that may have clung to it as a result of the hieroglyphic use of images. The falcon symbol used to spell the name Ra-Harakhti, which in this form would represent the sun-god, was changed to abstract signs. Thus the word 'Ra' no longer represented the god of Heliopolis but achieved a new abstract meaning, 'the Lord'. The name Aten had been placed in two cartouches to represent the ruling king. The second of these two cartouches was now altered, ridding it of the word *shu*, which could be a representation of the old Egyptian god of the atmosphere. *Shu* was now spelled alphabetically, giving it the meaning of 'light'. The new form of the God's name read: 'Ra (the Lord), the living Ruler of the Horizon, in his name the light which is in Aten.' This concept is, perhaps, difficult to grasp. However, we find a similar process in the Bible where Yahweh (Jehovah) has been established by archaeologists as having been an earlier Canaanite deity with a wife named Ashirah.† Nevertheless the name Yahweh is used in the Bible to indicate an abstract monotheistic power, the Lord.

The scholarly assault upon Akhenaten has not been confined to the nature of his religion. In an attempt at character destruction of the monotheistic king he has, in addition, been accused of having had a homosexual affair with his brother/

---

† This has been established from both the Aramaic texts found on the Nile island of Elephantine, opposite Aswan in Nubia, where a Jewish community lived from the 5th century BC, and also from texts found in Sinai by Israeli archaeologists when the peninsula fell under their occupation after the Six Day War of 1967. They found the name of Yahweh associated with a wife goddess called Ashira(h).

co-regent/son-in-law Semenkhkare. The Scottish Egyptologist Cyril Aldred wrote:

An unfinished stele from Amarna which has been the subject of some discussion shows two kings seated side by side, the foremost being identified as Akhenaten and the other as his co-regent Semenkhkare. The homosexual relations between the elder and the younger monarch revealed by this monument have been likened to those subsisting between the Emperor Hadrian and the youth Antinous, and gives significance to the epithet 'beloved of Akhenaten', which Semenkhkare incorporated into both his cartouches. He also assumed the name of Akhenaten's chief queen Nefertiti, presumably on her death; and this, and the intimacy so frankly exhibited on the stele by the elder Pharaoh who chucks the younger under the chin, suggest that Akhenaten was the active partner in the relationship.

[*Akhenaten*, London, 1968, p. 139]

In fact the younger person depicted on the lap of Akhenaten in this scene (Plate 15) is not Semenkhkare, who was about 22 at the time, but one of the king's daughters, who was no more than 9 or 10.

Furthermore, although we have evidence of his having fathered six daughters, Akhenaten has also been described as impotent. The bizarre allegation of impotence was first voiced some 30 years ago by Cyril Aldred, based upon one of four colossi of Akhenaten that date from the time he set up his temple to Aten at Karnak during his early years in Thebes and are now to be seen in the Cairo Museum. Three of these enormous statues show Akhenaten wearing a kilt: the other is apparently a nude study in which he has no genitalia (Plate 16). This led Cyril Aldred to the conclusion that he must have been suffering from a distressing disease that rendered him impotent.

He wrote in *Akhenaten*:

All the indications are that such peculiar physical characteristics were the result of a complaint known to physicians and pathologists as Fröhlich's Syndrome. Male patients with this disorder frequently exhibit a corpulence similar to Akhenaten's. The genitalia remain infantile and may be so embedded in fat as not to be visible. Adiposity may vary in degree, but there is a typical feminine distribution of fat in the region of the breasts, abdomen, pubis, thighs and buttocks. The lower limbs, however, are slender and the legs, for instance, resemble plus-fours.

Aldred goes on to say: 'There is warrant for thinking that he suffered from Fröhlich's Syndrome and wished to have himself represented with all those deformities that distinguished his appearance from the rest of humanity.'

Whether or not Akhenaten suffered from Fröhlich's Syndrome has since engaged the attention of some of the world's leading physicians and inspired several million words of learned debate. It was Julia Samson of University College, London, who put an end to this fiction by establishing that what was missing from the fourth, supposedly nude, statue of Akhenaten was not his genitalia but his kilt. She explained in her book *Amarna, City of Akhenaten and Nefertiti*:

The belt is made by cutting back the surface of the abdomen to leave a ridge, and the linen folds of the kilt are then carved over the hips, curving up to the belt buckle. On the one unfinished colossal statue of Akhenaten found in Karnak, the only one that is nude, his kilt would have been added in this way, because the stone is already recessed around Aten plaques at the waist and would have been further cut back, as on the finished colossi, to make the ridge for the belt.

112

> *There would have been [then] no necessity for further delineation of the king's figure, about which there has been so much conjecture . . . This underlines the fallibility of theories about his physical build and condition being based on unfinished statues. Rather than . . . his choosing to be represented as unable to father his children, the probability is that the one nude, unfinished statue was never raised to a standing position. It is unlikely that the Amun priests left in Thebes after the royal removal to Akhetaten (Amarna) would have exerted every effort to finish the Aten temple . . .*

The co-regency crown did not sit easily on the head of Akhenaten even after he had removed himself and his family from Thebes to distant Amarna. From that time he relied completely on the army's support for protection and, possibly, as a future safeguard against the confrontation that would be inevitable once his father died and he became sole ruler.

He seems not to have been physically strong – alone among Tuthmosside rulers he is not represented in activities at which his forebears excelled such as horsemanship, archery and seamanship – but, to impress his subjects, he appears to have gone to considerable lengths to stress his military power. In the vast majority of his representations, he is shown wearing either the Blue Crown or the short Nubian wig, both belonging to the king's military headdress, rather than the traditional ceremonial crowns of Lower and Upper Egypt. Alan R. Schulman, the American Egyptologist, has also pointed out in an article on the military background to the Amarna period that 'scenes of soldiers and military activity abound in both the private and royal art of Amarna . . . the city was virtually an armed camp . . . Everywhere we see parades and processions of soldiers, infantry and chariotry with their massed standards. There are soldiers under arms standing guard in front of the palaces, the temples and in the watchtowers that bordered the city, scenes of troops, unarmed or equipped with staves, carrying out combat exercises in the presence of the king.'

He goes on to say: 'Just as Amarna had its own military garrison which stood ready to enforce the will of the king, so the other cities of Egypt must also have had their garrisons and the army, loyal to the throne, carried out its will. That the army was so loyal to the throne and to the dynasty was almost assured by the person of its commander, . . . Aye (Akhenaten's maternal uncle) . . .'

The hostility of the Establishment and Theban priesthood towards Akhenaten had worsened during his co-regency years because, as a response to his rejection by the Amun priests as a legitimate ruler, he had snubbed Amun by abolishing his name and names of all ancient deities from walls and inscriptions of temples and tombs in his new city of Amarna. This campaign intensified later when he came to the throne as sole ruler in his Year 12 (1367 BC) upon the death of his father. By that time his monotheistic ideas had developed to the point where he took the view that, if Aten was the only God, he, as Aten's sole son and prophet, could not allow other gods to be worshipped at the same time in his dominion.

He therefore abolished throughout Egypt the worship of any gods except Aten. He closed all the temples, except those of Aten, dispersed the priests and gave orders that the names of other deities should be expunged from monuments and temple inscriptions throughout the country. Units were despatched to excise the names of the ancient gods, particularly Amun, wherever they were found written or engraved. Even the plural word *netaru* for gods was proscribed.

Alan R. Schulman makes the point that this religious campaign must have weakened Akhenaten's support among both the army and his subjects:

The persecution of first Amun and then the other gods, which must have been exceedingly hateful to the majority of the Egyptians, would certainly also be hateful to the individual members of the army. This persecution, which entailed the closing of the temples, the despatch of artisans who entered everywhere to hack out his name from inscriptions, the presumed banishment of the clergy, the excommunication of his very name, could not have been carried out without the army's active support. Granting the fact that the theoretical fiction of the divine kingship was accepted by the mass of the Egyptian people, it is, nevertheless, hardly credible that they would just sit by and acquiesce silently to the persecution of Amun. Some strong backing had to support the royal dicta. Each time a squad of workmen entered a temple or tomb to destroy the name of Amun, it must have been supported by a squad of soldiers who came to see that the royal decree was carried out without opposition. Ultimately the harshness of the persecution must have had a certain reaction even upon the soldiers who, themselves, certainly had been raised in the old beliefs, and rather than risk a wholesale defection and perhaps even a civil war, the army, through the agency of Aye, probably put pressure upon Akhenaten not only to cease the persecution, but to compromise with the old order by the elevation of Semenkhkare to the co-regency.

More information about the extent to which Akhenaten went on trying to eliminate the old forms of worship, as well as the consequent sense of complete loss felt by Egyptians, can be gathered from Tutankhamun's later Restoration Stele, which he erected in the Temple of Amun at Karnak after succeeding to the throne:

Now when his majesty appeared as king, the temples of the gods and goddesses from Elephantine [down] to marshes of the Delta [had] gone to pieces. Their shrines had become desolate, had become mounds overgrown

*with [weeds]. Their sanctuaries were as if they had
never been. Their halls were footpaths. The land was
topsy-turvy, and the gods turned their backs upon this
land. If [the army was] sent to Djahi [Palestine-Syria] to
extend the frontiers of Egypt, no success of theirs came
at all. If one prayed to a god to seek counsel from him,
he would never come [at all]. If one made supplication
to a goddess similarly, she would never come at all.*

Akhenaten appointed his brother, Semenkhkare, as his co-
regent around Year 15 (1364 BC) after giving him his eldest
daughter, Meritaten, the heiress, as his wife. Initially,
Semenkhkare and his queen lived with Akhenaten in the
royal palace at Amarna. In the face of the continuing hostility
throughout the country, however, Semenkhkare left Amarna
for Thebes where he reversed the trend of the religious
revolution, at least in the capital, by establishing a temple to
Amun, an action that indicates the extent to which
Akhenaten was isolated in his attempt to impose his religious
ideas upon the country.

The appointment of Semenkhkare proved to be only a
temporary sop. Within two years it had become clear to Aye,
despite his control of the army, that Egypt was on the brink
of revolution and Akhenaten was himself in danger of
assassination. Aye made another attempt to urge a compromise: Akhenaten refused. Aye must have then told him
that he could no longer guarantee the king's safety: the only
course open to him was to give up the throne and flee the
country.

Architectural evidence to support the claim that
Akhenaten (Moses) was forced to abdicate when threatened
by a military coup came to light as recently as the end of
1997 with another important discovery by Dr Alain-Pierre
Zivie, the French archaeologist, who had earlier found the
tomb of Aper-el, until then unknown, who had served as both
chief minister and high priest during the reign of Akhenaten
(Moses). In the same Saqqara region, ten miles south of

Cairo, he uncovered the tomb of Maya, Tutankhamun's wet-nurse. When first found, the tomb was almost completely full of mummified cats, placed there almost 1,000 years after the original burial. However, on the wall is a scene depicting Maya, protecting the king, who is sitting on her knee. The inscriptions describe her as 'the royal nanny who breast-fed the Pharaoh's body'.

Behind her, to the left, are six officials representing Tutankhamun's cabinet, two above, four below, each with different facial characteristics. Although none of the officials is named, Dr Zivie was able to suggest their identities from their appearance and insignia of office. With one exception, all are military men, four of whom came to the throne of Egypt after the death of Tutankhamun. Dr Zivie recognized the two above as Aye, who succeeded Tutankhamun, his great-nephew, and Horemheb, last ruler of the 18th Dynasty, who followed Aye. The four below are Pa-Ramses, first Pharaoh of the 19th Dynasty, his son, Seti I, who succeeded his father on the throne, and General Nakht Min, thought to be a relative of Aye. The sixth official, also named Maya like the wet-nurse, is described as a treasurer.

This is the first time in Egyptian history that we find the king's cabinet composed almost totally of army generals, who could have gained their positions of power, and later on the throne, only as the result of a military coup. It is clear that in his Year 17 Akhenaten faced an army rebellion led by Horemheb, Pa-Ramses and Seti. General Aye (as he then was), supported by General Nakht Min but unable to crush the rebellion, made a deal with them to allow the abdication of Akhenaten (Moses) and the appointment of his young son, Tutankhamun, as the new ruler over Egypt. Akhenaten (Moses), no doubt reluctantly, accepted the situation. The place he chose for refuge was the wilderness of Sinai, which he would choose again when he led the Israelites in their Exodus from Egypt – but that was a challenge he did not face until a quarter of a century later.

In the meantime, Aye had succeeded Tutankhamun after

his great-nephew's early death, only to disappear mysteriously, along with General Nakht Min, after a reign of only four years. Horemheb then seized power and appointed the other two leaders of the earlier threatened rebellion, Pa-Ramses and Seti, as viziers and commanding generals of the army, thus creating the situation which enabled them in their turn to come to the throne eventually as the first two Pharaohs of a new 19th Dynasty.

Chapter Eleven

The Brazen Serpent

If Moses and Akhenaten are the same person and Moses did not lead the Israelites in their Exodus from Egypt until a quarter of a century later, it follows that he must have survived the threat of revolution and possible assassination that caused him to abdicate and flee to the safety of Sinai. However, this has been the subject of as much scholarly debate as whether or not he shared a co-regency with his father, Amenhotep III.

The tomb prepared for Akhenaten, with the doorway facing roughly east, was found in a side valley at Amarna by the Italian archaeologist Alessandro Bassanti in December 1891. It had been desecrated by the king's enemies and later plundered by tomb robbers. Further investigations took place at Amarna in 1892 (Bassanti), 1894 (Mission Archéologique Française), 1931 (Egypt Exploration Society, the first British organization to be invited to carry out work on behalf of the Service des Antiquités) and in 1931 again (Service des Antiquités).

The items found – the sarcophagus (stone coffin) with its lid, *ushabti* (funerary statues) and the canopic chest (used for holding the royal entrails) – are all items normally placed in a tomb *before* a king's actual death. The great size of the sarcophagus, once it had been reconstructed with its lid from fragments found, suggests that this was the outermost of a series of coffins that would protect the royal mummy (the mummies of both Yuya and Tutankhamun, found later, were enclosed in three coffins). Yet, although the evidence indicates that Akhenaten's enemies smashed everything in

119

the tomb, no matter how large or solid, into small pieces after the end of the Amarna regime, no remains of other coffins were found, nor any remains of the usual shrine or canopy that were part of the normal burial furniture. The idea that Akhenaten was never buried in the tomb is reinforced by the fact that no trace was found of other items – chariots, chairs, boxes, magic bricks and amulets – that were normally buried in royal tombs only *after* the king's death.

John Pendlebury, director of the 1931 expedition, later made the important observation in his account 'Clearance of the Royal Tomb at Amarna': 'In view . . . of the demonstration that the so-called body of Akhenaten found in the cache of Tiye at Thebes' – he was referring to Tomb No. 55 where the skeleton of Semenkhkare had been found and was originally thought to be that of Akhenaten – 'is in reality not his at all, it was imperative to try and collect all the evidence as to whether Akhenaten was ever buried at el-Amarna, and, if so, whether in the Royal Tomb or elsewhere.' After giving a short account of what was found in the tomb, he went on to say: '. . . Akhenaten's magnificent alabaster canopic chest, with protecting vultures at the corners, together with pieces of the lids capped with the king's head . . . gives evidence of never having been used, for it is quite unstained by the black resinous substance* seen in those of Amenhotep II and Tutankhamun, and is additionally interesting in that it is inscribed with the early form of the Aten name' – shortly after the start of the co-regency – 'while the sarcophagi all have the later.'

Pendlebury is here remarking that as the burial rituals required some parts of the funerary furniture, including the canopic chest, to be anointed by a black liquid, and he was unable to see any traces of such staining on the fragments he found, he concluded that the tomb had never been used. This would mean that Akhenaten was never buried in his Amarna

* Used to preserve the heart, lungs and other parts taken from the body during mummification.

tomb, a view supported by the fact that no trace of such anointing was found of any fragments of the canopic jars themselves, usually placed in position at the time of burial. This idea is further reinforced by the use of the early Aten name, which suggests that the canopic chest was made and placed in position very early in the king's reign, before Year 9 when the Aten received his new name, the abstract writing for *shu* and Ra.

Pendlebury's conclusions were later confirmed by the Egyptian archaeologist Muhammad Hamza, who in 1939 restored Akhenaten's canopic chest from the fragments found by Pendlebury and commented subsequently in an article, 'The Alabaster Canopic Box of Akhenaten': 'As the box is quite unstained by the black resinous unguents to which those of Amenhotep II, Tutankhamun and Horemheb were subjected, it seems probable that it has never been used for the king's viscera.'

As a result of the archaeological evidence presented by Pendlebury and Hamza, most Egyptologists accepted the conclusion that Akhenaten could not have been buried in his Amarna tomb; nevertheless they still believed that he died in his Year 17 (1361 BC), the year he fell from power. Some, like Alan H. Gardiner, the British Egyptologist, took the view that he had never been buried at all and his 'body had been torn to pieces and thrown to the dogs': others, like Arthur Weigall and Cyril Aldred, thought that he must have been buried at Thebes or somewhere else.

In the absence of any evidence of his death in his Year 17, the central issue is: What positive evidence is there to suggest that Akhenaten actually survived? A good deal exists in one form and another. Much of it has been the subject of scholarly argument, often acrimonious, that has led in one instance to accusations of dishonesty. It will help to simplify matters if we summarize briefly – assuming that Akhenaten (Moses) survived – what one might expect to be the subsequent course of events in the light of Egyptian customs of the time.

When we say that Akhenaten abdicated in his Year 17, we use a modern term expressing a modern practice. However, Egyptian Pharaohs did not gain power from the people or the parliament, but from the gods. From the time of his birth the king was regarded as the Son of Amun-Ra, the principal state god, and destined to rule. On being crowned he took possession of his inheritance, the lands given to him by the gods, and retained possession until the day he died.

For his part, Akhenaten ruled in the name of Aten, whom he regarded as his father. However, even in exile, as long as he lived he would still have been regarded as the legitimate ruler by the followers of Aten. After the abdication, his successor Semenkhkare, the co-regent appointed in Akhenaten's Year 15, is thought to have ruled for only a few months, perhaps even days, before being assassinated at Thebes. He was succeeded in his turn by Akhenaten's son, the young king Tutankhamun, then named Tutankhaten. If his reign as Pharaoh began while his father was still alive and regarded as the legitimate ruler, he could be said to have taken his authority from the old king. The situation changed in his Year 4 (1358 BC), however, when he abandoned Amarna for Thebes and changed his name to Tutankhamun.* The Amun priesthood accepted this return to the old ways with a new coronation celebration. Thus, at this point Aten had no longer any ruling power in Egypt, no land to give, and Akhenaten, from this moment, could no longer be regarded as the legitimate king.

Egyptians calculated the years of each king separately and, if there was no co-regency, the first year of the new king began only after the last year of his predecessor. If Akhenaten abdicated in his Year 17 but did not cease to be looked upon as the king until four years later, his Year 21, one would expect to find some written evidence confirming this course of events.

---

* He changed his name when he decided to reopen the old temples of Egypt. As Amun was the official deity of the 18th dynasty, every member of the family was regarded as a son of Amun.

A hieratic (cursive script) docket,* No. 279, found by excavators at Amarna, bears two different dates – Year 17 and Year 1. This was explained by H. W. Fairman, the British Egyptologist, in the following terms: 'It records, therefore, the first year of an unnamed king which followed the seventeenth year of another unnamed king. There cannot be any doubt that the latter was Akhenaten. Year 1 can hardly have been that of Semenkhkare since . . . his Year 1 was probably Year 15 of Akhenaten. Thus the docket must be assigned to the first year of Tutankhamun.' This is the first time, as far as I am aware, that a king placed his own date on the same text as that of a predecessor after the latter's rule had come to an end. How, therefore, is it that Akhenaten's Year 17 was also regarded as Year 1 of Tutankhamun unless there was a co-regency – that is, Akhenaten was still alive when Tutankhamun came to the throne?

Another hieratic docket found at Amarna resulted in a charge of dishonesty being levelled at certain scholars. The essence of the dispute is whether this docket refers to Year 11 of Akhenaten or to Year 21. A facsimile of this docket was made and published in 1923 by Battiscombe Gunn, the British archaeologist, who, as he admitted, dated the docket to Year 11 because of 'the absence of other evidence as to the reign [of Akhenaten] extending beyond Year 17'.

The hieratic sign for the figure 10 is an upside-down 'V' and for 20 two upside-down 'Vs' above each other and, in this case, the figure 1 written alongside them. The docket shows a complete 'V' with the remains of another 'V' above it, which convinced the American scholar Keith C. Seele, correctly, that the date should be read as 'Year 21'. He even went as far as to accuse British scholars of avoiding the evidence intentionally: 'While the actual fate of Akhenaten is unknown, it is evidence that he must have disappeared in his twenty-first year on the throne or even later. Some Egyptologists, including the Egypt Exploration

---

* The docket is an inscription, in this instance, on pottery.

Society's excavators at Amarna, allow him but seventeen years.'

Although many scholars all over the world became convinced by Seele's arguments, debates over the matter have rumbled on down the decades, only one of many unidentified example of scholars' preconceptions standing in the way of impartial evaluation of the evidence. Fairman himself disclosed later in an article in an archaeological journal that a member of the Egyptian Exploration Society team that worked at Amarna during the years 1930–31 was able to read the date Year 18 on one of the ostraca (pottery figures) he was responsible for copying. However, Fairman took the arbitrary view that this 'ostracon of Year 18 . . . may be dismissed as being untrustworthy, and without value'. He then goes on to explain that 'the ostracon was not kept, but according to a rough facsimile this reading is certainly wrong'. Fairman is not telling us that the disputed ostracon was lost: he is saying that it was 'not kept', that it was thrown away. One would, in contrast, have expected, as this ostracon gives a different reading, that it would have been guarded carefully for further examination. Instead, we now have only Fairman's judgement to rely on for whether the original reading was right or wrong.

Further evidence of Akhenaten's survival was provided by Professor D. E. Derry, Professor of Anatomy at Cairo University, who examined the remains in Tomb No. 55, originally thought, wrongly, to have been those of Akhenaten, and eventually identified as being those of his co-regent, Semenkhkare, as no other suggested candidate has sufficient supporting evidence. In the subsequent notes about his investigation he made the point that the reign of Akhenaten had been 'extended to the nineteenth year by Pendlebury's recent discovery at el-Amarna of a monument bearing that date and with the further possibility that this may be lengthened to the twentieth year. Mr Pendlebury has very courteously permitted us to make use of these hitherto unpublished facts.' Pendlebury was captured and shot by the

Germans in Crete during the Second World War before he could publish the source of his information.

Another significant piece of evidence is provided by four bricks of dried, gritty mud found *in situ*, distributed around Tomb No. 55. Although they had suffered, like everything else in the tomb, from the effects of damp, Akhenaten's name could be read on at least two of the bricks, whose function was to protect the dead person from intruders. The four bricks form a complete set, each having to be placed in a certain position in relation to the mummy in order to fulfil their protective function (i.e. through magic, to prevent evil beings from interfering with the burial area).

That these magical bricks belonged originally to Akhenaten is not the subject of dispute, and the fact that they were found *in situ* in Tomb No. 55 was one of the strong points that led Egyptologists to believe initially that the remains in the coffin were his rather than Semenkhkare's. Why, then, was no attempt made either to erase Akhenaten's name or adapt the text to suit Semenkhkare? It is now agreed that Akhenaten's reign ended a few months, if not a few days, before the death of Semenkhkare. In this case, had Akhenaten's reign ended with his death, his funerary arrangements, which would have taken seventy days, might not even have ended when the arrangements for Semenkhkare's burial began. How, then, does one explain that Akhenaten's original magical bricks, that formed an essential part of the funerary rituals, were found *in situ* in Semenkhkare's tomb? The only possible conclusion is that they were not needed by Akhenaten who, although he had fallen from power before Semenkhkare's death, was himself not dead but alive.

We are told in the Old Testament that Moses fled to Sinai after killing an Egyptian – after abdicating as a king, as we saw earlier in the Talmud account – and lived there until his return after the Pharaoh of the Oppression, Horemheb, had died. Although we do not have conclusive evidence that

Akhenaten followed a similar course, there are many indications that point to this being the case.

Sinai, beyond the eastern boundary of Egypt proper, is in the form of a triangle with its apex to the south between the two arms of the Red Sea, the Gulf of Suez and the Gulf of Aqaba. At its northern base runs the road from Egypt to Asia, from Kantarah to Gaza along the Mediterranean coastline. Beneath this low northern land is a lofty limestone plateau, crossed only by a few narrow passes. The southern triangle, between the two arms of the Red Sea, is a mountain mass including Mount Sinai or Mount Horeb (modern name, Gebel Musa, which means the Mount of Moses). En route from the Eastern Delta, through the valleys, before arriving at Mount Sinai we come to another important site, Serabit el-Khadim, which is rich in deposits of turquoise as well as being a holy place.

Sinai had an appeal as a place of refuge beyond the fact that the terrain made it a 'wilderness'. Although it had been regarded as part of Egypt from the early days of Egyptian history, no army garrison was stationed there. Nor did it have a resident governor. Instead, during the 18th and 19th Dynasties the area was placed under the control of two officials, The Royal Messenger in All Foreign Lands and The Royal Chancellor, who was responsible for turquoise mining operations in Sinai.

Neby, the Troop Commander and Mayor at Zarw, was also The Royal Messenger in All Foreign Lands. As we have seen, Zarw was Tiye's city, given to her as a summer residence by her husband, Amenhotep III (Solomon), and there are indications that Zarw remained faithful to Aten during the reigns of the two Amarna kings who came to the throne after the disappearance of Semenkhkare – Tutankhamun and his great-uncle successor, Aye (Ephraim). It was only later, when Horemheb, the last ruler of the 18th Dynasty, who was an implacable enemy of the Amarna regime and of worship of Aten, appointed Pa-Ramses (later Ramses I) to the posts previously held by Neby that the climate changed. At least

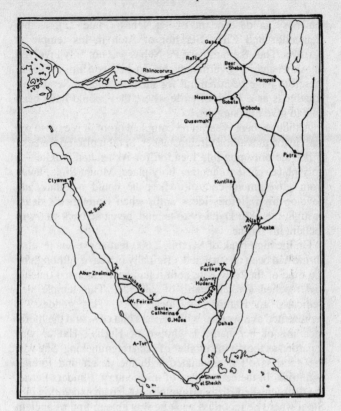

Sinai

until that time, therefore, Akhenaten could count on being able to live in peace in his chosen refuge.

Nor was he under any threat from The Royal Chancellor. We know from inscriptions found in Sinai and other sources that, up to the time of Amenhotep III, the treasury was placed in the hands of one family, that of Pa-Nehas, for three generations. Akhenaten himself also appointed the priest

127

Panehesy, a descendant of Pa-Nehas (Plate 22), as his chancellor and Chief Servitor of Aten in his temple at Amarna. Thus the family of Pa-Nehas was not only involved in Akhenaten's government, but in his worship. It would therefore have been natural for them to suggest Serabit el-Khadimas as a place of exile where they would have been able to give him support.

Although there is as yet no complete proof, it is easy to see that, in the prevailing circumstances, Serabit offered the best, if not the only possible location for Akhenaten's exile – a holy place, close to another holy place, Mount Sinai, away from government control, where he could meditate and develop his religious ideas until, when Horemheb's death brought the 18th Dynasty to an end, he came back to try to reclaim his throne.

On the high peak of Serabit, 2,600 feet above sea level, a shrine had been constructed, originally in a cave, although by the time of the New Kingdom it had been extended outside and reached a total length of 230 feet. This temple was dedicated to Hathor, the local deity. This goddess is represented as a woman with the ears of a cow, and the literal meaning of her name is 'house of Horus'. Hathor was regarded as the divine mother of each reigning king. She was the goddess often associated with the desert and foreign countries. In the early years of this century, Flinders Petrie, the distinguished British Egyptologist, led an expedition into Sinai where he recorded what he was able to find of ancient inscriptions. One of his surprising discoveries at the Serabit temple was a dark green head, executed in the Amarna style, all that remained of a statuette of Queen Tiye, Akhenaten's mother. The complete statuette must have been about a foot high. Why should it be at Serabit? 'It is strange that this remotest settlement of Egypt has preserved her portrait for us, unmistakably named by her cartouche in the midst of the crown,' Petrie remarked in his subsequent book *Researches in Sinai*. 'The haughty dignity of the face is blended with a fascinating directness and personal appeal. The delicacy of the surfaces round the eye and over the cheek shows the greatest delicacy in handling. The curiously drawn-down lips with their fullness and yet delicacy, their disdain without malice, are evidently modelled in all truth from the life.'

Petrie also found evidence indicating that the rituals performed in the temple at Serabit were Semitic in their nature. Under the temple lay more than fifty tons of clean white ash, which he took to represent the remains of burnt sacrifices over a long period. This practice is known from the Bible to have been Israelite. ('When Abraham was about to sacrifice Isaac, Abraham lifted up his eyes, and looked, and behold behind him a ram caught in a thicket by his horns, and Abraham went and took the ram, and offered him up for a burnt offering in the stead of his son' [Genesis 22:13].) Two cones of sandstone, alike in shape and size, were found in the temple. Stones of this type were used in certain forms of Syrian ritual and are not to be found in Egypt. Three rectangular tanks and a circular basin were placed to be used at four different stages of entering the temple. This makes it clear that ablutions played a great role in the form of worship at Serabit as they do in both Judaism and Islam.

Scattered over the area around the temple Petrie came across many slabs of sandstone, set upright. The slabs ranged in height from a few inches to a couple of feet, propped up by other stones if necessary to make them stand on end. Similar piled stones were found around Mount Sinai, indicating that both areas were regarded as sacred places. Petrie noted that this piling of stones is part of a well-known system of sacred stones, set upright for adoration, that is not Egyptian, and for him the only explanation for this ritual would be the custom of sleeping at or near a sacred place in order to obtain some vision from the deity, which he compared with what the patriarch Jacob is said to have done:

And Jacob went out from Beersheba, and went towards Haran. And he lighted upon a certain place, and tarried there all night, because the sun was set; and he took of

*the stones of that place, and put them for his pillows,
and lay down in that place to sleep. And he dreamed,
and behold a ladder set up on the earth, and the top of
it reached to heaven: and behold the angels of God
ascending and descending on it. And, behold, the Lord
stood above it . . .*

[Genesis 28:10–13]

The Ten Commandments, said to have been given by the
Lord God of Moses to the Israelites in Sinai, clearly derive
from an Egyptian tradition and would seem to have roots in
common with the Egyptian *Book of the Dead*. Egyptians
believed that, after their death, they faced a trial in the
underworld before Osiris and his 42 judges in the Hall of
Judgement. Spell 125 of the *Book of the Dead* contains a
Negative Confession that the dead person has to recite on this
occasion, containing such assurances as 'I have done no
falsehood' and 'I have not killed men'. It therefore seems
likely that (Moses) Akhenaten, who did not believe in Osiris
or his underworld, turned the moral code according to which
the Egyptians believed their dead would be judged into an
imperative code of behaviour for his followers in this life –
the Ten Commandments. Now I shall compare the two in
detail.

Chapter 20 of the Book of Exodus contains the Ten
Commandments of God given to the Israelites at the foot of
Mount Sinai. Except for the first two commandments which
forbid them from worshipping other gods or bowing down
for images of any kind, and a third that demands them to
honour their parents, the remaining seven are found in
Chapter 125 of the *Book of the Dead*:

Thou shalt not take the name of the Lord thy God in vain.
I have not acted deceitfully.

Remember the sabbath day, to keep it holy.
I have not committed any sin against purity.

130

Thou shalt not kill.
I have not slain man or woman.

Thou shalt not commit adultery.
I have not defiled the wife of a man.

Thou shalt not steal.
I have not committed theft.

Thou shalt not bear false witness against thy neighbour.
I have not uttered falsehood.

Thou shalt not covet thy neighbour's wife.
I have not defiled the wife of a man.

My conclusion, on the weight of the foregoing evidence, and more that will follow, is that (Moses) Akhenaten fled at the time of his abdication to Sinai, which was not merely a safe refuge, but a holy place. Furthermore, as a quarrying region it provided the materials he needed for the tabernacle (large tent) that, according to the Old Testament, he built at the foot of Mount Sinai, the holy mountain, where St Catherine's monastery stands today (Plate 27).

When (Moses) Akhenaten sought refuge in Sinai he seems from later evidence to have taken with him one of the sceptres of the king's power – a rod in the shape of a serpent, either made of, or covered with, brass. The very last mention of Moses in the Old Testament serves through an oblique reference to this symbol of power as another link identifying him as a Pharaoh. It occurs in the second Book of Kings, which gives an account of various rulers, more than five centuries after the Exodus, some of whom tried to keep to the Lord's teachings, some of whom did not. Among the former, we are told, was Hezekiah:

'And he did that which was right in the sight of the Lord,

according to all that David his father did.
He removed the high places and brake the images, and cut
down the groves; and brake in pieces the brasen serpent
that Moses had made: for unto those days the children of
Israel did burn incense to it . . .'

[II Kings 18:3–4]

(Moses) Akhenaten was also accompanied on his journey
into exile by some of his closest and most faithful followers.
Among them was Panehesy, his chancellor and Chief
Servitor of Aten at Amarna, who – as we shall see – would
be named in the Talmud many centuries later as the priest
who killed Jesus.

Part II
Christ the King

... they hanged Jesus
(the Nazarene) ... because he
hath practised magic and led
astray Israel ... [And] everyone
who passed to and fro said:
'It seems that the king is
crucified.'

Talmud, B. Sanh., 43a
T. Sanh., 9.7

Chapter Twelve

The Gospel Makers

The statement that the historical Jesus was killed by a priest named Panehesy in the 14th century BC will be greeted with varying emotions by the millions of Christians throughout the world who accept the orthodox belief that he lived, suffered and died in the 1st century AD. As we shall see in the next chapter, the early Church Fathers believed that Jesus appeared twice in two different periods of time. The first appearance, which they construed as a spiritual pre-existence, they state to have occurred in the form of Joshua, son of Nun, the Israelite leader who followed Moses: the second, historical appearance took place under Roman rule at the time of John the Baptist. Although I accept these two appearances, I regard the first as the historical appearance and the second as the spiritual one. However, while it is certain that his disciples have claimed that he appeared to them at this time, not a shred of evidence exists to support the orthodox view that this was the historical Jesus, while, disturbing as the thought may be, substantial evidence – from the Bible itself and the teachings of the early Church Fathers as well as Egyptian history – points to his having lived, suffered and died many centuries earlier.

Two thousand years ago, at the time Jesus is said to have lived, Palestine was part of the Roman Empire. Yet no contemporary Roman record exists that can bear witness, directly or indirectly, to the physical appearance of Jesus. Even more surprising is the absence of any reference to Jesus in the writings of Jewish authors living at that time in Jerusalem or Alexandria, although we know from Talmudic writings that the Jews did know of Jesus, even if they refused to accept either that he was the Messiah (Christ) or that he was descended from the House of David.

The orthodox Christian view, based on the gospels of Matthew, Mark, Luke and John, whose earliest versions were written several decades after the events they describe, is that Jesus was born in Galilee or Judaea during the time of Herod the Great (40–4 BC), that his ministry began when he was 30 years of age and that his suffering and crucifixion took place three years later when Judaea had become a Roman province and Pontius Pilate was its procurator (AD 26–36). Subsequently, during the 4th century AD when Christianity had become the official religion of the Roman Empire, a date was fixed for his birth, and AD 1 became accepted as the dawn of the Christian era.

Yet when we attempt to match the four gospels of Matthew, Mark, Luke and John against the facts of history we cannot escape the implication that with the gospels themselves we are dealing with a false dawn. We find no agreement about when Jesus was born or when he was put to death. But first let us look at the established historical facts.

Pompey, the Roman general, defeated the Greek rulers of Asia Minor and Syria in 64 BC and made the territories into new Roman provinces. At this time Judaea was allowed to remain an independent client state under local rulers. However, in 40 BC, the Roman Senate granted Herod the Great control over Judaea, plus Idumea to the south, Samaria and Galilee to the north, and Peraea to the east of the Jordan. Mark Antony, the Roman soldier and statesman, subsequently appointed Herod the Great (not to be confused with his son, Herod Antipas, tetrarch of Galilee and Peraea at the supposed time of the Crucifixion) as governor, and three years later he became *de facto* king. His position was confirmed in 31 BC by Octavian after the latter's defeat of Mark Antony and Cleopatra, the Queen of Egypt with whom Mark Antony had fallen in love, at the naval battle of Actium. Four years later, the Senate gave the victorious

Octavian the title Augustus Caesar. This was the point at which the Roman republic came to an end and the Roman Empire, encircling the Mediterranean and stretching as far north as Britain and Germany, began.

When Herod died in 4 BC his dominions were divided between his three sons. However, Archelaus, the son who ruled over Judaea, was deposed by the Romans in AD 6 and the territory came under direct Roman rule. From this time onward, Judaea was ruled by Roman procurators, of whom Pontius Pilate was the fifth, appointed during the reign of Tiberius Caesar (AD 14–37), Augustus's stepson, who had succeeded him.

Only two of the four gospel authors, Matthew and Luke, refer to the birth of Jesus, but their accounts do not agree. Matthew places his birth firmly in the time of Herod: 'Jesus was born in Bethlehem of Judaea in the days of Herod the king' (Matthew 2:1). This means that he was born before 4 BC, the date of Herod's death. Then we are told that Herod, learning that a king of the Jews – whom he saw as a rival – had been born, was troubled and 'exceeding wroth, and sent forth, and slew all the children that were in Bethlehem, and in all the coasts thereof, from two years old and under' (2:16). In the meantime, Joseph, the husband of Mary, had been warned by an angel: 'Arise, and take the young child and his mother, and flee into Egypt, and be thou there until I bring thee word' (2:13). Joseph remained in Egypt 'until the death of Herod: that it might be fulfilled' – a significant statement – 'which was spoken of the Lord by the prophet, saying, "Out of Egypt have I called my son"' (2:15).

After the death of Herod, the angel appeared to Joseph again and said: 'Arise, and take the young child and his mother, and go into the land of Israel: for they are dead which sought the young child's life. And he arose and took the young child and his mother, and came into the land of Israel' (2:20–21). The implication of this account is that we are dealing with quite a short span of time as Jesus, a baby when Joseph and Mary, his mother, fled with him into Egypt, was still a 'young child' when they returned to Judaea on learning of the death of Herod.

Luke, for his part, relates the birth of Jesus to that of John the Baptist, who was also born 'in the days of Herod, the king of Judaea' (Luke 1:5). We are told that John's father, Zacharias, was informed by an angel: 'Fear not, Zacharias . . . thy wife Elisabeth shall bear thee a son, and thou shalt call his name John' (1:13). The story goes on to relate that in the sixth month of Elisabeth's pregnancy 'the angel Gabriel was sent from God unto a city of Galilee named Nazareth, To a virgin espoused of a man whose name was Joseph, of the house of David; and the virgin's name was Mary . . . And the angel said unto her, Fear not, Mary: for thou hast found favour with God. And, behold, thou shalt conceive in thy womb, and bring forth a son, and shalt call his name Jesus. He shall be great, and shall be called the Son of the Highest: and the Lord God shall give unto him the throne of his father David' (1:26–27,30–32).

Here Luke goes on to tell the familiar Christmas story of the birth of Jesus in a Bethlehem stable because there was no room at the inn – and contradicts both Matthew and his own earlier account by placing these events a decade *after* the death of Herod the Great: 'And it came to pass in those days, that there went out a decree from Caesar Augustus, that all the world should be taxed. (And this taxing was first made when Cyrenius (Quirinius) was governor of Syria.) And all went to be taxed, every one into his own city. And Joseph also went up from Galilee, out of the city of Nazareth, into Judaea, unto the city of David, which is called Bethlehem; (because he was of the house and lineage of David)' (2:1–4). We know from Roman sources that this event could not have taken place before AD 6, the year in which Quirinius was appointed governor of Syria and Judaea became a Roman province. The purpose of the census in AD 6, attested from other non-biblical sources, was to assess the amount of tribute which the new province of Judaea would have to pay.

Up to this point we have been offered two possible dates

for the birth of Jesus – before 4 BC, the year of Herod's death, and AD 6, the year of the census. In the next chapter of Luke's narrative we are offered yet a third, when he describes John's baptism of Christ, which, as all four gospels record, immediately preceded the start of his mission: 'In the fifteenth year of the reign of Tiberius Caesar, Pontius Pilate being governor of Judaea . . . Annas and Caiaphas being the high priests, the word of God came unto John the son of Zacharias in the wilderness. And he came into all the country about Jordan, preaching the baptism of repentance for the remission of sins' (3:1–3) . . . 'Now when all the people were baptized, it came to pass, that Jesus also being baptized, and praying, the heaven was opened. And the Holy Ghost descended in a bodily shape like a dove upon him, and a voice came from heaven, which said, "Thou art my beloved son; in thee I am well pleased" ' (3:21–22).

As Tiberius became emperor in AD 14, this would place the baptism of Jesus in AD 29. Luke then goes on to say: 'And Jesus began to be about thirty years of age' (3:23) when he started his ministry. If he was about 30 in AD 29, he cannot have been born before the end of Herod the Great's reign in 4 BC or at the time of the census in AD 6, but during the last year before the end of the pre-Christian era. No doubt it was this account that persuaded the Roman Catholic Church to fix this year as the turning point in world history – the first year of our Lord.

Similar difficulties arise when it comes to trying to arrive at a precise date for the Crucifixion. All four gospels agree that it took place when Pontius Pilate was governor of Judaea (AD 26–36) and that the high priest of Jewish Jerusalem at the time was named Caiaphas, known from other sources as Josephus Caiaphas, who held the office from AD 18 until AD 37. The situation is further complicated by the fact that the gospels disagree about how long the ministry of Jesus lasted: Matthew, Mark and Luke favour one year, John indicates two or three years.

The majority of New Testament scholars agree that Jesus

met his death around AD 30. If this is the case, his age at the time would have been 36 or more, if he was born towards the end of Herod the Great's rule and we allow at least two years for the Holy Family's sojourn into Egypt and for Herod to have all children up to the age of two slain; 25 if he was born at the time of the AD 6 census; or 31 if one accepts Luke's account of his baptism and his age at the start of his ministry.

To summarize the argument so far, on the basis of known historical facts all we can be certain about concerning the figure presented to us in the gospels as Jesus is that he lived and died between 27 BC when the Roman Senate appointed Octavian as the Emperor Augustus, and AD 37, the year of the death of Augustus's successor, Tiberius. However, if the Jesus of the gospels lived, suffered and died during the period of Roman rule over Palestine, it is curious that his name does not appear in the writings of three distinguished contemporary authors – Philo Judaeus, Justus of Tiberias and Flavius Josephus.

This absence is particularly striking in the case of the 38 works left behind by Philo Judaeus, who was born in 15 BC and died some two decades after the supposed date of the Crucifixion. Philo was a man of eminence and importance. His brother was the head of the Jewish community living in Alexandria, his son was married to a grand-daughter of King Herod and Philo himself was chosen to head a mission to Rome to plead with Caligula, the third Roman emperor (AD 37–41), who believed he was divine, to withdraw an edict ordering the Jews to place the imperial image in their temple at Alexandria and worship it.

Although a Jew, Philo was also a follower of the Greek philosopher Plato and is known as the first of the neo-Platonists who tried to reconcile Greek doctrines with the revelations of the Old Testament. His works were recognized as having a close affinity with Christian ideas and many scholars have seen in him the connecting link between Greek thought and the New Testament. Some have even gone as far as to suggest that Philo's philosophy was similar to the thinking of St Paul.

Despite his close links with Christian thought, we find only one New Testament figure mentioned in Philo's works, Pontius Pilate, but nothing about Jesus. It is a similar story with Justus of Tiberias, a place on the west shore of the Sea of Galilee mentioned frequently in the gospels. Justus wrote a history of Herod the Great. Nowhere does he refer to Jesus or Herod's order to slaughter all children under the age of two. Although his work is now lost, it was known to Photius, Bishop of Constantinople in the 9th century AD, who confirmed the absence in it of any mention of Jesus.

No official report by Pontius Pilate about Jesus and his trial exists, although a few centuries later some writings called *Acts of Pilate* appeared. They included an account of Jesus of Nazareth. However, they have been proved forgeries, either by Christians who wished to confirm the historicity of their Lord or by enemies of Christianity who wished to attack the religion.

The first references to Christianity in Roman writings are found in the works of the historians Suetonius and Tacitus, and Pliny the Younger, who were friends and held posts under Roman emperors. The earliest was by Suetonius, who was born around AD 69, served as a secretary to Hadrian, the 14th emperor (AD 117–138), and thus had access to the imperial archives. His major historical work, *The Lives of the Caesars*, published about AD 120, gave accounts of the reigns of Julius Caesar and the 11 emperors who followed him. The mention of Christ occurs in the 25th chapter where the author is discussing events in the reign of Claudius (AD 41–54), who had succeeded as the fourth emperor after the assassination of Caligula. Suetonius makes a brief mention of riots that took place in Rome in AD 49: 'As the Jews, at the instigation of Chrestus, were constantly raising riots, he (Claudius) drove them out of Rome.' In the light of the gospels, this is a surprisingly early date, given the slow nature of travel at the time.

Chrestus, a common name in Rome, must have been substituted for the Greek Christus because the two names were pronounced alike and Suetonius thought – wrongly – that someone called Christ was in Rome at the time, instigating the riots. These troubles in Rome were not the result of Roman oppression but of internal conflicts within the Jewish community between Jews (Christians) who believed the Messiah (Christ) had already come and Jews who believed that he was still to appear. An echo of these troubles is found in the Acts of the Apostles (18:2–3) where we read of a Jew, Aquila, and his wife, Priscilla, who, having been driven from Rome by an edict of Claudius, went to start a tentmaking business in Corinth where they met Paul. Although the work of Suetonius is the oldest written testimony about followers of Christ in Rome, it does not refer to the historical Jesus.

In the circumstances it was a consolation to Christians to learn, once the work of Flavius Josephus had been translated from Greek into Latin, that the text included references not only to Pontius Pilate but to John the Baptist, Jesus and his brother James. Josephus, a Palestinian Jew of priestly family, was born in AD 37, shortly after the Crucifixion is said to have taken place. In the latter years of his life, he settled in Rome during the reign of Domitian (AD 81–96), the 11th emperor. There he wrote *Antiquities of the Jews*, a long historical work of 20 books that, in surviving copies, are in some cases the only source we have for details of events in Syria/Palestine during the 1st century of the Christian era.

In Book 18 we find an account of a war between Aretas, Arab king of Nabatea, to the south and east of the Dead Sea, and Herod Antipas, the tetrarch of Galilee and son of Herod the Great. The cause of the quarrel lay in the fact that Herod Antipas, who had been married to the daughter of Aretas, sent her back to her father and took a new wife – his sister-in-law, Herodias. In the subsequent hostilities, Herod's army was destroyed. The Jews took the view that this defeat was a punishment from God for what Herod had done 'against

John, that was called the Baptist; for Herod slew him, who was a good man, and commanded the Jews to exercise virtue, both as to righteousness towards one another, and piety towards God, and so to come to baptism . . .'

John the Baptist linked immersion in a flowing river to erasing sin. His baptism was a sign of divine pardon, and seems to have been a substitute for the practice of offering a sacrifice in atonement for sin. It differed, however, from the baptism of Jesus.

In the New Testament, Jesus is quoted as saying: '. . . John truly baptized with water; but ye shall be baptized with the Holy Ghost not many days hence' (Acts 1:5). In fact, according to the gospels the apostles continued to practise baptism by water of the type administered by John, but they emphasized the necessity of its being preceded by an inner conversion. Other followers of Jesus are also described as having known only the baptism of John: 'And it came to pass, that . . . Paul having passed through the upper coasts came to Ephesus: and finding certain disciples, he said unto them, Have ye received the Holy Ghost since ye believed? And they said unto him, We have not so much as heard whether there be any Holy Ghost. And he said unto them, Unto what then were ye baptized? And they said, Unto John's baptism' (Acts 19:1–3).

Therefore it seems that recognition of the Holy Spirit was the new element of early Christian baptism. Paul himself was the first to define its symbolic significance, joining the ritual to belief in the resurrected Christ. It was thus an initiation into the spiritual life with Christ: the stain of sin was not washed away by water, but by Jesus's death and belief in his resurrection. In this context it is curious that three of the gospels should give an account of Jesus being baptized by John.

Not surprisingly, John's promised forgiveness of sins made him extremely popular with the Israelites, and Herod became disturbed by the enthusiastic crowds that gathered to hear him preach: 'Herod, who feared lest the great influence

John had over the people might put it into his power and inclination to raise a rebellion (for they seemed ready to do anything he should advise), thought it best, by putting him to death, to prevent any mischief he might cause . . .' This account by Josephus, while establishing John the Baptist as a historical figure, contains no reference to Jesus and provides no support for the gospel statement that John was 'preparing the way' for him.

However, Josephus does provide evidence that the gospel story of Pilate sitting on his seat of judgment and, despite his wife's plea for mercy, handing Jesus over to the multitude in Jerusalem to be crucified (Matthew 27:19–23), can be regarded only as a piece of creative writing. Although a Roman garrison was stationed in Jerusalem, the governor's residence and seat of judgement was some seventy miles away in the port of Caesarea, an ancient city that had been restored and given its new name by Herod. From AD 6, two years after Herod's death, it became the seat of the Roman procurators of Judaea and remained the capital of Rome and Byzantine Palestine for many centuries.

Josephus also records in Book 18 that, shortly after taking office in AD 26, Pilate sent troops to the Jerusalem Temple by night, carrying military standards bearing the image of Emperor Tiberius. Pilate himself remained in Caesarea, however, and, once they discovered what had happened, a band of outraged Jerusalem citizens had to make the long journey to the coast to intercede with Pilate for removal of the standards. In fact, another incident in Book 18 is the only indication from any contemporary source that Pilate ever visited Jerusalem. His arrival, according to Josephus, was prompted by a scheme to bring water to the city from the vicinity of Hebron. The Jews, who opposed the scheme because it was to be financed with money from the Temple treasury, 'made a clamour against him'. Eventually, when the large throng refused to disperse, Pilate set soldiers armed with daggers upon them and the soldiers 'laid upon them much greater blows than Pilate had commanded'. The status of Caesarea is confirmed by the story in the later Book of Acts about the rescue of Paul by Roman soldiers in Jerusalem when Jews wished to kill him. The soldiers took Paul to Caesarea (Acts 23:24) and handed him over to Felix, the new procurator, who kept him in prison for two years while the rights and wrongs of the matter were examined.

In the circumstances, the subsequent discovery that Jesus *was* actually mentioned in the fourth chapter of Book 18 was a source of great consolation to Christians. The text reads:

> *Now, there was about this time Jesus, a wise man, if it be lawful to call him a man, for he was a doer of wonderful works – a teacher of such men as receive the truth with pleasure. He drew over to him both many of the Jews, and many of the Gentiles. He was (the) Christ; and when Pilate, at the suggestion of the principal men amongst us, had condemned him to the Cross, those that loved him at the first did not forsake him, for he appeared to them alive again the third day, as the divine prophets had foretold these and ten thousand other wonderful things concerning him; and the tribe of Christians, so named from him, are not extinct to this day.*

This passage was greatly valued during the Middle Ages as the only external testimony from the 1st century AD pointing to Jesus having lived at that time. Unfortunately, it has since become an embarrassment, having been exposed in the 16th century as a forgery, an interpolation placed in the work of Josephus by a Christian copyist or editor, frustrated by the historian's silence over the birth, suffering and death of Jesus. No mention was made of this passage until two and a quarter centuries after publication of Josephus's work. It is absent from the work of Origen (*c.* AD 185–254), a Father of the early Christian Church, whose writings covered every aspect of Christianity and who was familiar with the writings of Josephus. In his own writings, he referred to the account of John the Baptist's life and death to be found in Book 18 of *Antiquities of the Jews*, but made no reference whatever to Jesus, a curious omission by someone who believed in him, if Jesus was a contemporary of John the Baptist. The first person to mention this testimony was, in fact, Eusebius – another early Church Father who wrote an ecclesiastical history down to his own time – in his *Demonstration of the Gospel*, written about AD 320.

Literary criticism of the passage falls into three categories. In the first place, the clause 'if it be lawful to call him a man' looks like an attempt by an orthodox Christian to remind readers that Jesus was also divine; secondly, the sentence 'He was (the) Christ' is a straightforward confession of faith in Jesus as being the Jewish Messiah, but this could not be possible in the case of Josephus as Origen himself in one of his works, *Against Celsius*, describes the Jewish historian as 'not receiving our Jesus as Christ'; and, thirdly, the reference to the resurrection of Jesus would suggest that the author believed in it. Moreover, Josephus would not have called the followers of Jesus 'the tribe of Christians', for this was not how the Jews referred to them. As already noticed by the Revd Joseph Bingham in the 17th century, the Jews did not refer to the followers of Christ as 'Christians' but as 'Nazarenes': '. . . *Nazarenes*; a name of reproach given them (Christians) first by the Jews, by whom they are styled *the sect of the Nazarenes*, . . . both St Jerome and Epiphanius himself observe, the Jews termed all Christians, by way of reproach, Nazarenes; . . .' (*Origines Ecclesiasticae; or, The Antiquities of the Christian Church, The Works of Rev. Joseph Bingham*, v. I, Oxford, 1855, p.12). For these reasons, scholars have come to the conclusion that the passage must have been interpolated by some Christian copyist or editor between the time of Origen in the 3rd century and the time of Eusebius a century later.

There was further great excitement in 1906 when a long-forgotten medieval Slavonic (Old Russian) version of *The Jewish War*, another of Josephus's works, was found. *The*

Jewish War not only predated *Antiquities of the Jews* by 20 years, but included another reference to Jesus. He was described as the 'wonder worker' and portrayed as being pressed by his followers to lead a rebellion against Rome. It was thought at first that this Russian translation must have been made from the now-lost original Aramaic text of Josephus. However, after careful examination it became clear that it derived from the Greek text and had been made around the 12th century AD. No traces of Semitic Aramaic idiom have been found in it, and the opening of the section about Jesus is clearly an expanded version of the interpolated testimony quoted earlier in this chapter. F. F. Bruce, the British scholar, makes the point in his book *Jesus and Christian Origins outside the New Testament*: 'In fact, it is as certain as anything can be in the realm of literary criticism that they were not part of what Josephus wrote at all, but had been interpolated into the Greek manuscripts from which the Old Russian translation was made.'

Another mention of Jesus occurs in Book 20 of *Antiquities of the Jews* where Josephus relates how the Roman procurator Festus died suddenly in office around AD 62 and an interval of three months elapsed before the arrival in Judaea of his successor, Albinus. Then the high priest, Ananus, used this opportunity to rid himself of some of his opponents whom he accused of breaking the law, and, having assembled the *sanhedrim* (high court of justice), ordered them to be stoned to death. Among those executed was a man called James, who had a brother named Jesus. When the citizens complained to Albinus about this unlawful execution, he sacked Ananus and appointed Jesus as high priest in his stead. Realizing a good opportunity to enhance his argument, a later Christian copyist added 'who was called Christ' to the phrase 'James, the brother of Jesus'.

As we saw previously, some writings called *Acts of Pilate*, which included an account of Jesus of Nazareth, have similarly been exposed as forgeries, produced either by Christians who wished to confirm the historicity of their

Lord, or enemies of Christianity who wished to attack the religion. We therefore have the situation that, while the account of the life and execution of John the Baptist in Josephus is accepted by scholars as a description of actual historical events, there is nothing to link him with 'preparing the way' for Jesus in the accepted sense, and once we remove the insertions made to the Jewish historians' texts, we have no contemporary evidence whatever about his life, suffering and death. *No* contemporary record, Roman or Jewish, testifies to the presence of Jesus in Palestine at the beginning of the 1st century AD. Nevertheless, we do have testimonies from this period reporting the appearance of Christ, *in his spiritual form*, to his disciples, such as St Paul.

This raises the question, examined in the third section of this book, of the circumstances under which seemingly false accounts of the life of Jesus came to be written and the motives that inspired them.

Chapter Thirteen

The Suffering Servant

If Jesus is not a mythical figure – and it has never been suggested that he appeared physically *after* the first half of the 1st century AD – it follows that we must seek his historical identity in an earlier century. In this quest it is possible to follow two paths, one a documentary trail that includes the Bible, the teaching of the early Christian Church and Jewish literature; the other the mass of evidence available today about Egyptian history as a result of the work in recent times of explorers and, in particular, archaeologists and scientists.

A convenient starting point on the documentary trail is *The Dead Sea Scrolls*, the remains of the library of the Essenes, a secret Jewish sect that separated itself from the Jewish community at large and from the Jerusalem priesthood, whose beliefs and teachings they regarded as false. Some of the manuscripts, found in a series of caves at Qumran early in 1947, were in Hebrew and Aramaic, the vernacular language of Judaea at the time the Christian era began, and some in Greek, have been dated between 200 BC and AD 50 and include biblical and sectarian texts. They include also Jewish literature and other documents.

As the scrolls came from the Holy Land and covered the period before and after the years when Jesus is generally accepted to have lived, it was widely hoped that they would provide first-hand evidence to support the gospel stories and shed new light on Jewish and Christian history. Far from confirming accepted ideas about the origins of orthodox Christianity, however, the texts contradict them. They provide positive witness to a Saviour and a Christian Church that predates the accepted start of the Christian era by at least two centuries.

The Messianic leader of the Essenes was named simply 'The Teacher of Righteousness', who, like Jesus, had met a violent end at an unspecified time in the past, in his case at the hands of someone referred to as 'The Wicked Priest'. As texts of the scrolls began to be published, scholars became divided about their significance. One school disclaimed any serious link between the Essene community and the early Christian Church, the other saw the Essenes as the earliest Christians. For instance, W. F. Albright, one of the most highly qualified American Orientalists, who had himself carried out a great deal of archaeological work in the Holy Land, has been quoted as saying: 'The new evidence . . . bids fair to revolutionize our approach to the beginnings of Christianity.'* Dr J. L. Teicher, himself a Jew and a distinguished Cambridge scholar, went so far as to argue that the Dead Sea manuscripts 'are quite simply Christian documents'. Although the manuscripts come from as early as 200 BC he also maintained that the leader of the Essenes, the Teacher of Righteousness, was none other than Jesus Christ himself.

The French scholar André Dupont-Sommer, after reading one of the scrolls, the *Commentary on Habakkuk*, came to the conclusion that Jesus now seemed an 'astonishing reincarnation of the Teacher of Righteousness'. Like Jesus, he said, the Teacher was believed by his disciples to be God's Elect, the Messiah, the Redeemer of the world. Both were opposed by the priesthood; both were condemned and put to death; both proclaimed judgement on Jerusalem; both established communities whose members expected them to return to judge the world.

The significance of the scrolls received fresh impetus

* *The Jewish Sect of Qumran and the Essenes*, André Dupont-Sommer, London, 1954, p. 150.

when the biblical scholar Hershel Shanks published a fragment in his Washington-based magazines *Biblical Archaeological Review* and *Bible Review* in 1990. This fragment reads: 'He shall be great upon the earth . . . he shall be called the Son of God and they shall call him the Son of the Most High.' The intriguing aspect of this fragment is the uncanny resemblance to the account of the Annunciation to the Virgin Mary that we find in the first chapter of St Luke's gospel: 'He shall be great, and shall be called the Son of the Highest . . . that holy thing which shall be born of thee shall be called the Son of God' (1:32,35).

The very name 'Essenes' indicates that they were followers of Jesus. Philo Judaeus, who wrote the earliest account of the sect around AD 30, called them Essaeans from the Greek *Essaios*, but made it clear that this was not originally a Greek word. Josephus, who, half a century later, included them among the Jews of his time, called them Essenes, the same term that is used in English. However, it was recognized that the word 'Essene' must have had a Semitic origin. Surprisingly, amid many unsatisfactory suggestions about its source, the obvious one was overlooked – *Essa*, the Arabic name for Jesus and the name for him used in the Koran. *Essaiois* would therefore mean 'a follower of *Essa*'. This meaning may in itself have been the main reason for its having been ignored: if the Essenes existed *before* the dates given in the gospels for the life of Jesus, they could not be looked upon by the early Church as his followers.

The Revd Joseph Bingham, a 17th-century Presbyter of the Church of England, confirms that this name was one of the names of the early Christians: 'When Christianity was first planted in the world, they who embraced it were commonly known among themselves by the names of *disciples, believers, elect, saints, and brethren*, before they assumed the titles and appellation of Christians. Epiphanius says they were also called *Iessaioi, Jesseans*, . . . from the name of the Lord Jesus. (*Origines Ecclesiasticae; or, The*

Antiquities of the Christian Church, The Works of Rev. Joseph Bingham, v. I, Oxford, 1855, p. 1).

The Essenes (Judaeo-Christians) were not, however, the only followers of Jesus who were flourishing at the start of the Christian era. Another group of sects, sharing many of their beliefs, were the Gnostics (Gentile-Christians), later to be persecuted and wiped out because of their opposition to the Church of Rome's organized form of orthodox Christianity that developed in the first four centuries AD. Until the end of the Second World War we had to rely almost entirely on their enemies for knowledge of the Gnostics. This situation changed with the discovery in 1945, two years before *The Dead Sea Scrolls* were found, of the remains of the Gnostic library that had been hidden in a cave at Nag Hammadi in Upper Egypt. In all there were 52 manuscripts in Coptic, the liturgical language of Egyptian Christians that was written using the Greek alphabet. Among several previously unknown gospels was the Gospel of Thomas, which contained 114 sayings attributed to Jesus and which has since been established as probably predating the gospels of Matthew, Mark, Luke and John.

The Gnostic writings make it clear that they believed Jesus had lived a long time in the past and that many of them were awaiting his Second Coming. It is also clear that they looked upon themselves as the true interpreters of Christianity. In the Nag Hammadi gospels, no date or place is given for the birth of Jesus. Although he is described as a Nazarene, no mention is made in these gospels of such locations as Nazareth, Galilee, Bethlehem, or even Jerusalem. None of the appearances of Jesus reported in these writings represents a *historical physical appearance*; he always appears to his disciples as a *spiritual* being, although in different forms. Characters of the New Testament gospels, such as Joseph husband of Mary, Joseph of Arimathea, John the Baptist, Caiaphas the high priest of Jerusalem, King Herod, and Pontius Pilate the Roman governor of Palestine, are not found in the gospels of Nag Hammadi. And although no specific time is given for his *earlier* historical life, the indication is that it was *not* in the immediate past.

The Christian Gnostic sects, in their turn, developed from an earlier group of sects, the ascetic Therapeutae. Our sole authority for the history of the Therapeutae is the philosopher Philo Judaeus, who lived at the time of the events narrated in the gospels and died in the middle of the 1st century AD. We know from his work that the Therapeutae shared many characteristics with both the Gnostics and the Essenes although they differed – particularly from the latter – on a number of important points. In his account of *The Contemplative Life*, the most important of all his works, Philo records that, like the Gnostics, the Therapeutae sect 'is to be found in many parts of the civilized world (the Roman Empire) . . . But it is numerous in Egypt throughout each of the districts called nomes, and particularly around Alexandria.' Eusebius, the outstanding theologian of the 3rd century AD and the 'father of Church history', regarded the Therapeutae as the first Christian Church in Egypt.*

The writings of the prophet Isaiah (Esais)† take us back several more centuries. Isaiah lived during the second half of the 8th century BC, but biblical scholars have come to the conclusion that the Book of Isaiah had at least two authors, Isaiah (I) (Chapters 1–39) and Isaiah (II), and possibly a third, who penned the last eleven chapters, which have been dated to the second half of the 6th century BC.

The dominant role given to Jesus in the gospels is that of someone sent by God as a light to the nations and a Redeemer, who is to suffer and be sacrificed like a lamb in order to wipe out the sins of his transgressing people. Such a figure is found in The Suffering Servant, described in the Songs of Isaiah that form part of Isaiah (II): 'All we like

---

* These sects and their significance are examined in greater detail in the third section of this book, which deals with events that followed the dawn of the Christian era.

† So called in John 12:41.

153

sheep have gone astray . . . and the Lord hath laid on him the iniquity of us all . . . he was oppressed, and he was afflicted, yet he opened not his mouth: he is brought as a lamb to the slaughter, and as a sheep before her shearers is dumb . . . he was cut off out of the land of the living: for the transgression of my people was he stricken. And he made his grave with the wicked (the sense is that he had his grave made for him by the wicked), and with the rich (among kings and nobles) in his death . . .' (53:6–9).

Isaiah was the first Israelite prophet to present the Suffering Servant (Christ) as the divinely appointed Saviour. Hitherto the Hebrew Saviour was expected to be the victorious son of David, a living king who would defeat the nation's enemies, and the Israelites believed that life came to an end when a person went to Sheol, the underworld or grave. The account of the Servant in the Songs of Isaiah, however, presents us for the first time in the Old Testament with the idea of a second life although it is presented only for the Servant, not for those who believe in him. The rising of the Servant from the dead is very clear in the words that follow the above passage: '. . . he shall see his seed, he shall prolong his days, and the pleasure of the Lord shall prosper in his hand. He shall see of the travail of his soul, and shall be satisfied: by his righteousness shall my righteous servant justify many; for he shall bear their iniquities . . . he shall divide the spoil with the strong; because he hath poured out his soul unto death . . . he bare the sin of many, and made intercession for the transgressors' (53:10–12).

Fluctuations of tenses are common in Isaiah. This arises because Hebrew does not have tenses (old forms of Semitic languages used only one form of a verb, and indicated time separately), and whether Isaiah is writing about the past, present or future depends upon what interpretation the translator put into his words. The death of the Servant, the divinely appointed Saviour, is clearly in this passage an event that has already taken place and, although we must assume from the manner of his report that Isaiah accepted the truth of what he was saying, the belief in life after death can only have originated with the Servant himself. Isaiah could not have invented it.

The Songs of Isaiah were written at a disastrous time for the Israelites. The Babylonians destroyed Jerusalem in 587 BC and brought the Jewish kingdom to an end. Most of its population became exiled in Babylon, a situation that continued until 538 BC when the Persian king, Cyrus, defeated Babylonia, freed the Jews and allowed them to rebuild the Jerusalem temple. Isaiah (II) represented the Israelite defeat and humiliation as a punishment by God for a crime committed a long time previously.

Isaiah's Suffering Servant is to be found in the New Testament as well as in the work of the prophet himself. In Acts, for example, when an Ethiopian eunuch, after a visit to Jerusalem, asks one of the apostles, Philip, who was meant by the Servant, '. . . Philip . . . preached unto him Jesus' (8:35). Again, Peter, in his first epistle, does not give any hint about his personal relation with Christ or about his life, teaching or death, but simply repeats the part of the Songs of Isaiah that relates to the Servant: '. . . Christ . . . Who did no sin, neither was guile found in his mouth: Who, when he was reviled, reviled not again; when he suffered, he threatened not; but committed himself to him that judgeth righteously: Who his own self bare our own sins in his own body on the tree, that we, being dead to sins, should live unto righteousness: by whose stripes ye were healed. For ye were as sheep going astray . . .' (2:21–25).

Luke, in his account of Jesus reading in the synagogue, has Jesus himself quoting Isaiah: 'And when he had opened the book [of the prophet Isaiah] he found the place where it was written. The Spirit of the Lord is upon me, because he hath anointed me to preach the gospel to the poor; he hath sent me to heal the broken-hearted, to preach deliverance to the captives, and recovering of sight to the blind, to set at liberty them that are bruised, To preach the acceptable year of the Lord' (Luke 4:17–19). Insertion of the word 'anointed' in this use of the original Isaiah quotation is significant because there is no other reference in the gospels to Jesus having been anointed, a completely different rite, with different implications, from baptism. Its use here, together with Jesus having been identified in the opening verse of Matthew as 'Jesus Christ, the son of David' and being addressed frequently as 'son of David' by ordinary people, provides a strong indication that the historical Christ was of royal descent.

Yet again, John, after using a reference to Isaiah to report some of the activities of Jesus, goes on to say in his gospel: 'These things said Esaias (Isaiah), when he saw his glory, and spake of him' (John 12:41). Here the evangelist is saying that the prophet Isaiah, who lived several centuries before the start of the Christian era, saw the glory of Christ and spoke of him. This indicates that Isaiah, like St Paul on the road to Damascus later, had an encounter with the spiritual Christ.

In order to reconcile such texts with the gospel story of the life of Jesus in the 1st century AD the early Church Fathers put forward the explanation that Jesus must have been a spiritual, pre-existent Christ, not to be confused with the Jesus of the New Testament. This explanation has been accepted by many modern scholars. However, the evidence we have examined so far – with more to follow – suggests that we are not dealing here with a spiritual, 'pre-existent' Christ, but that *Jesus himself lived many centuries earlier* and believers were wont to experience some kind of spiritual encounter with him. This is clear from Paul's account of his own experience in the 1st century AD: '. . . I conferred not with flesh and blood' (Galatians 1:16). In the same way, John is quoted above as saying that Isaiah saw the 'glory' of Jesus. The 'glory' of Christ indicates an eternal spiritual character, for Jesus is said to have achieved 'glory' only after his death and resurrection: '. . . God, that raised him up from the dead and gave him glory . . .' (I Peter 1:21), and again: '. . . the sufferings of Christ and the glory that should follow' (I Peter 1:11).

There are also strong indications in the New Testament

1. A priest of Serapis, the Egyptian god whose cult was based at Alexandria. This painting, from the Fayyum area in the Western desert, dates from the mid second century AD, well before all traces of Egyptian influence were eradicated by the Roman Church in the early fifth century.

2. Tuthmosis III, the historical David, who established the first empire that extended from the Nile to the Euphrates.

3. An aerial view of the mound Tell el-Sultan at Jericho, showing trenches dug by Kathleen Kenyon's expedition 1952–8. The evidence of this excavation work shows that the location was virtually uninhabited during the time of Joshua. The battle of Jericho is therefore sheer invention.

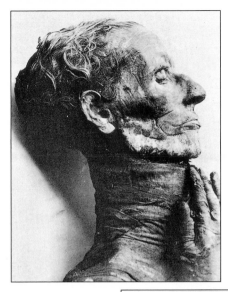

4. Head of the mummy of Yuya, the historical Joseph. His strong, aquiline features and hooked nose suggested at once to those who examined the mummy that he was of foreign, possibly Semitic origin.

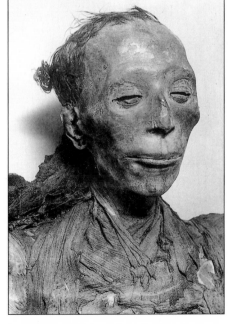

5. Mummy of Tuya, the Egyptian wife of Yuya.

6. (*Left*) The marriage scarab of Amenhotep III and his Queen Tiye, Yuya's daughter.

7. (*Right*) Tablet of sun-dried clay impressed with cuneiform signs, one of the despatches from Tushratta, King of Mittanni, to Amenhotep III, the historical Solomon.

8. (*Left*) Merenptah's great victory stele, known as the Israel stele. In the second from last line occurs the only reference to Israel in Egyptian literature. (*Below*) The hieroglyphic name for Israel.

9. Amenhotep III, the historical Solomon.

10. Head of Queen Tiye, daughter of Yuya, the historical Joseph, and mother of Akhenaten, the historical Moses.

11. An icon at
St. Catherine's monastery,
Mount Sinai, depicting Moses
as a young man receiving the
tablets of the Law at the
Burning Bush from which the
Lord spoke to him.

12. Akhenaten, the
historical Moses, and Nefertiti,
the historical Miriam, with their
three eldest daughters.

13. A portrait head of Akhenaten, the historical Moses.

14. The famous bust of Nefertiti, the historical Miriam, in the Berlin Museum.

15. Unfinished statue of Akhenaten kissing one of his daughters. This statue was believed by those who claimed that the younger figure portrays Semenkhkare, the king's brother, to be evidence that Akhenaten was homosexual.

16. Two statues of Akhenaten as Osiris. The one on the right lacks the royal kilt. The Egyptologist Cyril Aldred interpreted this as evidence that Akhenaten possessed no male genitalia. However, since the statue is unfinished, this assumption is incorrect. The pelvic area would eventually have been carved (as in the statue on the left) to show the kilt.

17. The painting on the north wall of the burial chamber of Tutankhamun, the historical Jesus, includes three scenes. The first scene shows Aye, the historical Ephraim and Tutankhamun's successor, as king, dressed in the priestly leopard skin, performing the ritual of 'the opening of the mouth', to resurrect the dead king.

18. The second scene shows Tutankhamun entering the heavenly realm of the gods, being greeted by the sky goddess, Nut.

19. The third scene shows Tutankhamun, the god-king, in his three forms: as Osiris, the father; as Horus, the son; and as Ka, the (holy) spirit. The manner in which the three embrace one another, as well as their identical profiles, emphasizes that they are three in one and one in three – the original, Egyptian Trinity.

20. Christ as Ruler of the Universe. This icon was painted in the first half of the sixth century and is one of the earliest icons in St Catherine's monastery. Christ was always represented as a king in Egyptian tradition, and was never shown dying on a Roman cross.

21. Tutankhamun being anointed by his wife Ankhsenpa-amun. This scene is found on the back of the King's throne chair, found in his tomb. The anointing of Jesus by Mary Magdelene echoes this ritual.

22. Panehesy, the historical Elias, the Chief Servitor of the Aten temple, from his tomb at Amarna.

23. The prophet Elias (Ilia), a painted panel at St Catherine's monastery, Mount Sinai.

24. & 25. Isis nurses her son Horus, whose father is the god Osiris. At St Catherine's monastery, Mount Sinai, the Virgin Mary, also enthroned, holds Jesus, the son of God, in her lap. More than a thousand years separate these two portrayals, but the comparison is striking.

26. The scene of the transfiguration at its original site, the main church of St Catherine's monastery. Christ in the centre, with Moses on the right and Elias (Ilia) on the left. Here Tutankhamun, Akhenaten and Panehesy, the historical originals of Jesus, Moses and Elias respectively, are shown, rightly, to be contemporaries. Beneath are Jacob, Peter and John.

27. (Right) The monastery of St Catherine, at the foot of Mount Sinai, where the historical Jesus was hanged on a tree by Panehesy.

Biblical and Koranic accounts indicate that this area at Mount Sinai (Gabal Musa, Horeb) had been holy ground even before the time of Moses. Archaeological and traditional evidence also confirm that this site of the Burning Bush remained sacred, visited by pilgrims and occupied by monks, until the monastery of St Catherine was built by Emperor Justinian in the sixth century AD. It was in the library of St Catherine that the Codex Sinaiticus, now in the British Museum, was found. This earliest New Testament text contains the Gospel of Mark, which makes no mention of the resurrection.

28. A representation of St Peter, at St Catherine's monastery.

29. A representation of St Paul, who was an initiate of the Egyptian Mysteries, at St Catherine's monastery.

30. (*Above left*) A unique scene from the Coptic Monastery of St Macarius at Wadi el-Natrun in the Western desert, showing Christ being embalmed according to Ancient Egyptian customs. As the gospel writers tell us, spices and ointments were used to anoint Jesus's body, and John says that Nicodemus 'brought a mixture of myrrh and aloes' and describes Jesus's body being bound 'in linen clothes with the spices'.

31. (*Above right*) Another scene from the Monastery of St Macarius showing the mummified Christ carried away by the priests.

32. (*Left*) The Egyptian god Serapis is shown as an angel on the walls of the Coptic monastery of St Paul at the Red Sea. This is confirmation of the teaching of Tutankhamun when reopening the old temples. It was then that he regarded the old gods as angels and saints, while Aten remained the one god.

33. Limestone fragments from the entrance to an Egyptian house dating from the fifth century AD, now in the Coptic Museum, Cairo, each depicting a fish. The fish was a symbol of Christ during the early years of the Church.

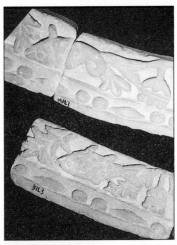

34. St Paul's Monastery, Red Sea. St Paul was regarded as an important disciple by the Egyptians, and the building of this monastery confirms the belief that Paul himself must have visited this area near Mount Sinai when he went into Arabia.

35. (*Right*) The obelisk of Tuthmosis III, now in the Piazza San Giovanni in Laterano, Rome. Obelisks together with the hieroglyphics inscribed upon them became a powerful symbol of the Roman universal church at the time of the Counter-Reformation, and signify Rome's acknowledgement of Egypt as the source of faith and theology.

that the historical Jesus was present with the Israelites in the wilderness of Sinai. Paul makes this clear in another of his letters, his first epistle to the Corinthians: 'Moreover, brethren, I would not that ye should be ignorant, how that all our fathers were under the cloud, and all passed through the sea; And were all baptized unto Moses in the cloud and in the sea; And did all eat the same spiritual meat; And did all drink the same spiritual drink: for they drank of that spiritual Rock that followed them: and that Rock was Christ' (I Corinthians 10:1–4). This left no doubt in the minds of biblical scholars about what Paul was trying to say: 'It is much more likely that Paul here means that the Rock really was Christ . . . That is to say, he believed that the Messiah was in some form present with the people during this critical period in the wilderness . . .' (*Jesus in the Old Testament*, Anthony T. Hanson, the former Professor of Theology at Hull University).

The idea of the presence of Jesus with the Israelites in the Sinai wilderness is reinforced by Paul in his epistle to the Hebrews where, after referring to the disobedient Israelites 'who left Egypt under Moses', he says: 'For unto us was the gospel preached, as well as unto them: but the word preached did not profit them, not being mixed with faith in them that heard it' (Hebrews 4:2). The point Paul is making here is that the Christian gospel preached in the 1st century AD had been preached before. John also confirms that Jesus was a contemporary of Moses when he quotes Jesus as telling the Jews of Jerusalem: 'For had ye believed Moses, ye would have believed me: for he wrote of me' (John 5:46). Therefore, Moses, according to John, did not prophesy concerning Jesus, but wrote about him in the Pentateuch, the first five books of the Old Testament.

The Book of Joshua, which describes his conquest of the Promised Land through a swift military campaign in the 13th century BC, takes us back another five centuries from the time of Isaiah. Although archaeological evidence has made it clear that this account is a work of fiction (as will be explained in detail later), the name Joshua is important.

Greek translators of the Old Testament did not – and their Greek Bible, the Septuagint,* still does not – use the name Joshua, but Jesus. Thus their account of the conquest of the Promised Land appears in The Book of Jesus. Many early Church Fathers of the 2nd and 3rd centuries AD, too, identified Joshua as Jesus, including Justin Martyr, Irenaeus (Bishop of Lyon), Tertullian, Eusebius (Bishop of Caesarea and 'the father of Church history') and Origen, the most brilliant theologian of his time.

For example, Eusebius, Bishop of Caesarea, who wrote the history of the early Church, says that Christ and Christianity were older than the appearance of the Church: '. . . both the antiquity and the divine character of Christian origins will be demonstrated to those who imagine them to be recent and outlandish, appearing yesterday for the first time. . . The Holy Spirit Himself says in prophecy: "His generation who shall declare?" (Isaiah 53:8)' (HE 2). He then goes on to say: 'The extreme sanctity and glory of the name Christ was first proclaimed by Moses himself . . . Never yet heard by human ears till it was made known to Moses, the title Jesus was bestowed by him for the first and only time on the man who – again as a pattern and symbol – he knew would after his own death succeeded to the supreme authority. His successor had not hitherto used the designation Jesus . . . but Moses calls him Jesus, conferring the name on him as a priceless honour . . . for Joshua the son of Nun himself bore the image of our Saviour, who alone, after Moses and the completion of the symbolic worship given to men by him, succeeded to the authority over the true and most pure religion' (HE 3).

The identification is particularly striking in the case of

---

* The earliest extant Greek translation of the Old Testament from Hebrew. It was made in Alexandria by 70 Jewish scribes in the 3rd century BC, during the reign of Ptolemy II.

Origen. Commenting on the passage (Exodus 17:9) where Moses is first mentioned with Joshua, he wrote: '. . . let us observe what instructions Moses gave when war was imminent. It says: "He said to Jesus" – the King James Bible here gives Joshua with Jesus as a marginal note – "choose for yourself men and go and fight with Amalek* tomorrow." Up to this point nowhere has there occurred a mention of the blessed man Jesus. Here first the brilliance of this name shone forth.' Jesus and Joshua are also linked by various references to the latter in the Pentateuch as the 'son of Nun'. These are the only references in the Bible to 'Nun', a word that means 'fish', the traditional symbol of Christ. In fact, Eusebius, Bishop of Caesarea, makes it very clear that both the name of Jesus and his looks appear for the first time in the son of Nun, successor to Moses.

The Old Testament does not merely identify Joshua (Jesus) as a contemporary of Moses but as his successor as the leader of the Israelites: 'And Joshua the son of Nun was full of the spirit of wisdom; for Moses had laid his hands upon him: and the children of Israel hearkened unto him . . .' (Deuteronomy 34:9).

In the early centuries of the Christian era, Jesus was the only name to be found in secular works as well as Greek translations of the Old and New Testaments. For example, we find in the 20-volume *Antiquities of the Jews* by the 1st century AD historian Flavius Josephus, a number of references to Jesus and his relationship with Moses. He writes of 'Jesus, the son of Nun' becoming the successor to Moses (Book 3). When Moses was grown old, he says later, he 'appointed Jesus for his successor, both to receive directions from God as a prophet, and for a commander of the army' (Book 4). He then goes on to confirm that 'Jesus also prophesied while Moses was present' (Book 4).

It was not until the 16th century AD, when a new

---

* Amalek was an ancient tribe, enemies of the Israelites, which dwelled in the area south of Judaea extending into northern Arabia.

159

translation was made of the Masoratic* Hebrew text of the Old Testament, that the English translator – in an attempt, not entirely successful, to resolve problems of biblical chronology – substituted the name Joshua for Jesus whenever he encountered the epithet 'son of Nun'. The similarity of the names Joshua (*Ye-ho-shua* in Hebrew) and Jesus (*Ye-shua* in its short form), both of which have the same meaning, 'Yahweh (the Lord) is salvation', must have influenced his choice.

What of the Jews, as they were known after their return from exile in Babylonia? The gospel account describes how Caiaphas, the Jewish high priest, and other chief priests and elders of the time were deeply involved in the accusations against Jesus and his subsequent arrest, trial and condemnation. They are even said to have gone so far as to refuse Pilate's offer to release him for the occasion of the Passover feast, commemorating the liberation of the Israelites from Egyptian bondage, demanding instead the release of another prisoner, Barabbas. In the circumstances, we should expect to find that Jewish literature has kept some memory of him.

Rabbinical Scriptures, which date from the first five centuries AD, make it clear that the Jews *did* know Jesus, but did not wish to reveal *all* that they knew about him. His name, Yeshu, the Hebrew form of the Greek Jesus, is found at least twenty times in the Talmud, the Jewish commentaries and interpretative writings that were written during this time and are looked upon as only second in authority to the Old Testament, although there is a tendency to refer to him as 'a certain person' rather than use his name. In some passages he is also named as Balaam or Ben Pandira, 'the son of Pandira' (see below). As the Jews disputed the claim that Jesus was the Son of God, they put forward the view that Pandira was a lover, not the husband, of Mary, but they confirm her name: 'Miriam (Hebrew for Mary, and identified in an earlier

---

* The Masoratic Text Old Testament is the Hebrew text supplied with diacritical marks in the 10th century AD to enable correct pronunciation.

chapter as the same person as Queen Nefertiti) ... the mother of "a certain person" ' (b. Hag., 4b).

This is only one of many points of agreement between the four gospels and the Talmud and the *Midrash*, the ancient Jewish commentary on part of the Hebrew Scriptures. At the same time, there are important areas of contradiction, particularly those that may help to establish when Jesus actually lived. To deal first with some of the important areas of agreement:

The Royal Descent of Jesus. Jesus's mother 'was the descendant of princes and rulers' (b. Sanh., 106a).

The naming of Jesus as 'the son of Pandira' also points to his having been an Egyptian king. As Pandira is not a Hebrew word, various explanations of its origin have been put forward. In fact, the word Pandira is simply a Hebrew form of an ancient Egyptian royal epithet. That the rabbis kept the word without knowing what it means supports its authenticity. The word in Hebrew is *Pa-ndi-ra*. In Egyptian, its original form, this becomes *Pa-ntr-ra* - that is, *Pa-neter-ra*, the god Ra. Son of Ra was an essential title for all Egyptian kings from the time of the builders of the pyramids during the 4th Dynasty, 27 centuries before the Christian era.

Jesus in Egypt. The Talmud says that Jesus, in his early manhood, was in Egypt where he 'practised magic and led astray and deceived Israel' (b. Sanh., 107b).

Condemned to Death by the Priesthood. Although no mention of a trial of Jesus is found in the Talmud, Jewish rabbis accepted that the Nazarene had been executed: '. . . they hanged Jesus (the Nazarene) . . . because he hath practised magic and deceived and led astray Israel' (b. Sanh., 43a).

Jesus Died Young. 'Men of blood and deceit shall not live out half their days' (b. Sanh., 106b, quoting Psalm 55:23).

Jesus the King. When Jesus was executed 'everyone who passed to and fro said: "It seems that the king is crucified"' (T. Sanh., 9.7).

Here at last we find Jewish confirmation of many of the essential points in the life of Jesus that are related in the four gospels. Yet the Talmudic rabbis, who compiled the interpretation of Jewish laws as well as legends and commentaries in the early centuries after the supposed date of the life and death of Jesus, would not have relied simply on the Christian traditions of the time, but referred to their previous Jewish authority, both for the details they do not dispute and those they disagree with. One or two points need clarification, however.

In terms of establishing when Jesus actually lived, it is a significant aspect of the Rabbinical writings that at no point do they refer to his execution as having taken place during the reign of Herod or when Caiaphas was high priest, despite the fact that they must have been aware of the account given in the four gospels. Nor do we find any reference within the pages of the Talmud to personalities who lived in the era of Herod, such as John the Baptist.

The Talmud also contradicts the gospels in some essential points concerning Jesus. For instance, it never mentions that he was a Galilean or came from the city of Nazareth. Although it refers to him as being a Nazarene, this is a word (Greek, *Nazoraios*) used to indicate a religious sect, not a geographical location. This meaning is clear from Acts 24:5 where the Jews address Felix, the Roman procurator, accusing Paul of stirring up trouble among Jews throughout the world and describing him as 'a ringleader of the sect of the Nazarenes'. In fact, Paul himself always referred to Jesus as 'the Nazarene' and never mentions that he came from Nazareth. Yet, elsewhere in Acts, Nazarene is always translated in the English version of the New Testament as 'of Nazareth', which is incorrect and has become a cause of misunderstanding among English readers. The Nazarenes were one of a number of secret Judaeo-Christian sects like the

Essenes, and the term 'Nazarene' is still the designation given to Christians both by Hebrew Jews and by Muslims to this day. The Semitic word is derived from the root *nsr*, which means to 'guard' or 'protect' and indicates 'devotee'. The existence of the Nazarene sect is confirmed by both classical and Christian historians.

The name Nazareth is not found in the Book of Acts, the letters of the Apostles, any books of the Old Testament, the Talmud or the works of Josephus, who was himself given command in Galilee at the time of the Jewish revolt against the Romans in AD 66. The first time we hear of this location is in the writings of Mark, regarded by scholars as the earliest of the gospel authors. After the section dealing with John the Baptist, we find this verse: 'And it came to pass in those days, that Jesus came from Nazareth of Galilee, and was baptized of John in Jordan' (1:9). Mark's example was followed by Matthew and Luke.

We have no definite knowledge of when the Gospel of Mark was written, but it is believed by biblical critics to have been about AD 75 (because it contains a reference to the destruction of Jerusalem, which happened in AD 70). At this time no geographical record of Nazareth exists anywhere. The fact that the gospel of Mark chose to relate the word 'Nazarene' to a geographical location rather than a sect was a consequence of his attempt to place the account of the life and death of Jesus in a Roman framework. It was later to have the effect that the location was identified as a place, which was then turned into a place of pilgrimage, but not until the 6th century AD.

The Cross is identified as the symbol of Christ. The four gospels are consistent in saying that Jesus was crucified: 'And they crucified him . . .' (Matthew 27:35); 'And when they had crucified him . . .' (Mark 15:24); 'And when they were come to the place, which is called Calvary, there they crucified him . . .' (Luke 23:33); 'Then the soldiers, when they had crucified Jesus . . . (John 19:23). Paul, too, describes this as the means by which Jesus met his death: '. . . Jesus, whom ye have crucified . . .' (Acts 2:36). This is what one would expect if Jesus had been tried and condemned to death in Roman times. Crucifixion – nailing someone to a cross – was a Roman, not an Israelite, form of execution. The Israelites hanged the condemned person from a tree: 'And if a man have committed a sin worthy of death . . . thou hang him on a tree' (Deuteronomy 21:22). This will be elaborated later.

The Talmud, as we saw, refers to Jesus as having been both crucified and hanged. This would appear to be a serious contradiction but for the fact that we find also in the New Testament references to Jesus having been hanged rather than crucified. The account of Jesus's death given by Peter, for instance, reads: '. . . whom they slew and hanged on a tree' (Acts 10:39), and Paul, having in an earlier reference used the term 'crucified', is now found declaring: '. . . they took him down from the tree, and laid him in a sepulchre' (Acts 13:29).

Thus, in terms of the words used, it is possible to suggest that there is not necessarily a contradiction between the Talmudic and gospel versions of how Jesus met his death, and that 'crucifixion' and 'hanging' can be looked upon as synonymous. Later, however, a more positive attempt was made in the gospels to adapt the story of Jesus to the Roman era. John, the most theological and the least historical of the evangelists, added more details that favoured the Roman practice of nailing to a cross rather than the Israelite punishment of hanging. These details are to be found in the story of doubting Thomas, who sought physical proof of Christ's resurrection: '. . . he (Thomas) said unto them, Except I shall see in his hands the print of the nails, and put my finger into the print of the nails, and thrust my hand into his side, I will not believe' (John 20:25).

Adapting the story of Jesus to fit into the Roman period has resulted in conflicting accounts not only of how he met his death, but of who was responsible for condemning him –

Israelite priests or the Roman authority. However, the rabbis are quite specific about the identity of the man responsible for the death of Jesus: 'Pinhas . . . killed him' (b. Sanh., 106b) – and Pinhas has been identified as having the same rare Egyptian name as Panehesy*, chancellor and Chief Servitor of the Aten at Amarna, one of the group of followers who fled with Akhenaten (Moses) when he sought exile in the safety of the Sinai wilderness.

The contradictions between the writings of the rabbis, who denied that Jesus was the Messiah, and the gospel accounts of his life, suffering and death should not be looked upon as anti-Christian propaganda. The authority on which the rabbis relied in compiling the Talmud was the Law of Moses and the Pentateuch, the first five books of the Old Testament, which the Jews call the Torah. Their laws did not allow them to make any changes, even of the smallest kind, in the account, although they were free to explain the significance of the older traditions, which had originally been passed orally from generation to generation, and to offer interpretations of obscurities and inconsistencies. They could not have invented the name Ben Pandira or that of Pinhas. Despite confusion resulting from a long oral tradition, the rabbis must have had knowledge of Jesus and his execution through old traditions dating from the time of Moses and Joshua.

---

*Such differences in names are explained by the fact that we are dealing with three languages – Hebrew, Aramaic and Egyptian.

Chapter Fourteen

The Sacrificial Victim

The two paths we have followed until now – the documentary evidence on the one, back through the centuries from the start of the Christian era, the Egyptian historical evidence on the other, down through the centuries – have both brought us to the same point in history, the 14th century BC. This was the time of Moses receiving the Lord's commandments and appointing Joshua to be his successor, on the one hand, and Akhenaten leading the Amarna religious revolution and appointing Tutankhamun to succeed him on the throne of Egypt, on the other.

As we saw earlier, no evidence exists to support the view that the four Christian gospels give an historical account of the life, suffering and death of a physical Jesus. According to the Gospels, nobody saw Jesus, *they only saw Christ*, which means his *spiritual not physical* element.* In contrast, we have examined a great deal of evidence indicating that he lived many centuries earlier. Who was he?

In order to identify him we need to seek someone of whom it is said that, like Jesus (Joshua), he succeeded Akhenaten (Moses) as leader of the Israelites; was present with him in the wilderness; had a mother who was 'the descendant of princes and rulers'; was himself a descendant of the House of David (Tuthmosis III), a son of Pandira (the god Ra), from whose line the Bible assures us repeatedly the promised

---

* When Jesus asked his disciples whom did they think he was, 'Simon Peter answered and said, Thou art the Christ, the son of the living God' (Matthew 16:16).

Messiah would come; was an anointed king; spent his early manhood in Egypt; died young; and was hanged because he was accused, rightly or wrongly, of having 'led astray and deceived Israel'.

Of all the prominent figures who graced the 14th century BC, of only one can it be said that all of the above criteria are to be found in his life – the charismatic Tutankhamun, murdered in Sinai when he made his way there on an ecumenical mission to preach peace and tolerance of the fact that not all men share the same perception of God.

It is, I believe, an unconscious recognition of the truth about his identity that impels millions to visit his tomb in the Valley of the Kings each year in what might be described as a form of pilgrimage, and more millions to queue for hours to view, whenever they are on international display, the treasures recovered from the tomb by Howard Carter and his workers after he discovered it in 1922.

There is little to be seen in the tomb itself. After walking down a short tunnel, whose wall-paintings have suffered some damage from the moist breath of the endless millions of tourists, one is simply left facing a wall behind which lies an enclosed coffin containing the skeleton of the young king. In the course of this short walk one comes to a wall-painting whose profound significance had escaped me until November 1997 when I was invited by General Mohamed Yusef, the then governor of Luxor, to speak in the city hall as part of the 75th anniversary celebrations of the tomb's discovery. Afterwards I was privileged to have a private visit to the tomb. As I stood alone, gazing at the painting of the burial chamber on the north wall of the tunnel, I realized for the first time that I was looking at the strongest pictorial evidence linking Tutankhamun and Jesus.

The painting, unique in all my experience (no similar representation has ever been found in Egypt), is divided into three separate scenes. To appreciate their profound significance it is necessary to understand the conventions of royal pictorial art in ancient Egypt. The ruling Pharaoh was depicted during his life as Horus, who was looked upon as the embodiment of the divine and protector of the reigning king. After death he was shown as a mummified, risen Osiris, god of the underworld and the father of Horus. Statues and paintings also depicted the *ka* – the spirit – of a king, which came into existence at the moment of birth and survived his death.

The first of the above scenes, on the right (Plate 17), shows Aye (Ephraim, who was the second son of Joseph the Patriarch as well as the great-uncle of Tutankhamun). He also served as the young king's vizier and succeeded him on the throne. Aye is wearing a crown, with his cartouche above him, indicating that he had already assumed the role of a ruling Pharaoh. Nevertheless, at the same time as being depicted as a king, Aye is shown as officiating as a priest, dressed in a priestly robe of leopard skin and performing the ritual of 'the opening of the mouth' for resuscitation of the dead Tutankhamun, who faces him as a risen Osiris.

The middle scene (Plate 18) shows Tutankhamun entering the realm of the gods and being welcomed there by Nut, the goddess of heaven. It was the ultimate scene on the left of the north wall, however, that aroused my wonder. Here I saw three different representations of Tutankhamun, linked as one person. On the left of the scene (Plate 19) stood Tutankhamun as the risen Osiris and a second Tutankhamun, facing him as the ruling king, Horus. Behind him is a third Tutankhamun depicted as his *ka*. The most remarkable feature of this scene is the fact that the risen Osiris, although shown in the conventional mummified form, with his hands folded across his chest, is reaching out to touch Horus, as is his *ka*.

Thus we have Tutankhamun as father, son and spirit – the same relationship that we find in the Christian Trinity of three persons in one God – Father, Son and Holy Spirit – finally established as orthodox belief after much acrimonious debate during the first four centuries of the Christian era. The fact that Aye, a ruling Pharaoh, was officiating as a priest also indicates that we are in the presence of a theology that was beyond the powers and understanding of priests of the state god Amun-Ra.

Sigmund Freud is not the only distinguished scholar to have come to the conclusion that there is more to the biblical story of Jesus than meets the eye. Attempts to establish his identity date back to the 18th century, the Age of Enlightenment, when scholars sought to apply critical and rational thought to assumptions previously taken for granted. By 1906, when Albert Schweitzer, the French theologian, organist and surgeon-missionary, wrote his classical – and critical – study *The Quest of the Historical Jesus*, it had already become clear that many scholars who had embarked upon this quest had portrayed a Jesus based largely upon their personal presuppositions or the widely accepted beliefs held by the society in which they lived.

Schweitzer's study, in which he argued that the Jesus recognized in Protestant liberal theology of the 19th and early 20th century bore little resemblance to the Jesus of history, had a profound effect. Many New Testament scholars refused to produce lives of Jesus or to attempt studies of the orthodox – that is, generally accepted – account of his ministry.

This situation has changed since the Second World War. Renewed scholarly interest in the matter has produced many new books, with more in the pipeline, that have presented Jesus in a variety of guises – a political revolutionary, a gay magician, a Galilean rebel, a Pharisee, an Essene, an apocalyptic (revelatory) fanatic or an eschatological prophet, putting forward doctrines about death, judgement, heaven and hell. It is remarkable that one historical figure should inspire so many conflicting identifications. If, charitably, one assumes that the authors involved were trying sincerely to establish the truth, their failure to arrive at broadly similar conclusions may lie in the fact that they were trying to reconcile facts that, on closer analysis, prove to be theological rather than historical facts.

Tutankhamun, the 10-year-old son of Akhenaten (Moses), came to the throne of Egypt as sole ruler in 1361 BC after the abdication of his father and the disappearance of Semenkhkare. Some doubts have been expressed – as seems to be common about any aspect of the Amarna period – about the parenthood of the young king, who at this time bore the name Tutankhaten. These matters are not difficult to resolve. A linen shirt, found in his tomb and dated to Year 7 of Akhenaten (1372 BC), indicates that this was the year of his birth. Akhenaten (Moses) had a co-regency with his father, Amenhotep III (Solomon), for 12 years, then ruled alone for five. The birth of Tutankhamun in his father's Year 7 would make him 10 years of age when he came to the throne and 19 when he died at the end of his short reign. These dates are confirmed by anatomical examination of his body as well as by the dating of objects found in his tomb. As for his mother, some scholars have suggested, without any evidence to support their argument, a different mother from Queen Nefertiti for the young king. It has been argued that he was Akhenaten's son by another wife named Kia. However, the late German Egyptologist Hans Wolfgang Helck was able to show – at the 6th International Congress of Egyptology, held in Turin in 1991 – that Kia was another name given to Queen Nefertiti and produced a scene showing her depicted under this alternative name. Before the birth of Tutankhamun, she had three daughters, and another three afterwards. No evidence of other sons has been found. The archaeological remains of Amarna's northern palace offer strong evidence of her parenthood. They indicate that Nefertiti did not accompany Akhenaten into exile in Sinai but remained with her son, Tutankhamun, in Egypt at least until the time of his early death. During his brief reign, Tutankhamun – who married his sister, Ankhsenpa-aten, in order to inherit the throne – was able to rely for guidance and support, as had his father before him, on his great-uncle, Aye (Ephraim), the second son of Yuya (Joseph). Aye was the most powerful man in Egypt – the young king's vizier and the strong military presence behind the throne as Commander of the Chariots, Master of the King's Horses and Chief of the Bowmen.

For the first four years of his reign, Tutankhamun continued to live at Amarna, the capital city built by his father. However, he stopped all attempts to enjoin worship of Aten on his subjects. Nefertiti was still referred to as the 'Great Royal Wife', further confirmation that Akhenaten was still alive and regarded, at least by some of his followers, as king. During this period the young king also began building activities at Thebes, where he made additions to the older Aten temples, constructed originally by his father. Further confirmation that Akhenaten was still alive at this time is provided by the fact that none of the ancient gods of Egypt feature in these constructional changes at Thebes, only the name of Aten.

The second stage of Tutankhamun's reign, starting at some point in his Year 4, saw the young king, now about 15 years of age, move his residence from Amarna to Memphis, south-west of modern Cairo. It was then that he allowed the temples of the ancient gods of Egypt to reopen and the gods to be worshipped alongside Aten. The popular response brought home to him the fact that the majority of his people did not share his own beliefs. He therefore, in this third stage of his reign, changed his name – in recognition of the state god Amun – from Tutankhaten to Tutankhamun while his queen became Ankhsenpa-amun. The priesthood was given formal recognition, temple income was restored and work was begun on making good the ravages wrought by years of neglect.

As sovereign over the whole of Egypt, Tutankhamun was looked upon as beloved of Amun of Thebes, Ra of Heliopolis, Ptah of Memphis and all the other deities. Nevertheless, the king himself remained an Atenist until the very end. This can be seen clearly from the scenes on the back panel of the throne (Plate 21) found in his tomb in the Valley of the Kings. This wooden panel – overlaid with gesso and gold, silver leaf, and inlaid with coloured glass and faience – shows the king and queen in an intimate scene. Both are wearing coronation crowns and garments of silver. The standing queen is anointing the seated king with perfume from a vessel held in her left hand.

Although it is clear from one of the cartouches placed behind his crown that the king used this throne after he had changed his name, it is obvious that he still adhered completely to the Aten faith for, top centre, we see the symbol of the Aten with its extending rays that give the *ankh*, the Egyptian key of life, to the royal pair.

Aten is here represented as the sole God, with his two cartouches of a ruling king of the universe dominating the scene. Howard Carter, who was struck by this fact, commented in his book *The Tomb of Tutankhamun*: 'It is curious, to say the least of it, that an object which bore such manifest signs . . . should be publicly buried in this, the stronghold of the Amun faith . . . It would appear that Tutankhamun's return to the ancient faith was not entirely a matter of conviction.' This is confirmed from a text found on other objects in the tomb furniture which, after mentioning some of the important Egyptian deities, ends with the statement that Tutankhamun was the 'eldest son of Aten in Heaven'.

Yet, despite his efforts to heal the religious wounds inflicted upon Egypt by his father's introduction of the monotheistic God, Aten, Tutankhamun was murdered.

The violent nature of his death is attested by the state of his mummy. It was the subject of a detailed examination, including the use of X-rays, in the king's tomb in 1968 by Professor R. G. Harrison, the late Professor of Anatomy at Liverpool University, and A. B. Abdalla, Professor of Anatomy at Cairo University. They reported:

When the bandages around the remains were removed, it was immediately obvious that the mummy was not in one piece. The head and neck were separated from the rest of the body, and the limbs had been detached from *the torso . . . The resin exuded a sweet smell which soon pervaded all through the tomb and became a noticeable feature of the remainder of the examination.**

Further investigation showed that the limbs were broken in many places as well as being detached from the body. The right arm had been broken at the elbow, the upper arm being separated from the forearm and hand . . . The left arm was broken at the elbow, and in addition at the wrist . . . The left leg was broken at the knee. The right leg was intact . . . The heads of the right humerus [bone of the upper arm] and both femora [thigh bone] had been broken off the remains of the bone . . . The head and neck had been distracted from the torso at the joint between the seventh cervical and first thoracic vertebrae.

Their account goes on: 'The tissues of the face are contracted on the skull so that the cheekbones appear very prominent . . . The teeth are tightly clenched together . . . The radiographs of the thorax confirmed the fact that the sternum and most of the ribs on the front of the chest had been removed.' The age at the time of death is thought to have been about 18 and the height of the body 5ft 6½ in.: 'It is of interest that the heights of the two statues of the young king, which stood on either side of the sealed door leading to the burial chamber, are within a few millimetres of the height estimated above.' The examination also confirmed the refined looks reflected in his golden mask: 'All present at the exposure of the king's remains agreed with Howard Carter's description of a "refined and cultured face" and a "serene and placid countenance".'

The examination failed to find any evidence of disease as

---

* Although it can be only a matter of conjecture after the passage of so many centuries, this sweet scent is reminiscent of the odour of sanctity said to emanate from the body of many men of exceptional holiness, such as Padre Pio, whose saintly qualities made San Giovanni Rotundo a place of renewed pilgrimage in modern times.

the cause of death, and it is clear from the state of his remains that Tutankhamun did not die of natural causes but must have been exposed to severe physical torture, then hanged.

When in 1992, in my book *The House of the Messiah*, I concluded, relying on this report by Professor Harrison, that Tutankhamun had been killed, no one seemed to agree. Nevertheless, after examining Dr Harrison's X-rays, many scholars have come recently to accept my view. Bob Brier, Professor of Egyptology at the Long Island University, New York, studied X-rays of Tutankhamun's fractured skull, following the publication of my book, and accepted my conclusion that the young king was killed. In his book *The Murder of Tutankhamun*, published in 1998, though, he identified Aye (the king's vizier and Commander of the Chariots) as the one who killed him rather than Panehesy. His reason for this identification, he argued, was Aye's motive to replace Tutankhamun on the throne. On the contrary, I regard Aye, Queen Tiye's brother, as the *protector* of his nephew Akhenaten as well as his son Tutankhamun, whose main motive was to save the Amarna rule from collapse.

The Old Testament contains two garbled accounts of the death of Tutankhamun, one featuring Moses and Joshua, the other the priest Panehesy/Pinhas under yet a third form of his name, Phinehas.

The first of these accounts, which places the events as having taken place *after* the Exodus rather than during the earlier period of exile of Akhenaten (Moses), describes how Moses was summoned to meet the Lord on Mount Sinai to receive tablets of stone bearing the Ten Commandments, and 'Moses rose up, and his minister Joshua (Jesus): and Moses went up into the mount of God' (Exodus 24:13). In his absence, the Israelites are said to have gathered together all their earrings, made a golden calf and worshipped it. We find an indication of conflict in the words said to have been used by the Lord when he subsequently instructed Moses and

Joshua to return to the foot of the mountain: '. . . I have seen this people, and, behold, it is a stiffnecked people. Now therefore let me alone, that my wrath may wax hot against them . . .' (32:9,10). As they descended from Mount Sinai, Moses and Joshua heard the noise of celebrations and Joshua commented that 'the noise of them that sing do I hear' (32:18). Moses was so angry over what had happened while he was away that he cast down the tablets bearing the Ten Commandments and shattered them (32:19). The Lord therefore summoned him to a second meeting on the mountain to replace the broken tablets.

On this second occasion we are told – in an apparent attempt to remove him, at least temporarily, from the scene – that Joshua (Jesus) 'the son of Nun, a young man, departed not out of the tabernacle' (33:11). Immediately after the return of Moses with the new tablets, however, we learn that the Lord was inside the tabernacle of worship Moses had built at the foot of Mount Sinai and Moses went in and out a number of times, serving as a go-between for his Israelite followers. During these proceedings, when 'all the children of Israel saw Moses, behold, the skin of his face shone . . . and till Moses had done speaking with them, he put a vail on his face. But when Moses went in before the Lord to speak with him, he took the vail off until he came out. And he came out, and spake unto the children of Israel that which he was commanded . . .' (34:30,34–35). Support for the view that this is where and when Jesus met his death is to be found in rabbinical tradition, which says of the occasion: 'According to Bava Batra (121a) it is the day on which Moses came down from Mount Sinai with the second tablets of the law.'*

If Jesus lived 14 centuries earlier than the time his disciples claimed to have seen him, it would throw new light on events described in the New Testament gospels of Matthew, Mark and Luke – the meeting of Jesus and Moses at the time of what has become known as his Transfiguration:

* *The New Jewish Encyclopaedia.*

'And after six days Jesus taketh with him Peter, and James, and John, and leadeth them up into an high mountain apart by themselves: and he was transfigured before them. And his raiment became shining, exceeding white as snow; so as no fuller on earth can white them. And there appeared unto them Elias (Elijah – Plate 23) with Moses: and they were talking with Jesus . . . And there was a cloud that overshadowed them: and a voice came out of the cloud, saying, This is my beloved Son: hear him. And suddenly, when they looked round about, they saw no man any more, save only Jesus with themselves . . .' (Mark 9:2–4,7).

Elijah, Elias of the New Testament, is a mysterious figure presented in the Book of Kings of the Old Testament. Although he is believed to have lived during the time of King Ahab of Israel in the 9th century BC, we know nothing of him or his family. He is believed never to have died but to have gone to heaven in a chariot. It is this mysterious character, who is thought to have been a mythical representation of Phinehas the priest, who is mentioned by the New Testament gospels as having been with Moses when he met Jesus on the top of the mountain. The New Testament account indicates that the return of Elias from heaven would usher the appearance of the Messiah. (Incidentally, the name Phinehas derives from the Egyptian *panhysy*, meaning 'the southerner', but is also employed in Egypt as a proper name.)

Christian authors avoided trying to interpret the meaning of this account until the 19th century. It was then explained away as not being a description of actual historical events, but rather a matter of the psychology of Jesus and His disciples or having been a 'spiritual experience'. However, the factual nature of the gospel narratives themselves does not permit this interpretation.

Unlike the confrontation with Satan, when Jesus was alone with a fallen angelic being, the Transfiguration cannot be interpreted as symbolic or a description of a vision. Here we have three disciples who are said to be witnesses to a meeting between Jesus and Moses, an event that is the only clue in the gospels to the era in which Jesus lived.

That there was more than one 'tradition', separated by many hundreds of years, about when the Transfiguration occurred is indicated by a mosaic in the monastery church of St Catherine, built at the foot of Mount Sinai in the last years of the 6th century AD (Plate 26). In the sanctuary apse off one of its chapels, the Chapel of the Burning Bush, we see contrasting depictions of the Transfiguration. Christ is portrayed, with black hair and beard, in an oval glory, between Moses and Elijah. At his feet stand three apostles, Peter, James and John. In the accompanying medallion the three apostles have been replaced by three other apostles, Paul, Thaddaeus and Matthias.*

That an Israelite leader was killed in Sinai at around this time is not a new idea. It was, as we saw much earlier, voiced by Sigmund Freud, who identified Moses, wrongly, as the victim. The same is true of Ernest Sellin, the German biblical scholar. In his book *Moses and His Significance for Israelite-Jewish Religious History* he described the killing as 'the scarlet thread' running through Israelite history. Sellin based his conclusion on a chapter in the Book of Numbers that features Phinehas.

The story in Numbers tells how, after Israel had been locked in combat with the tribes of Moab and Midian, a number of Israelites began 'to commit whoredom' (25:1) with Moabite women, who invited them to 'the sacrifices of their gods: and the people did eat, and bowed down to their gods' (25:2). This, it is said, angered the Lord (25:3). Then 'one of the children of Israel came and brought unto his brethren a Midianitish woman in the sight of Moses, and in the sight of all the congregation of the people of Israel, who

---

* At a meeting with me in June 1996 Archbishop Damianos of St Catherine's monastery confirmed this as the site of the Transfiguration scene.

were weeping before the door of the Tabernacle of the Congregation. And when Phinehas, the son of Eleazar, the son of Aaron the priest, saw it, he rose up from among the congregation, and took a javelin in his hand; and he went after the man of Israel into the tent (tabernacle), and thrust both of them through, the man of Israel and the woman . . .' (25:6–8).

For these actions, Phinehas is presented to us as a hero. As a result, a 'plague' that had cost the lives of 24,000 people was brought to an end, and the Lord spoke to Moses, saying: 'Phinehas, the son of Eleazar, the son of Aaron the priest, hath turned my wrath away from the children of Israel, while he was zealous for my sake among them, that I consumed not the children of Israel in my jealousy. Wherefore say, Behold I give unto him my covenant of peace. And he shall have it, and his seed after him, even the covenant of an everlasting priesthood; because he was zealous for his God, and made an atonement for the children of Israel' (25:11–3). A few verses later the victims are identified as minor figures – Zimri and Cozbi, the son and daughter respectively of two chiefs.

If one analyses this account, it is easy to see why Sellin suspected that it had been subjected to some priestly sleight-of-hand in the editing in order to cover up what had actually happened. An ordinary Israelite would not have taken a foreign woman into the inner room of the tabernacle, where only a king or high priest was allowed; there is no mention of the man in this case worshipping another god; making love to a woman was not punishable by death; Moses, the Israelite leader, did not give any orders for action against the man, and, if the male victim was a minor figure, why would it require revenge in the form of the death of 24,000 people? It is no wonder that Sellin commented that 'despite the efforts of the priests to suppress the sordid story, it nevertheless lived in prophetic circles'.

It is clear that, as what is described as a plague is mentioned only *after* Phinehas had committed the killing, it was a punishment for the assassination, not for worshipping false gods. Paul had this in mind when, after indicating that Christ was present with the Israelites in Sinai, he went on to say: 'But with many of them God was not pleased . . . and fell in one day three and twenty thousand' (Corinthians 10:5,8). This understanding is reinforced by the evidence available from *The Dead Sea Scrolls*. The *Commentary on Habakkuk*, one of the Qumran texts, tells us that, after The Wicked Priest had killed The Teacher of Righteousness, 'he (the Teacher) appeared before them to swallow them up'.* 'Swallow up' is a Hebrew metaphor for 'do away with' or 'kill'. As for the appearance of the Teacher after death, 'the Hebrew verb used here may also be translated as "he revealed himself to them" – indicating a spiritual rather than an historical appearance.

Further support for the theory that the 'plague' that followed the Sinai assassination was a form of punishment – and for the moment in history at which the assassination took place – is to be found in the Book of Hosea, where this punishment is said to have been carried out by Ephraim (Aye, Tutankhamun's vizier and head of the chariotry): 'When Ephraim spake trembling (the sense here, given in other translations, is caused others to tremble), he exalted himself in Israel . . .' (13:1). It is also curious that Phinehas should have been rewarded with 'the covenant of a perpetual priesthood to him and his descendants after him' when we know from the previous book in the Pentateuch, Leviticus, that this promise had already been made to Aaron and his descendants.

Establishing the truth about these events at the foot of Mount Sinai is difficult because, as we shall see, elaborate efforts were made down the centuries to conceal that truth. In the meantime, what was the 'crime' of Tutankhamun that brought him to such a violent end? In other words, why was he killed?

---

* *The Essene Writings from Qumran*, André Dupont-Sommer.

Chapter Fifteen

The Holy Family

Tutankhamun was described in his tomb, as we saw earlier, as 'the eldest son of Aten in Heaven'. The young king-to-be was given the name Tut-ankh-aten when he was born. The three elements in his birthname – Tut (image), ankh (the Egyptian cross, the symbol of life) and Aten (the Egyptian equivalent of Adonai, 'the Lord' in Hebrew) – mean that it is to be translated as 'the living image of the Lord'. Thus he was looked upon as the Son of God from the time of his birth – or perhaps even before it, as it was the custom of Egyptian kings to choose names for their children before they were born.

After the religious reforms of his early years – opening the temples, allowing the ancient gods of Egypt to be worshipped again and changing his name to Tutankhamun and his wife's to Ankhsenpa-amun in honour of the state god Amun-ra – Tutankhamun embarked in his Year 9 on an ecumenical mission to Sinai to try to persuade his father, Akhenaten (Moses) and his followers to return to Egypt where they could live in peace if they accepted the religious changes he had made, and that other people could have their own form of worship.

We find an echo of this mission on behalf of tolerance and peace in Matthew's gospel account (Chapter 5) of the Sermon on the Mount given by Jesus: 'Blessed are the peacemakers: for they shall be called the children of God . . . Think not that I am come to destroy the law, or the prophets: I am not come to destroy, but to fulfil . . . Agree with thine adversary quickly . . . Ye have heard that it hath been said,

An eye for an eye, and a tooth for a tooth: But I say unto you, that ye resist not evil: but whosoever shall smite thee on thy right cheek, turn to him the other also . . . Ye have heard that it hath been said, Thou shalt love thy neighbour, and hate thine enemy. But I say unto you, Love your enemies, bless them that curse you, do good to them that hate you . . . That ye may be the children of your Father which is in Heaven.' One can also sense the supplication of Tutankhamun, ruling over two peoples divided by race and religion, in the words of the Lord's Prayer that follows: '. . . forgive us our trespasses as we forgive those who trespass against us . . .'

However, instead of his pleas being accepted, he was accused of betraying his faith and killed – at a time when the vast majority of Israelites were still at Goshen in Egypt and cannot be said to have had any responsibility for, or even any possibility of being aware of, events that have since haunted the Jewish people for more than 3,000 years.

Despite various efforts to mask the truth about these events, memories of them – and of many of the personalities involved – survived down the centuries and were echoed in the New Testament gospels of Matthew, Mark, Luke and John when they retold the story as if the life, suffering and death of Jesus had taken place in the 1st century AD, the start of the Christian era.

Mary, the Mother of Jesus. Two women named Mary are placed in a close relationship with Jesus in the New Testament – his mother and Mary Magdalene. The Greek version of the name is Maria, the Hebrew is Miriam, but its origins lie in Ancient Egypt where the word *mery* means 'the beloved'.

This epithet is also applied to Nefertiti, the mother of Tutankhamun, and to Ankhsenpa-aten, his wife. His mother's name, Nefertiti, means 'the beautiful one who has come'. From her celebrated head in the Berlin Museum it is clear that she was indeed a beautiful woman. It is also known that she had a beautiful voice: she used to sing the evening prayers at the Aten temple in Amarna (see Plates 24 & 25).

Before the birth of Tutankhamun, she had three daughters, and another three afterwards. No evidence of other sons has been found. In the tombs of Amarna Nefertiti assumed many qualities of Isis, the Ancient Egyptian mother-figure and mother of the falcon god Horus, and Nefertiti's figure replaced that of the goddess on the Amarna sarcophagi. For instance, it is to be found instead of the image of Isis on the sarcophagus of Akhenaten. Furthermore, there are statues in Rome, originally made in the 1st century AD to represent Isis and her son, which were used by the early Church to represent Mary and her son.

The other Mary, apparently related emotionally to Jesus, appears to be a younger woman, Mary Magdalene. Her first appearance in the gospels is as an unnamed sinner: 'And being in Bethany in the house of Simon the leper, as he sat at meat, there came a woman having an alabaster box of ointment of spikenard very precious; and she brake the box and poured it on his head' (Mark 14:3). For his part, Luke has her anointing the feet of Jesus: 'And she stood at his feet behind him weeping, and began to wash his feet with tears, and did wipe them with the hairs of her head, and kissed his feet, and anointed them with the ointment' (Luke 7:38) (see Plate 21). Subsequently, the name of Mary Magdalene appears among those who followed Jesus and remained close to him until after his death. Although no satisfactory explanation is given, she was clearly very attached to him. She remained by the temporary burial place where he was placed after his death and is described as having encountered Jesus after the Resurrection: 'Jesus saith unto her, Mary. She turned herself, and saith unto him, Rabboni; which is to say, Master. Jesus saith unto her, Touch me not, for I am not yet ascended to my Father; but go to my brethren, and say unto them, I ascend unto my Father, and your Father; and to my God, and your God' (John 20:16–17).

This Mary can only have been Ankhsenpa-aten, Tutankhamun's queen. Alabaster ointment jars were found in the king's tomb and she is represented at the back of the royal throne anointing him with perfume, exactly as the evangelists say. In four other scenes found on objects in the tomb, the couple are represented together, always in relaxed, romantic scenes. We can see how closely she was attached to his person in the very same manner that Mary Magdalene is described in the gospels.

The epithet 'Magdalene' has been explained by saying that she belonged to the city of Magdala, an unidentified location on the western shore of the Sea of Galilee. On the other hand we know from both biblical and Egyptian sources of such named locations at the time of Tutankhamun. The Hebrew word *migdol* means 'watch-tower' and indicates a fortified city. Such a city is recorded as having been the second military post to the east of Zarw on the Road of Horus, leading from Egypt to Gaza. This location is shown on Seti I's road map in his Hypostyle Hall at Karnak and is mentioned in many Egyptian texts.

The *Gospel of Mary*, one of the Gnostic gospels found in a cave at Nag Hammadi in upper Egypt in 1945,* depicts Mary Magdalene as the one favoured with visions and insight: 'Peter said to Mary, "Sister, we know that the Saviour loved you more than the rest of women. Tell us the words of the Saviour which you remember . . ." Mary answered and said, "What is hidden from you I will proclaim to you." . . . "I," she said, "saw the Lord in a vision and I said to him, 'Lord, I saw you today in a vision.' He answered and said to me, 'Blessed are you, that you did not waver at the sight of me. For where the mind is, there is the treasure.' I said to him, 'Lord, now does he who sees the vision see it [through] the soul [or] through the spirit?' The Saviour answered and said, 'He does not see through the soul nor

* The significance of the Nag Hammadi documents (touched upon earlier) is dealt with in a later chapter.

through the spirit, but the mind which [is] between the two"' (*The Gospel of Mary*, 10–15).

The *Dialogue of the Saviour*, another Nag Hammadi text, praises Mary Magdalene as the apostle who excels all the rest. The *Gospel of Philip*, a third document, speaks of the intimate relationship between Jesus and Mary Magdalene: 'There were three who always walked with the Lord: Mary his mother and Magdalene, the one who was called his companion. His sister and his mother . . . were each a Mary' (59: 6–10). It goes on to say: 'And the companion of the [Saviour is] Mary Magdalene. [But Christ loved] her more than [all] the disciples and used to kiss her [often] on her [mouth]' (63: 34–35). Here we find three women named Mary – his mother, his sister and his companion – but it seems that both his sister and his companion are one person, his sister-wife.

Apart from a visit to Jerusalem when he was 12 (Luke 2:42–43), the gospels do not tell us anything about the childhood of Jesus. Two of them, as we have seen, do not even mention his birth. However, there is no reason to supposed that he could not have married during this time. The evangelists were mainly concerned to convey his teachings and message rather than give details of his personal life. Even details of his mother's life are absent from the New Testament: this does not mean that she had no life to be reported, but simply indicates that it was outside the scope of the gospels. In fact, John's account of Mary Magdalene and the Resurrection reflects a verifiable historical event. Ankhsenpa-aten, being both the wife and queen of Tutankhamun, was the only person who could attend his funerary rites, see him as he was declared risen from the dead by the priests during their mummification ritual and bear the news to the 'disciples'. The fact that Jesus's disciples at the time of John the Baptist are the ones mentioned in the gospels does not mean that the historical Jesus did not have disciples during his lifetime. In every generation from the time he lived there was a group of followers and disciples who kept his memory and teachings alive until they were brought into the open through John the Baptist's death.* The first 12 could have been his ministers.

As for brothers, we know from evidence of diplomatic communications with the Hittite kingdom of Asia Minor that Tutankhamun died without an heir. Howard Carter makes the point in his book *The Tomb of Tutankhamun*: 'Tutankhamun died without [male] issue, which accords with the claim [made by his widow] that she had no son to succeed to the throne.'

The Two Josephs. The gospels feature two Josephs. One is described as a carpenter, descended from the House of David, and the stepfather of Jesus. Of the four gospel authors, only Matthew and Luke mention this Joseph, who disappears from the scene before the ministry of Christ. Nothing is said about his fate. The second person bearing the name is Joseph of Arimathaea, who is said to have been rich, a man of authority, a disciple of Jesus, and to have appeared suddenly after the Crucifixion to demand the body of Jesus for burial. I believe they are to be identified as the same person – Aye (Ephraim), Tutankhamun's great-uncle, vizier and successor on the throne (whom we met in Chapter 5).

The disappearance of the first Joseph, completely un-explained, is matched only by the sudden appearance of the second Joseph: 'When the even was come, there came a rich man of Arimathaea, named Joseph, who also himself was Jesus's disciple: He went to Pilate, and begged the body of Jesus . . . And when Joseph had taken the body, he wrapped it

---

* The Baptist, according to his behaviour, was a member of the Essene, Jewish-Christian sect of Qumran, which also indicates the early Jerusalem Christian Church of Peter and James. The reason he came into the open in this period was the Roman occupation of Jerusalem and the new tax they forced on the Jews, which is the same reason for the rebellion of Judas in AD 6. The Baptist was a contemporary person to these events, and his account was not included in the gospels before the 2nd century AD, as part of the Orthodox effort to turn the spiritual appearance of Christ into history.

in a clean linen cloth, And laid it in his own new tomb, which he had hewn out in the rock . . .' (Matthew 27:57–60). Mark gives us a little more information about him: 'Joseph of Arimathaea, an honourable counsellor, which also waited for the kingdom . . . went in boldly unto Pilate, and craved the body of Jesus . . . And he bought fine linen, and took him down, and wrapped him in the linen, and laid him in a sepulchre which was hewn out of a rock' (15:43,46). From these passages we know that Joseph arrived on the scene on the evening of Christ's death; he was a follower of Jesus; he was also a member of the Israelite leadership; he had sufficient authority to demand the body and have his wish granted; he 'waited for' – that is, 'was near to' – the kingdom.

This mysterious character has much in common with Aye, who also had authority and was near to the kingdom. It is also significant that Ephraim is identified in the Book of Hosea as the avenger responsible for the 'plague' to punish Phinehas and his followers after the Sinai assassination: 'When Ephraim spake trembling' – the sense here, given in other translations, is caused others to tremble – 'he exalted himself in Israel . . .' (13:1).

These passages, if taken in conjunction with the statement in Isaiah that The Suffering Servant 'made his grave with the wicked, and with the rich', indicate that Aye took the body of Tutankhamun after his death at the foot of Mount Sinai and buried him in a tomb – a second tomb, not the one later usurped by Horemheb – that was not originally his but was meant for Aye himself, hewn out of the rock in the Valley of the Kings. The archaeological evidence supports this view. Certainly there is no doubt that Aye supervised the young king's burial. Donald Redford makes the point in his book *Akhenaten the Heretic King*: 'It was King Aye, Tutankhamun's successor, who buried our monarch, for there, on the inner walls of Tutankhamun's tomb-chamber, Aye, as king, has caused himself to be represented among the religious scenes, officiating before Tutankhamun, a scene unprecedented in the royal tombs of this necropolis.'

We find many echoes of those distant days in Christian beliefs, traditions and ritual:

Resurrection. From as early as the 31st century BC, Egyptians believed that a human being consisted of spiritual as well as physical elements. They regarded death as the departure of the spiritual element from the body, but also believed that, if the physical being could be kept safe and protected by magic formulas, the spirit would return to the body at some point in the future and the person concerned would lead a second life. That is why they devoted such care to preserving a dead body by mummification and building secure tombs to keep it safe. Osiris, whom they looked upon as one of their ancient kings, was said to have been killed by his brother Set, who dismembered the body of Osiris in order to deny him a second life. However, his wife, Isis, was able to collect the various members and, with her magic, restore him to life three days later – not on earth but in the underworld, where he became the god and judge of the dead. The account of the Resurrection of Jesus is in many ways similar to that of Osiris. Like Osiris, he is said to have been killed on a Friday and risen on the third day. The Osiris worshippers of ancient Egypt believed, as did the early Christians, that man cannot be saved by a remote omnipotent deity, but by one who has shared the experience of human suffering and death. Osiris became the saviour to whom men and women turned for assurance of immortality.

Akhenaten (Moses) abolished the worship of Osiris as well as other ancient Egyptian gods and never spoke of an after-life. However, followers of Christ, the Essenes among them, believed – unlike the rest of the Jews – in life after death. This revived belief in the eternal existence of the spirit and judgement after death can be traced to the historical Jesus himself. Tutankhamun accepted the Osiris belief in an after-life and made Aten the God of both life and death. This is reflected in his tomb where, in complete contrast to the teachings of Moses, he is shown resurrected and alive, facing Aye.

Tutankhaten's Change of Name. This change of name is referred to in both the Old and New Testaments. In the Book of Isaiah we find three references to Immanuel, including 'Therefore the Lord himself shall give you a sign; Behold, a virgin shall conceive, and bear a son, and call his name Immanuel' (7:14). Opinions differ about the significance of the name. The Jewish interpretation is that the reference does not indicate the Messiah and is not even a proper noun. However, the evidence of *The Dead Sea Scrolls* shows that the Qumran Essenes looked upon it as a name. The evangelist Matthew also considered it a name, a synonym for Jesus: 'Now all this was done, that it might be fulfilled which was spoken of the Lord by the prophet, saying, Behold, a virgin shall be with child, and shall bring forth a son, and they shall call his name Emmanuel, which being interpreted is, God with us' (1:22–23).

As we saw earlier, because Hebrew has no tenses, the way a statement is translated often reflects the beliefs of the translator. An early Christian such as Matthew, who believed that the Virgin Birth had taken place in the 1st century AD, would therefore take the view that Isaiah, writing several centuries earlier, was making a prophecy rather than recording an event that had already taken place. Matthew is also mistaken in his interpretation of the name Emmanuel,* which is arrived at by dividing the word into two elements – Emma-nu (with us) and El (Elohim, God). While this reading is possible, another is here intended: Imman-u (his Amun) El (is God). Use of the word 'virgin' in the translation is also a distortion of what Isaiah was actually saying.

The Egyptian word *amun*, as well as being the name of the state god, means 'hidden' or 'unseen': the Hebrew equivalent is *alam*. Isaiah used *alma*, the feminine form of *alam*, in his verse about the birth of Immanuel. While *alma* can be translated as either 'a young girl' or 'virgin' it is also a

---

* As this is a Semitic name, it is sometimes written with an I, and sometimes with an E.

feminine form of 'the hidden one' (God). The reason why both the Essenes and early Christians insisted on relating the verse to the Messiah is that they interpreted correctly the sense in which Isaiah was using the word – to indicate a feminine aspect of the hidden power of God. God is presented as three persons, God the Father, God the Mother and God the Son. To make this clear, I believe that the following translation is closer to the literal sense of the Hebrew text: 'Therefore Adonai (Aten) gives himself to you as a sign. Behold, Alma (the hidden one) conceived, a son is born, and she (the hidden one) called his name Amun-u-el.' Thus the word *Amun* was used here to indicate an aspect of the 'hidden' Adonai (Lord).

Although Matthew, as well as later Christian writers, took the view that Immanuel is a synonym for Jesus, no clear explanation has hitherto been given, and it is only when we examine the events in the life of Tutankhamun, the historical Christ, that the meaning becomes clear.

It has been suggested that part of the reason for proclamation of the Virgin Birth, based upon the words of Isaiah, was to popularize Christianity among the Gentiles. The Greeks, for instance, believed that the human Semele, the mother of Dionysos, was impregnated by their chief god, Zeus. Thus we find Justin Martyr, one of the early Church Fathers, explaining to them in the middle of the 2nd century AD: 'In saying that the word . . . was born for us without sexual union, as Jesus Christ our teacher . . . we introduce nothing new beyond [what you say of] those whom you call sons of Zeus.'

Amen. In his book about Isis and Osiris, Plutarch, the Roman historian of the second half of the 1st century AD, states that 'when the Egyptians name the supreme God, whom they believe to be one with the universe, they call him Amun.'

The word *amen*, used as a response to prayers, almost certainly has as its source the word 'amun', used by Isaiah to mean 'the hidden one'. Both words were written *amn* in ancient Egyptian. The word 'amen' is found in the Old Testament ('And Ezra blessed the Lord, the great God. And all the people answered, Amen, Amen, with lifting up their hands; and they bowed their faces to the ground' [Nehemiah 8:6]) and the New Testament, where it appears 77 times and St Paul uses it in prayer ('. . . when thou shalt bless with the spirit, how shall he that occupieth the room of the unlearned say Amen at thy giving of thanks, seeing he understandeth not what thou sayest' [I Corinthians 14:16]). The word, frequently rendered as 'verily' or 'truly' in English, is used as a response to both Christian and Jewish prayers and by Muslims after every recital of the first Sura (chapter) of the Koran.

Angels and Saints. Realizing that most ordinary people could not grasp the abstract idea of a God who does not manifest himself in a seen image, or favour one nation more than another, Tutankhamun allowed the return of the old deities. Close examination of his religious reforms shows that he did not regard them as gods, but as angels in the heavenly world of Aten.

Although Tutankhamun still regarded Aten as the one and only God who had no image, he realized that his people needed some visual representation of the deity to communicate with. So he allowed the old temples to be reopened and old deities to be worshipped. But, as Aten was confirmed in his unique position, these deities were but *mediators* between him and ordinary people, angelic beings in the heavenly world of God. In fact this was the starting point for the recognition of angels, and gradually the word 'gods' in the plural was replaced by the word 'angels'. Tutankhamun made another very important development in the Aten cult, when he accepted Osiris and his underworld as part of the Aten belief. Neither Moses nor Akhenaten was ever reported to have spoken of life after death and the underworld, which was at the centre of all ancient Egyptian religious belief.

A fragment of the Song of Moses in Deuteronomy 32,

found in a cave at Qumran, includes a text of Verse 43 which mentions the word 'gods' in the plural: 'Rejoice, O heavens, with him; and do obeisance to him, ye gods.' William Brownless, the American biblical scholar, makes the point in his book *The Meaning of the Qumran Scrolls for the Bible*: 'When the passage is quoted in the New Testament (Hebrews 1:6), the phrase is appropriately rendered "angels of God".' The immediate popular response to Tutankhamun's reformation was fantastic, as ordinary Egyptians welcomed the change. But it was not given enough time for its true significance to be absorbed, as his death meant the complete dismissal of Aten, which in turn meant that the deities were once more recognized as gods.

Ritual. Howard Carter also reported that he found a great many ritual links with Christianity in the tomb of Tutankhamun. Among them were two gala robes and a pair of gloves similar to those later used by priests of the Roman Catholic Church: 'The two garments, which I have chosen to call gala robes, recall official vestments of the character of priestly apparel, such as the dalmatic worn by deacons and bishops of the Christian church, or by kings and emperors at coronations . . . They take the form of a long, loose vestment, having richly ornamented tapestry-woven decoration with fringes on both sides . . .

'Perhaps they were worn on special occasions . . . and . . . they were a symbol of joy, very much in the manner of the dalmatic placed upon a deacon when the holy order was conferred, whereby the following words are repeated: "May the Lord clothe thee in the Tunic of Joy and the Garment of Rejoicing." Moreover, these robes may well have had the same origin as the Roman garment, whence the liturgical vestment – the dalmatic – of the Christian church derives.'

The pair of gloves, according to Carter, were in a much better state of preservation, 'neatly folded, also of tapestry-woven linen. They were possibly intended to go with the robes (a Roman Catholic bishop wears gloves when pontificating – also buskins, tunic and dalmatic under his chasuble) and are similarly woven with a brilliant scale-pattern and have a border at the wrist of alternate lotus buds and flowers.' Other objects included 'a number of ostrich-feathers, recalling the flabella still used at a papal procession in Rome, such as was witnessed in the Eucharistic procession of His Holiness the Pope in July 1929. These fans, like the pontifical flabella, were carried by grooms-in-waiting in Pharaonic processions, or were held beside the throne, and appear always on either side of the king or immediately behind him.'

Transfiguration. The shining face of the Transfiguration is ascribed to Tutankhamun on one of the objects found in his tomb. A royal sceptre, used in connection with offerings, bears this text: 'The Beautiful God, beloved, dazzling of face like the Aten when it shines . . . Tutankhamun.'

The Crown of Thorns. The tomb contained fruits and seeds of Christ-thorn, a tree like a hawthorn, native to Ancient Egypt, used for food, medicine and timber, and also believed to have had religious significance. It is said to have been used for Christ's crown of thorns: 'And the soldiers platted a crown of thorns, and put it on his head . . .' (John 19:2).

The Three Wise Men. Evidence discovered elsewhere in the Valley of the Kings throws light on the story found in Matthew about the three wise men who came from foreign countries to offer presents as well as pay homage to the new-born king. This is a story of Egyptian origin. During the time of the Empire, when Egypt had control over most of western Asia as well as Nubia and part of northern Sudan, such visits and gifts were common.

A box, found in a room to the north of the tomb of Horemheb in the Valley of the Kings, contained several pieces of gold leaf bearing the names of Tutankhamun and Aye, clues that eventually contributed to discovery of the young king's tomb as well as pointing to the source of the story of the three wise men. One of these pieces of gold leaf had the two royal cartouches of Aye on the left side, faced on the right side by three foreigners whose arms are raised in a position of adoration towards the king's names.

'The first has a large beard and thick hair falling on the neck; his garment is ornamented with dotted designs forming circles above and squares below; the cape and broad girdle are also decorated,' wrote Gaston Maspero and George Daressy in their book *The Tombs of Haramhabi and Toutankhamanou*. 'This is the typical type of the Syrian from the Mediterranean coasts. The second has the hair arranged in tiers and surmounted by a feather, the collar fits closely to the neck, the scarf crosses the breast, and the robe falls in straight folds. He is undoubtedly a negro of the Sudan. The third wears a pointed beard; in his flowing hair are fixed two plumes; a large cloak envelops the body, leaving the limbs bare. It is in this way that, in the tombs of the kings and other ethnological pictures, are represented the . . . white-skinned races of the North, Libyans of Marmrica and inhabitants of the Mediterranean islands. Here, then, is a representation of the three biblical races, Shem, Ham and Japhet' – and the source of the story of the three wise men, who represented different peoples of the ancient known world.

Summary

Although the Glory of Christ appeared to his disciples in the early part of the 1st century AD, historical Jesus had lived and died 14 centuries earlier. Up to the 16th century AD, when the Old Testament books were translated from the Masoretic Hebrew text into modern European languages, Jesus was the name of the prophet who succeeded Moses as leader of the Israelites in Egypt. Since the 16th century we started to have two names, Jesus and Joshua, which confused people into the belief that they were two different characters. All those who spoke of Jesus in the early history of the

Church recognized in this name only one person, who (according to John 1:45) was the name 'of whom Moses in the law, and the prophets, did write'. As this Jesus of history was put to death at the foot of Mount Sinai, at the same position as the present monastery of St Catherine, his followers kept his memory alive over the centuries, awaiting his return. And he did return when he appeared in his glory to his disciples in Egypt and Palestine in the early years of the 1st century AD.

Tutankhamun's tomb was discovered, with his body inside his coffin, about 2,000 years after the appearance of Christ. Like him, he was killed at the foot of Mount Sinai when he attempted to reconcile those who believed in one God without an image and those who needed an image to mediate between them and the unseen deity. He was accused of being a deceiver who tried to turn the Israelites to worshipping other gods, and was hanged on a tree (according to ancient Israelite law) by Panehesy, the high priest of Akhenaten.

Chapter Sixteen

Exodus

Tutankhamun was succeeded in 1352 BC by Aye (Ephraim), his great-uncle, protector and, ultimately, the avenger of his death. It was only four years before Aye, too, disappeared mysteriously from the scene, to be replaced by Horemheb (*c.* 1348–1335 BC), an army general, who secured his right to the throne by marrying Mutnezmet, the sister of Nefertiti.

We find Horemheb mentioned in the Old Testament as 'a new king over Egypt which knew not Joseph' (Exodus 1:8), a description that cannot be applied to any of the four Amarna rulers, Akhenaten, Semenkhkare, Tutankhamun and Aye, all descendants of Joseph the Patriarch (Yuya), who brought the tribes of Israel down from Canaan to live in Egypt.

Horemheb inherited the religious revolution begun by Akhenaten, to which he was totally opposed. Worship of the Aten was abolished, and the names of the Amarna kings were excised from king-lists and monuments in a studied campaign to try to remove all traces of their rule from Egyptian memory. The task was carried out thoroughly, as was made clear once hieroglyphics were finally deciphered in comparatively modern times. A brilliant young French philologist, François Champollion (1790–1832), translated various Egyptian texts that had hitherto been a complete mystery to historians. Among them were the cartouches of the Kings-list on the walls of the Osiris temple at Abydos in Upper Egypt. The list, which included the names of the kings of the 18th Dynasty, made *no mention of the four Amarna rulers*. In the circumstances it is not surprising that when, in the middle of the last century, archaeologists came across the strangely drawn figure of Akhenaten at Amarna they were not sure initially what to make of him. Some thought that, like Queen Hatshepsut, this newly discovered Pharaoh was a woman who disguised herself as a king. Further cause for conjecture arose from the fact that Akhenaten had ascended to the throne as Amenhotep IV and later changed his name. Were they dealing with one Pharaoh or two?

Horemheb also made it a crime, punishable by death, even to mention the name of Akhenaten (Moses). I believe that the origin of the name Moses lies in this ban. Freud, as we saw earlier, pointed out that *Mos* was an Egyptian word meaning 'child', but it also had a wider legal meaning, 'the rightful son and heir'. This is clear from the inscriptions in a tomb at Sakkara about a dispute over a piece of land that lasted over a long period during reigns of different kings of the 18th and 19th Dynasties. The plaintiff in the case was a scribe named Khayri, who having been named once is afterwards referred to as *Mos* to indicate his claim to be the rightful inheritor. Consequently, it seems to me that an alternative, a type of codename, had to be found in order that followers of Akhenaten (Moses) could refer to him. Therefore they called him *Mos*, the son, to indicate that he was the legitimate son of Amenhotep III and the rightful heir to his father's throne. Later, the biblical editor, who may not have had any knowledge of the original name of the greatest Israelite leader, attempted to put forward a Hebrew explanation of the Egyptian word Moses in order to sever any possible link between Moses and Egypt.

As we saw earlier, from a philological point of view, in Ancient Egyptian, which had no vowels, the written word meaning a child or son consists of two consonants, *m* and *s*, although the vowels were pronounced. It is consequently easy to see that the Hebrew word came from the Egyptian word. As for the final 's' of Moses, this derives from the Greek translation of the biblical name.

By the time Horemheb came to the throne, many

Egyptians had adopted the Atenist faith and, as a result, were looked upon, in the words of Manetho, the native Egyptian historian of the 3rd century BC, as 'polluted persons'. Horemheb persecuted them. He turned the area around the fortified frontier city of Zarw, where Akhenaten (Moses) had been born, into a prison. There he gathered the mass of Akhenaten's followers, both Israelite and Egyptian, plus a variety of criminals, who lived in villages outside the city walls. Horemheb appointed Pa-Ramses (later Ramses I, the first ruler of the 19th Dynasty) as his chief minister, Commander of the Troops, Overseer of Foreign Countries, Overseer of the Fortress of Zarw and Master of the Horse. Pa-Ramses was therefore the most powerful man in Egypt after Horemheb, and it was he, on Horemheb's orders, who inflicted harsh labour on the Israelites and other prisoners by forcing them to rebuild Zarw as well as a new residence for himself, known later as Pi-Ramses, which, according to the Old Testament, was the starting point of the Exodus.

The length of Horemheb's reign has been the subject of considerable dispute, with estimates ranging from as low as eight years to as high as 59. Manetho assigned 12 years and three months to Horemheb's reign. Support for Manetho's view is provided by two large storage jars, which bear hieratic dockets and were found in fairly recent times in Horemheb's tomb. One of them is dated to 'Year 13, third month of Inundation' and is said to have contained 'very good quality wine from the vineyard of the estate of Horemheb, beloved of Amun . . .' As this is the last sure date we have for him and it agrees with the Manethonian tradition, it should be accepted as indicating the time he died.

The death of Horemheb in 1335 BC, aged about 70, left Egypt without a legitimate heir to the 18th Dynasty. Pa-Ramses, his chief minister, by now an old man, therefore prepared to claim the throne for himself as the first ruler of a new dynasty, the 19th. It was at this point that Akhenaten (Moses), who had been in exile in the wilderness for about a quarter of a century, decided to try to reclaim his throne – at a time when, according to the Old Testament, the Lord assured him that 'all the men are dead which sought thy life' (Exodus 4:19).

The biblical account of these events begins with the appearance of the Lord to Moses in a burning bush on the mount of God, Mount Sinai. The Lord said to him: '. . . I have surely seen the affliction of my people which are in Egypt, and have heard their cry by reason of their taskmasters . . . And I am come down to deliver them out of the hands of the Egyptians, and to bring them up out of that land . . . unto a land flowing with milk and honey . . . Come now therefore, and I will send thee unto Pharaoh, that thou mayest bring forth my people the children of Israel out of Egypt . . . (Exodus 3:7–8,10).

Moses protested that the Israelites would not listen to him. The Lord said to him: 'What is that in thine hand? And he said, A rod. And he said, Cast it on the ground. And he cast it on the ground, and it became a serpent . . . And the Lord said unto Moses, Put forth thine hand, and take it by the tail. And he put forth his hand and caught it, and it became a rod in his hand . . . And the Lord said furthermore unto him, Put now thine hand into thine bosom. And he put his hand into his bosom: and when he took it out, behold, his hand was leprous as snow. And he said, Put thine hand into thine bosom again. And he put his hand into his bosom again; and plucked it out of his bosom, and, behold, it was turned again as his other flesh. And it shall come to pass, if they will not believe thee, neither hearken to the voice of the first sign, that they will believe the voice of the latter sign. And it shall come to pass that, if they will not believe also these two signs, neither hearken unto thy voice, that thou shalt take of the water of the river, and pour it upon the dry land: and the water which thou takest out of the river shall become blood upon the dry land' (4:2–4,6–9).

Moses was still unwilling to undertake the mission. He protested that he was 'slow of speech and of a slow tongue' (4:10). However, the Lord replied '. . . Is not Aaron the

Levite thy brother? I know that he can speak well. And also, behold, he cometh forth to meet thee . . . he shall be thy spokesman unto the people . . . he shall be to thee instead of a mouth, and thou shalt be to him instead of God. And thou shalt take this rod in thine hand, wherewith thou shalt do signs' (4:14,16–17).

Moses and Aaron made their way to Egypt where 'Aaron spake all the words which the Lord had spoken unto Moses, and did the signs in the sight of the people. And the people believed . . . they bowed their heads and worshipped' (4:30–31). However, the oppression begun by Horemheb continued under his successor, Ramses I. When Moses and Aaron sought permission for the Israelites to spend three days in the wilderness to hold a feast to their God, Pharaoh not only refused but increased the harsh treatment of the Israelites: '. . . Behold the people of the land now are many, and ye make them rest from their burdens. And Pharaoh commanded the same day the taskmasters of the people, and their officers, saying, Ye shall no more give the people straw to make bricks, as heretofore: let them go and gather straw for themselves. And the tale [number] of bricks, which they did make heretofore, ye shall lay upon them; ye shall not diminish ought thereof: for they be idle; therefore they cry, saying, Let us go and sacrifice to our God' (5:5–8).

Faced with this hostility, Moses and Aaron sought permission for the Israelites to leave Egypt altogether. It was refused, whereupon the Lord told Moses that when Pharaoh asked him to perform a miracle he was to instruct Aaron to 'take thy rod, and cast it before Pharaoh, and it shall become a serpent . . . Then Pharaoh also called the wise men and the sorcerers: now the magicians of Egypt, they also did in a like manner with their enchantments. For they cast down every man his rod, and they became serpents: but Aaron's rod swallowed up their rods . . .' (7:9–12).

When permission to leave Egypt was still withheld Aaron 'lifted up the rod, and smote the waters that were in the river, in the sight of Pharaoh, and in the sight of his servants, and all the waters that were in the river turned to blood. And the fish that was in the river died; and the river stank, and the Egyptians could not drink of the water of the river; and there was blood throughout all the land of Egypt' (7:20–21). The white-hand ritual is not mentioned in this biblical account of events after the return of Moses to Egypt although it appears in the Koran. However, we are told how his 'magic rod' was used to cause a whole series of plagues on the country – frogs, lice, flies, the death of cattle, boils, hail, flooding, locusts and darkness – that resulted eventually in the granting of permission for the Exodus.

The events that inspired this fanciful biblical account are much more mundane. On learning of the death of Horemheb, the implacable enemy of the Amarna kings and the monotheistic Aten, Akhenaten (Moses) decided to return to Egypt to reclaim his throne. If he was born in 1394 BC he would have been rising 60 years of age at the time. As he was 'slow of tongue' – unable to address Israelites in their Hebrew language – he enlisted the aid of Aaron, his 'feeding brother', both of whose parents were Israelites, to help him. He made his way to Zarw, his birthplace, where his challenge as *Mos*, the rightful ruler, had to be decided by Egyptian priests and elders. In support of his case he took with him his symbol of Pharaonic power – a sceptre topped by a brass serpent. This was the 'magic rod' of the biblical account. The Hebrew word used in the Bible to indicate the rod of Moses is *nahash*, which has the meanings of both 'serpent' and 'brass'. In addition, the Haggadah, the legendary part of the Talmud, confirms the royal character of Moses's rod: 'The rod which Moses used . . . was shaped and engraved in the image of a sceptre [a staff borne as a symbol of personal sovereignty].'

Akhenaten (Moses) did not simply produce his rod in support of his claim, but performed before the priests and elders some secret rituals – secret, that is, from ordinary people – used by Pharaohs in their *sed* festivals for the purpose of rejuvenating their power, usually in their Year 30.

Among them were the use of the serpent rod and the hand ritual described – with some embellishments – in the Exodus account of these events. For instance, in the tomb of Kheruef, one of Queen Tiye's stewards, a throne scene shows the queen with her husband, Amenhotep III. Under the dais of the throne we see Kheruef and other officials, each holding something that he is about to hand to the king so that he can use it during the *sed*-festival celebrations of his Year 30. In one scene, Kheruef is followed by eight palace officials, the first of whom is wearing an apron. He puts his right arm across his chest and his hand over his left shoulder while he holds his own forearm with the left hand. The fourth of these officials holds a bundle of clothes in his right hand and a curved sceptre with serpent's head in his left.

The Koranic account of events after the return of (Akhenaten) Moses to Egypt gives more details than are to be found in the Book of Exodus, since the biblical narrator had a different interpretation of these events. It also presents the confrontation in such a precise way that one wonders if some of the details were left out of the biblical account deliberately. Here Moses sounds less like a magician, more like someone who presents evidence of his authority that convinces the wise men of Egypt, who throw themselves at his feet and thus earn the punishment of Pharaoh. One can only suspect that the biblical editor exercised care to avoid any Egyptian involvement with the Israelite Exodus, even to the extent of replacing Moses by Aaron in the performance of the rituals:

> Moses said: 'O Pharaoh!
> I am an apostle from
> The Lord of the Worlds, –
> 'One for whom it is right
> To say nothing but truth
> About Allah. Now have I
> Come unto you (people), from
> Your Lord with a clear (Sign)

So let the Children of Israel
Depart along with me.'

(Pharaoh) said: 'If indeed
Thou hast come with a Sign,
Show it forth,
If thou tellest the truth.'

Then (Moses) threw his rod,
And behold! it was
A serpent, plain (for all to see)!
And he drew out his hand
And behold! it was white
To all beholders!
Said the Chiefs of the people
Of Pharaoh: 'This is indeed
A sorcerer well-versed.

'His plan is to get you out
Of your land: then
What is it ye counsel?'
They said: 'Keep him
And his brother in suspense
(For a while); and send
To the cities men to collect –

'And bring up to thee
All (our) sorcerers well-versed.'
So there came
The sorcerers to Pharaoh:
They said, 'Of course
We shall have a (suitable)
Reward if we win!'

He said: 'Yea, (and more), –
For ye shall in that case
Be (raised to posts)

Nearest (to my person).'

They said: 'O Moses
Wilt thou throw (first),
Or shall we have
The (first) throw?'

Said Moses: 'Throw ye (first).'
So when they threw,
They bewitched the eyes
Of the people, and struck
Terror into them: for they
Showed a great (feat of) magic.

We put it into Moses's mind
By inspiration: 'Throw (now)
Thy rod': and behold!
It swallows up straightaway
All the falsehoods
Which they fake.

Thus truth was confirmed,
And all that they did
Was made of no effect.

So the (great ones) were vanquished
There and then, and were
Made to look small.

But the sorcerers fell down
Prostrate in adoration,
Saying: 'We believe
In the Lord of the Worlds, –

'The Lord of Moses and Aaron.'
Said Pharaoh: 'Believe ye
In Him before I give

You permission? Surely
This is a trick which ye
Have planned in the City
To drive out its people:
But soon shall ye know
(The consequences).

'Be sure I will cut off
Your hands and your feet
On opposite sides, and I
Will cause you all
To die on the cross.'
[Sura 7:104–124]

So Akhenaten (Moses) was not using magic but seeking to establish his royal authority, and the biblical story relates a political challenge for power in a mythological way. As for the promise that the Nile would turn red, this should be seen as indicating the time of the year. During the season of Inundation, the Nile waters become reddish, and, if these events took place in the Eastern Delta, this would suggest the late days of summer, by which time this change of colour would have begun to affect the lower reaches of the river. Similarly, the various plagues said to have been inflicted on Pharaoh and his country are to be seen as natural occurrences that would manifest themselves in the course of an Egyptian year.

Once they saw the sceptre of royal authority and Akhenaten had performed the *sed*-festival rituals, the wise men 'fell down prostrate in adoration', as the Koran puts it, confirming that his was the superior right to the throne. However, Pa-Ramses, who controlled the army, used his power to frustrate the verdict of the priests and elders and retained the right to rule by a kind of *coup d'état*. Akhenaten (Moses) was left with no choice but to flee from Egypt with his followers – the Israelites and those Egyptians who had embraced the Atenist faith. So began the Exodus, the first stage of what would prove a long journey to the Promised Land of Canaan.

Akhenaten (Moses) and his followers made their way to Sinai via the marshy area to the south of Zarw and north of Lake Temsah and present-day Ismaelia. This watery route was chosen to hinder pursuit: Egyptian chariots would become stuck in the mud whereas the Israelites, travelling on foot, would be able to cross safely. This is the possible time and location for the biblical account of the pursuing Pharaoh who was drowned. Egyptian sources provide no evidence of this event, but it is certain that the short reign of Ramses I (*c.* 1335–1333 BC) came to an end with his death at this very time.

Now faced with the problem of a large number of followers in need of food and water, Akhenaten abandoned his plan to head for Mount Sinai, and instead, went north on the ancient Road of Horus that connected Zarw on the borders of Egypt with the Canaanite city of Gaza. Along the road were settlements with water wells, guarded by military posts. According to the Book of Deuteronomy, Moses was eventually not allowed to enter the Promised Land and was killed by the Lord because 'ye trespassed against me . . . at the waters of Meribah-Kadesh in the wilderness . . .' (32:51). Moses had not been forbidden to obtain water for his followers, which cannot in any case be regarded as a sinful act. The implication is that Akhenaten secured water from the wells along the Road of Horus. This could have been done easily by force although it seems more likely that force was not necessary: he still had his brass sceptre of authority, and it is hardly to be imagined that a garrison commander would challenge the wishes of a former king whom he regarded as the Son of Ra.

Realizing that a fertile land was needed to feed his large following, Akhenaten next marched north towards Gaza and attempted to storm the city, seemingly joined by some of his bedouin Shasu allies (the Midianites of the Bible) in the assault. News of these events was reported to Egypt. Seti I (*c.* 1333–1304 BC), the son and successor of the elderly Ramses I, did not even wait for his late father's mummification before marching against Akhenaten, the Israelites and the Shasu. He met and defeated them at many locations on the Horus road as well as central Sinai. There was great slaughter among the Shasu, large numbers of whom were also captured and taken back to Egypt to be sacrificed at the feet of the god Amun-Ra at the Karnak temple. It is likely that Moses was killed by Seti himself in the course of these military operations (with the body either buried in the sand at the place of death, or left there to rot), and that it was his quest for water and food that much later, when the first five books of the Old Testament were written, inspired the waters of Meribah-Kadesh story.

Chapter Seventeen

Conspiracy of Silence

The slaying of Jesus at the foot of Mount Sinai on a spring evening in 1352 BC was later the subject of an elaborate conspiracy to try to conceal the truth about his death. Not the least element of this conspiracy was the 'resurrection' of Jesus in order to furnish graphic details of how he conquered the Promised Land in a swift military campaign a century after his death.

After the account in the Book of Exodus of the events at the foot of Mount Sinai when Jesus was killed, Joshua disappears entirely from the scene until the Book of Deuteronomy, the last of the five books of the Pentateuch, where he is mentioned as the leader who succeeded Moses: 'And Joshua the son of Nun was full of the spirit of wisdom; for Moses had laid his hands upon him: and the children of Israel hearkened unto him . . .' (34:9). This is followed by an entire book devoted to his exploits, including his conquest of Canaan at the head of the united tribes of Israel. Although this account has gained popular acceptance, it is a work of fiction that cannot be supported by either biblical criticism or archaeological evidence.

The Book of Joshua is the first of what are known as the Former Prophets or Historical Books. It consists of three main sections – the conquest of Canaan (Chapters 1–12); division of the conquered territory between the twelve tribes of Israel (13–21); and negotiations with tribes to the east of the Jordan, followed by a covenant at Shecham (22–24). The swift military campaigns ascribed to Joshua cannot have taken place in the latter part of the 13th century BC because two of the

207

cities said to have been sacked by him had been destroyed earlier and the other two were not destroyed until later.

The account of these campaigns tells us that the Israelites began by crossing the River Jordan from east to west opposite Jericho, which was in a state of siege. They took it and 'utterly destroyed all that was in the city' after, in a seemingly miraculous manner, its walls came tumbling down (Joshua 6:20–21). Jericho was a very ancient city, dating back as far as 8000 BC. In the course of its long history, the city and its massive fortifications were destroyed and rebuilt many times. The Hyksos, who invaded Egypt around 1683 BC, ruled for slightly more than a century and had Jericho under their control at this period, then were expelled by the kings of Egypt's 18th Dynasty, who pursued them into western Asia and destroyed Jericho and its fortifications during the 15th century BC. There is no evidence that the city itself or its walls were rebuilt for many centuries after this destruction: 'Thus there was settlement from about 1400 to 1325 BC, or even for a generation or so longer. Thereafter the earliest evidence for renewed settlement is isolated pottery vessels dating from *the 11th into the 10th century BC* '* (my italics). So, at the time of the supposed invasion by Joshua in the second half of the 13th century BC, neither the city of Jericho nor its walls existed (Plate 3)

Another ancient Canaanite city, Ai, west of Jericho and north of Jerusalem, became the next target of the Israelite invaders. At the first attempt, when about 3,000 men tried to take the city, they were defeated and forced to flee. Joshua then resorted to another plan. He divided his army into two. Part of it lay in ambush between Bethel, another fortified city a few miles north-west of Ai, and Ai itself. In the ensuing battle, Joshua, pretending that his forces had been defeated, withdrew, pursued by the men of Ai. At a signal, the army waiting in ambush fell upon the city, entering from the west through the open and now unprotected gate, set it on fire and

---

* *The Bible and Recent Archaeology*, Kathleen M. Kenyon.

sacked it. In the meantime, Joshua advanced to renew the battle with the King of Ai's army and defeated them (Joshua 8:21).

Excavations have shown that a large city existed at Ai (modern el-Tell) in the early Canaanite period, but it was destroyed in the Early Bronze Age, in about 2350 BC, and was not resettled until the Early Iron Age (12th century BC) when a village was established on the site. The newcomers were then mainly farmers, trying to secure a living in the inhospitable hills of central Canaan: 'This discovery indicates that, in the time of Joshua, the site was waste (also implied by the name Ai, literally "ruin"). Scholars explain the discrepancy in various ways. Some consider the narrative of the conquest of Ai contained in the Book of Joshua an aetiological (causal) story which developed in order to explain the ancient ruins of the city and its fortifications.'*

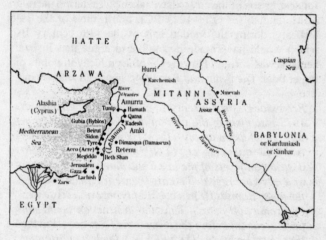

Canaan during Joshua's wars

* *Encyclopaedia Judaica.*

After this campaign, Joshua is said to have been approached to make a peace covenant with the Hivites, who dwelt in four cities to the south-west of Ai and north-west of Jerusalem. Once this covenant had been completed, however, Joshua found himself facing a new threat from Adoni-Zedek, the King of Jerusalem, who arranged an alliance of five Amorite kings of the Judaean hills and lowland – Jerusalem, Hebron, Jarmuth, Lachish and Eglon – to fight the united Israelite tribes. Joshua marched against the alliance in another successful campaign, which included the destruction of Lachish. He took the city 'on the second day, and smote it with the edge of the sword, and all the souls that were therein . . .' (Joshua 10:32)

Following early excavation of the site of Lachish (modern Tell el-Duweir) in southern Canaan between 1932 and 1938 it was thought that the evidence unearthed made it possible for destruction of the city to have taken place during the reign of Merenptah (*c.* 1237–1227 BC), fourth ruler of the 19th Dynasty, during the second half of the 13th century BC, which would have made it possible to argue that Joshua's account was correct. However, Kathleen Kenyon points out in her book *The Bible and Recent Archaeology* that when

Professor Ussishkin renewed excavations at Lachish in 1973 establishing the correct date for this destruction was one of his main objectives. He was to be unusually lucky in this respect. In 1978 a deep probe into destruction levels of the last Canaanite town at the site of a city gate revealed a cast-bronze fragment bearing the name Ramses III in a cache of bronze objects sealed by production debris. Thus the destruction could not have occurred before the accession of Ramses III to the throne of Egypt (c. 1182 BC) . . . Such a substantial bronze fitting, likely to be from an architectural setting, even if allowed a minimum life, makes it likely that Lachish was devastated some time in the second quarter of the 12th century BC.

Joshua's battles were not yet over. He next found himself facing another alliance, this time of the northern kings of Hazor, Madon, Shimron and Achshaph: 'And when all these kings were met together, they came and pitched together at the waters of Merom, to fight against Israel' (Joshua 11:5). In the subsequent battle, Joshua recorded another distinguished victory in the course of which he 'took Hazor, and smote the king thereof with the sword: for Hazor before time was the head of all those kingdoms. And they smote all the souls that were therein with the edge of the sword, utterly destroying them: there was not any left to breathe: and he burnt Hazor with fire' (Joshua 11:10–11). The description of these battles concludes with a list of the conquered Canaanite cities and their kings, numbering in all 31, whose territory was divided among the tribes of Israel.

After defeating Jabin, King of Hazor and head of the coalition against the Israelites, Joshua is said to have burned his city – and his city alone (Joshua 11:10–13). Hazor (modern Tell el-Qidah) was a large Canaanite city nearly nine miles north of the Sea of Galilee and situated strategically to dominate the main branches of The Way of the Sea, the road leading from Egypt to Syria, Mesopotamia and Anatolia. The fact that Hazor was mentioned by Ramses III (*c.* 1182–1151 BC) in his Temple of Amun at Karnak indicates that the city was still in existence and under his control during his reign as well as the possibility that Hazor, like so many other sites in Syria/Palestine, was actually destroyed later by the Peoples of the Sea, the Philistines, against whom Ramses III fought a war in the same area. Therefore, two of the principal cities mentioned in Joshua's supposed campaign of conquest (Jericho and Ai) had been destroyed before the 13th century BC and the other two (Lachish and Hazor) were not destroyed until later. Modern biblical scholars have recognized that the military campaigns described in the opening 12 chapters of the Book of Joshua do not represent a single unified campaign but are a compilation of several ancient battle stories, originally not related and some of which predate the Israelite period.

Martin Noth, the German biblical scholar, was the first to expose the fact that there had been a priestly cover-up. He demonstrated in 1966 that the fifth book of the Pentateuch, Deuteronomy, and the books of the Former Prophets or Historical Books, from Joshua to Kings, are the product of a single priestly editor,* known to scholars as the Deuteronomic redactor, and date from the period of the Babylonian exile in the 6th century BC, about the same time that Isaiah (II) was claiming that the defeat, humiliation and exile of the Israelites was a punishment for their killing of the Servant of the Lord, their Messiah. What better way to refute this charge than to produce the Servant, still alive after the death of Moses, and present Jesus as the victorious conqueror of the Promised Land?

This tampering with the truth has been the cause of considerable scholarly confusion. The British scholar John Romer had this to say about the matter as recently as 1988 in his book *Testament*:

> *All of this was a serious blow to the historians who had long been carefully gathering up archaeological evidence of a systematic invasion and destruction of all the cities of Canaan, and keying their evidence in with biblical accounts of the Israelite invasion. Now it appeared that the destruction of these cities had been earlier and more random than had previously been imagined. Several attempts have been made to salvage their theory by what might best be described as moving the goalposts; the archaeology was re-dated so that Joshua and the Israelites would find someone to fight on their arrival. But most scholars were agreed that the known archaeological facts called for a fresh look at our understanding of these Bible stories.*

* Or possibly writer.

The doubts about Joshua's campaign have led some scholars to question whether he ever existed. However, what is to be doubted is the Deuteronomic account. The aim of Deuteronomic history has been explained as an attempt to show that God's promise, already found in the Pentateuch, of Israelite possession of the Promised Land, had been fulfilled. The compiler recalled ancient traditions to illustrate God's work through history, not to present history itself. It was a theological interpretation designed to renew faith at a time of great difficulty.

It is no wonder that the Qumran Essenes took the view that the Jerusalem priests were falsifying the Scriptures.

Israelite settlement in the Promised Land was a gradual process, not a matter of stirring battles and swift military conquest. All the evidence – the account of the Book of Judges and archaeological discoveries – indicates that after the Exodus, which took place some 20 years after the death of Joshua (Jesus), the Israelites dwelt in the area of Mount Seir in Edom – south and south-west of the Dead Sea – for a long time. Memory of those days can be found in the Song of Deborah: 'Lord, when thou wentest out of Seir, when thou marchedst out of the field of Edom, the earth trembled, and the heavens dropped, the clouds also dropped water' (Judges 5:4). It was only when Egypt lost control over Palestine in the second half of the 12th century BC that the Israelite tribes completed their infiltration of the Promised Land of Canaan, from Dan in the north, near the source of the River Jordan in Upper Galilee, to Beersheba in the Negeb desert to the south, where archaeological excavation has shown evidence of new settlement during this period. They were still semi-nomadic, living among the ruins of ancient cities or among other Canaanite inhabitants. The Philistines – the Peoples of the Sea – had already established their city states of south-west Canaan after a mass invasion and were attempting to expand towards the Dead Sea and the River Jordan when the Israelites, too, were trying to establish themselves in the area.

Thus conflict between the two new arrivals became the main preoccupation of both the biblical Saul and tribal David.

After their entry into the Promised Land the Israelites spent the better part of three centuries in small groups, dotted around Canaan without any central authority or central place of worship. During these years the great majority of Israelites forsook the God of Moses for Canaanite and Phoenician deities, and it is thought, by biblical scholars, that the Passover feast was not observed, as no mention of it is found in the Bible, although it must have been known to the priests and the prophets.

The need for protection, particularly against the Philistines, resulted towards the end of the 11th century BC in Saul establishing the state of Judah with a unified central government. The state was further strengthened by the tribal David. The conventional account goes on to describe how Solomon – who, as we have seen, was actually Amenhotep III, who lived five centuries earlier – developed Jerusalem as the state capital and built a grandiose Temple, measures that gave the state stability and a spiritual authority. However, so it is said, high taxation to pay for the Temple and other massive building projects resulted in ten northern tribes seceding from Judah and setting up their own state, Israel. Israel, rent by dynastic squabbles, was eventually conquered by the Assyrians in the 8th century BC and disappeared completely afterwards.

Judah suffered a similar fate at the hands of the Babylonians a century later. Jerusalem and its Temple were destroyed, and many Israelite leaders, including its king, Jehoiakim, the intelligentsia and the priesthood, were taken into exile. The Babylonian exile began in 586 BC and lasted 70 years until Babylon in its turn was conquered by Cyrus, the Persian king, who allowed the Israelites – known hence-forth as Jews – to return to Jerusalem and rebuild the Jerusalem Temple. During this period of exile, the Israelite priests and scribes, who had taken a collection of their sacred writings with them, decided on reflection to have some second thoughts about their past history. They put down in their present form the books of the Pentateuch, the first five books of the Old Testament, which had originated at the time of Akhenaten (Moses) – the second half of the 14th century BC – and in the editing process changed certain facts.

For example, when we read in the Old Testament about the Israelites waiting for their 'anointed Messiah' this meant that they were waiting for a king to rule them, unite them and defeat their enemies. It was not a messianic Redeemer, the concept introduced by the prophet Isaiah, writing at about this time (6th century BC), whose death the Jewish scribes wished to gloss over, but the death of the anointed king, Tutankhamun, 'the first-born of Pharaoh that sat on his throne'. Their efforts went far beyond 'resurrecting' Jesus. They were trying to disguise the fact that he had been killed at all.

This process of editing-with-intent included tinkering with the chronology and significance of the two principal events in the Israelites' religious calendar – the Passover and the Day of Atonement. Initially, from the time Akhenaten (Moses) was in exile in Sinai with some of his priestly followers, the Passover (in celebration of the Israelites' escape from Egypt) and the Day of Atonement (repentance for the death of their Messiah [king]) were observed in the same period, from the 15th to the 21st day of Abib (March–April), the first month of the Jewish year. As this double feast had not been celebrated for many centuries, when the feast was reinstated the priestly scribes in Babylonia gave two contrasting accounts of how and why it had been established. The first occurs in the Book of Exodus: 'Thou shalt keep the feast of unleavened bread: thou shalt eat unleavened bread seven days . . . in the time appointed of the month Abib; for in it thou camest out from Egypt . . .' (23:15). The same exhortation, with slightly different wording, occurs in the Book of Deuteronomy, but there we find that a new element has been added: 'Thou shalt therefore sacrifice the passover to the Lord thy God, of the flock and the herd . . .' (2:6). The text does not make it clear why such a sacrifice was called for although one would expect it to be a form of expiation for a sinful act.

In exile, the priests adopted the Babylonian lunar calendar in place of the solar calendar used previously. As a result, Tishri (September–October), originally the seventh month of the Israelites' year, became the first month of a new calendar and Abib (Babylonian Nisan) became the seventh month. About half a century after the return to Jerusalem the priests took advantage of the ensuing confusion to separate the Passover from the Day of Atonement. The Passover continued to be observed in Abib (Nisan), the old first month, while the Day of Atonement – Yom Kippur, the most solemn day in the Jewish year – was transferred to the tenth day of Tishri (September–October), the new first month, and its significance was changed from atonement for the killing of their Messiah by the Wicked Priest to repentance for sin in general. In support of this transfer biblical editors reverted to the old calendar, in which Tishri had been the seventh month, and added two passages to the Pentateuch: '. . . on the tenth day of this seventh month there shall be a day of atonement: it shall be an holy convocation unto you; and ye shall afflict your souls . . .' (Leviticus 23:27), and: 'And ye shall have on the tenth day of this seventh month an holy convocation; and ye shall afflict your souls . . .' (Numbers, 29:7).

All the indications are that Phinehas (Pinhas/Panehesy), presented as the hero of the assassination and subsequent massacre in Sinai, was actually responsible for those events – he is the one identified by the Qumran Essenes as the Wicked Priest – and paid for it with his life. Yet the Deuteronomic redactor chose to 'resurrect' him as well as Joshua. He is named as one of Joshua's followers in the account of the latter's conquest of the Promised Land a century later. His death was never reported and he even surfaces again in the Book of Judges, which deals with events that took place nearly *three and a half centuries* later: 'And Phinehas, the son of Eleazar, the son of Aaron, stood before it [the ark of the covenant of God] in those days saying, Shall I yet again go out to battle against the children of Benjamin my brother, or shall I cease? And the Lord said, Go up; for tomorrow I will deliver them into thine hand' (20:28).

Although more than seven centuries had passed since the death of Joshua (Jesus), the author of these words must have known of the traditions that lay behind Isaiah's account of the death of the Suffering Servant and the later claim of the Talmudic rabbis that 'Pinhas killed Jesus'. The rabbis of the Talmud, who could not even understand what this statement meant in a historical sense, preserved this tradition in the same way they received it from their predecessors. They also preserved the word 'Pandera' as the name of Jesus's father, which turned out to be the Egyptian title of Tutankhamun, 'The Son of Ra'.

Summary of Parts I and II

The Hebrew tribe of Abraham gained historical importance only when it established contact with the 18th ruling dynasty in Egypt, 15 centuries BC. The marriage that took place between Sarah, the poor Hebrew woman, and Pharaoh Tuthmose III, the mightiest of all the ancient kings, produced the tribe of Israel, fathered by the Egyptian king and adopted by Abraham the Patriarch. Events in the later life of Sarah's descendents show that they never forgot their royal ancestor. But it was the dreamer Joseph, arriving there as a slave, who soon became Pharaoh's minister and his Lieutenant of the Chariots, the strongest man in the country after the king.

Another marriage took place between a Hebrew descendant and a member of the 18th royal dynasty. Amenhotep III married Tiye, Joseph's daughter, and insisted on making her his queen, against the customs of his country. This marriage was to produce King Akhenaten who has been described as the first individual in history, recognized as Moses of the holy books, the first monotheist to claim one God with no image for all people. This doctrine, though, did not become popular amongst Akhenaten's followers, as it was a sudden change that needed more time to be absorbed by ordinary people. When the army attempted a coup against the monotheistic king, he was advised by Aye, brother of his mother Queen Tiye and Commander of his Chariots, to abdicate the throne in favour of his son Tutankhaten.

While Akhenaten was living in exile with a few of his close followers among the bedouin of southern Sinai, Tutankhaten was trying to reform the monotheistic doctrine

218

to bring it nearer to his people. The young king's reformation proved to be of historical importance, for their beliefs are still living with us until this day. He recognized the eternal Egyptian belief of the spiritual element in man's existence, which continues to live after his death. So Aten became the God of death, as he was the God of life. He also recognized the degrees of spiritual existence, recognizing the old deities as angels in the heaven of God, and mediators between man and the deity. Introducing his new reformation as he reopened the temples closed by his father, he even changed his name to Tutankhamun.

Neither Tutankhamun nor his religious teaching were given a chance to work. He was killed by Panehesy, the orthodox Atenite priest, when he attempted to bring his father back from his exile in Sinai and convert his followers to the new beliefs. Tutankhamun's death led to the collapse of the Amarna rule, and the end of its religious reformation, as many attempts were made, both in Egypt and among the Israelites, to wipe out the memory of Akhenaten and his successor Tutankhamun – or Moses and his successor Joshua/Jesus. While the Egyptian authorities forbade the names or deeds of these kings to be mentioned in any written document, the Israelite scribes who wrote the accounts of these events made a big effort to cover up the killing of Joshua as well as to hide any blood connection between Israel and the Egyptian royal family. What betrayed them, though, is the fact that they had to replace Abraham, the adopting father, by King David (Tuthmosis III), the real father of Israel. Writing the account of a minor tribal ruler who lived in Canaan in the early part of the 10th century BC and fought many battles with the invading Philistines, the Hebrew scribes included the account of the Israelite real ancestor, who established the only empire between the Nile and the Euphrates.

In spite of the attempts to cover it up, the memory of Joshua/Jesus lived through a series of Israelite prophets who eventually established the Essene community following the return from the Babylonian Exile. It lived also in Egypt within the Osiris and Hermes Trismegistus cults which produced the Gnostic Christian movement by the start of the Christian era.

Part III
The Keys of the Kingdom

... when it pleased God
... To reveal his Son in me that I
might preach him among the heathen,
immediately I conferred not with
flesh and blood: Neither went I
up to Jerusalem to them which
were apostles before me; but I
went into Arabia ...

Paul's Letter to the Galatians 1:15–17

Chapter Eighteen

The Earliest Christians

Nearly all Christians nowadays – Roman Catholic, Protestant or Orthodox – share three basic premises. They accept the canon of the New Testament, the apostolic Creed and a Church with an institutional, hierarchical structure. It was only towards the end of the 2nd century AD that these three aspects of Christian belief and observance emerged in this form.

The purpose of the first two sections of this book was to demonstrate – not simply on the basis of historical evidence but on the witness of biblical writers and the writings of early Fathers of the Church – that, although the resurrected Jesus is reported to have appeared to his disciples during the early part of the 1st century AD, his historical mission on earth took place in the 14th century BC. How can this statement of historical fact be reconciled with orthodox Christian belief? The first task is to bridge the gap of 14 centuries.

As the British scholar A. N. Wilson pointed out in his book *Jesus*: 'The Jesus of History and the Christ of Faith are two separate beings, with very different stories. It is difficult enough to reconstruct the first, and in the attempt we are likely to do irreparable harm to the second.' The historical truth about Joshua, the Teacher of Righteousness and the Wicked Priest (i.e. Phinehas), and the Suffering Servant was preserved throughout this long period principally by two groups of sects – the Essenes (Judaeo-Christians) and the Gnostics (Gentile-Christians), seekers after self-knowledge, which they regarded as knowledge of God – the God within. The Gnostics were to be condemned as heretics by the bishops of the early Church because they would accept neither the canon of the New Testament, nor the apostolic Creed, nor the authority of the Church.

Until the discovery of their library, *The Dead Sea Scrolls*, in caves at Qumran in 1947, the Essenes were known only from Greek sources (that is, sources written in Greek). In the 1st century AD they were written about by the Jewish philosopher Philo Judaeus, by Pliny the Elder, the geographer and naturalist, and by the historian Flavius Josephus. At this time, according to both Philo and Josephus, there were about 4,000 Essenes in numerous communities scattered throughout Palestine and Syria.

The Essenes were the principal among a number of secret Jewish sects who believed that the Saviour – their Teacher of Righteousness – had already lived, suffered and died at the hands of an assailant identified as The Wicked Priest, and they awaited his Second Coming. The Essenes separated themselves from the Jewish community at large and from the Jerusalem priesthood, whom they looked upon as 'ungodly men' whose teaching was false. The sects faced the threat of persecution – through being ostracized socially or, like their Teacher, killed – if their beliefs were known, and they imposed a vow of secrecy upon all those who joined them.

Josephus understood and explained in his writings that, in complete contrast to the Old Covenant of Moses, which was simply to 'keep my Commandments' and which made no promise of eternal life, members of the sect believed in immortality: '. . . It is a firm belief among them that, although bodies are corruptible, and their matter unstable, souls are immortal and endure for ever; that, come from subtlest ether, they are entwined with the bodies that serve them as prisons, drawn down as they are by some physical spell; but that, when they are freed from the bonds of the flesh, liberated, so to speak, from long slavery, then they rejoice and rise up to the heavenly world.'

The manuscripts found at Qumran, which date from 200 BC to AD 50, are written largely in Hebrew. A few are in

Aramaic, the common language of Palestine in New Testament times, and some in Greek. Among them are sections of every book of the Old Testament apart from the Book of Esther (which may have been written later; alternatively it may have come from another place, such as Persia, where she lived). The Essenes seemed to attach particular importance to the writings of Isaiah as no fewer than 18 copies of his work were found in the caves. The most informative material, however, consists of documents about the sect itself. Two in particular – *The Damascus Document* and *The Manual of Discipline* – give an account of the history of the sect, conditions for admission to its ranks and the sect's rules of conduct.

The Essenes, like the Jewish Temple priests, studied the Torah (the first five books of the Old Testament) and the law of Moses; observed the Sabbath strictly; obeyed the law of Moses and the Commandments; and held the name of Moses in high esteem. However, their beliefs went far beyond what might be regarded by modern standards as the simplistic views of the Temple priests.* Although their roots lay in Israelite history, the Essenes, feeling that they personally had no responsibility for the death of their Teacher of Righteousness, observed the Jewish Day of Atonement with a Messianic Banquet rather than the Temple's ritual of animal sacrifice. This banquet, at which they expected their Teacher of Righteousness to return and join them, has many similarities with the Last Supper when, on Maundy Thursday, the eve of the Crucifixion, Christ is said to have instituted the Christian sacrament of Communion. According to the Qumran text the priest '. . . [will bl]ess the first of the bread and win[e and will stretch forth] his hand on the bread first. And after[wards] the Messiah will str[etch forth] his

---

* Priestly worship was focused on cultic sacrificial ritual performed by priests at the Temple, on behalf of the congregation. No personal involvement was required of the laity, other than attending the Temple with their offering.

hands upon the bread, [and then] all the Congregation of the Community [will give bles]sings, each [according to] his rank. And after this prescription shall they act for every ass[embly where] at least ten men are assembled.'

Later Christians, too, rid themselves of animal sacrifice because they regarded Jesus himself as the sacrifice: 'For even the Son of man came not to be ministered unto, but to minister, and to give his life a ransom for many' (Mark 10:45) and '. . . Behold the Lamb of God, which taketh away the sins of the world' (John 1:29).

The Dead Sea Scrolls show that women were excluded from membership of this secretive Judaeo-Christian sect and only circumcised Jewish males admitted. Aspiring members received a hatchet and an apron for taking part in the sect's rituals, and a white garment, the normal wear of the Essenes. Initially they had to undergo a year of probation, followed by a further two years. At the end of this three-year period the initiate had to swear an oath of allegiance that bound him to piety towards God, justice to men, honesty to his fellow Essenes, faithful transmission of the sect's teachings and preservation of their secrecy. The Essenes practised community of property. New members turned their property over to the group whose elected members administered it for the benefit of all.

Members of the sect began their day with prayer, followed by purification rituals and a communal meal, before and after which a priest recited another short prayer. They then did their work, mostly farming the land for food, and prayed again at sunset before coming together for an evening meal.

The Essenes were a strictly hierarchical sect. It was divided into priests and laity. The priests were described as 'sons of Zadok'* with the laity grouped, after the biblical model, into 12 tribes. As the Last Supper, with the blessing of bread and wine, echoes the Messianic Banquet of the

---

* Zadoc(k) was a priest of David and it is believed that his descendants held the priesthood in Jerusalem till the Babylonian Exile in the 6th century BC.

Essenes, the 12 disciples mentioned in the gospels are an echo, long predating the Christian era, of the formation of the Essenes' ruling council, comprised of one representative from each of the 12 tribes.

Their *Community Rule*, one of the documents found at Qumran, says: 'In the Council of the Community [there shall be] twelve men and three priests' – the ambiguous text allows two meanings: either that three of the 12 should be priests or that three additional priests were to be included – 'to practise truth, righteousness, justice, loving charity, and modesty, one towards the other, to guard the faith upon the earth with a firm inclination and contrite spirit, and to expiate iniquity among those that practise justice and undergo distress of affliction, and to behave towards all men according to the measure of truth and the norm of the time.'

The Egyptian roots of these Essene practices were as follows. They were affected by the belief in the spiritual element of human beings, which they saw as eternal, and believed that their Teacher would rise from the dead at the end of days. Their hermetic way of life was similar to later Egyptian practice, but they did not go as far as believing in their own resurrection, as Egyptians did.

Every member of the Qumran sect had his rank, with the priests first in authority. Geza Vermes, Professor of Old Testament Studies at Oxford, points out in his book *The Dead Sea Scrolls in English*: 'In their hands lay the ultimate responsibility for decisions on matters of doctrine, discipline, purity and impurity, and in particular matters pertaining to "justice and property". It was also a basic rule of the order that a priest was required to be present at any gathering of ten or more meeting for debate, Bible study or prayer . . . One interesting feature of the priesthood at Qumran is that their precedence was absolute.' This 'interesting feature' of the Qumran priesthood was to have consequences for Christian belief that have endured for almost two thousand years. The Essenes (Judaeo-Christians) were not alone, however, in keeping alive the truth about the death of The Teacher of Righteousness (Christ).

The Essene belief that the Saviour had already lived, suffered and died for the sins of mankind was shared by the Therapeutae (Gentile Christians in Egypt), one of the Gnostic sects. Our sole authority for the history of the Therapeutae is the philosopher Philo Judaeus, who was born around 15 BC and died some two decades after the supposed date of the Crucifixion. Philo, who wrote admiringly of the Essenes and identified them as a dissident part of the Jewish community, did not name the Therapeutae as Jews. This is also true of Josephus, who did not include them in his division of Jewish sects, which he named as the Sadducees, Pharisees, Essenes and the followers of Judas, who led a rebellion against the Romans and priests after introduction of the Roman tax in AD 6.

Despite many similarities between the sects, the Gnostic Therapeutae, unlike the Essenes, did not exclude women.* Nor were they divided into a rigid hierarchy of laity and priests, who were entitled to absolute obedience: anyone of either sex could take responsibility for ritual and organiza- tion. In contrast to the Essene practice, the Therapeutae accepted both Jews and Gentiles as members of the sect and also practised celibacy. Philo explained that most of the women, though old, 'are still virgins, having kept their purity not from necessity – like some of the priestesses among the Greeks – but rather through their own choice, because of their zeal and eagerness for learning, in which, being eager to pass their lives, they despise the pleasures of the body . . .'

The Therapeutae were members of a contemplative sect

---

* In contrast to Essene practice, women were never excluded from religious activities in Egyptian history. From their early days they had priestesses and women temple servants; in some cases a woman could dedicate her life for this service. Nevertheless, the evidence of *virginity* comes only with the Therapeutae.

that embraced the simple life. On becoming members, they renounced the world completely, fleeing 'without ever turning to look back, abandoning brothers, children, wives, parents . . . they make settlements for themselves outside the walls, in gardens or in solitary places, seeking solitude'. Like the Essenes, the Therapeutae believed in communal property. They handed over what they owned to the sect and went to live in encampments of individual huts: 'The houses . . . are very cheap affairs, affording protection against the two most necessary things, the heat of the sun and the chill of the air. Nor are the houses close together as they are in cities, for close proximity would be troublesome to those who seek solitude. Nor yet are they far apart because of the fellowship they covet, and also in order that they may help one another should there be an attack of robbers.'

Their commitment to simplicity – 'regarding the false as the beginning of pride, but truth as the beginning of simplicity' – was reflected in the food they ate and the clothes they wore: 'They eat no costly food, but simple bread and, as a seasoning, salt.' Those with daintier palates formed in the years before they joined the sect were permitted to add a little spice to this spartan diet in the form of the aromatic herb hyssop. Spring water was their only drink. In summer the Therapeutae wore 'inexpensive' sleeveless jackets of linen, in winter thick cloaks.

They began each day with prayers around the time that dawn broke. More prayers followed towards evening. The hours in between were spent in their huts, which they called 'monasteries', where they devoted themselves to 'reading Holy Scriptures. They philosophize and interpret allegorically their native code of laws, since they regard the words of the literal interpretation as symbols of a hidden nature revealed only in such figures of speech.' They also studied writings of forebears, founders of the sect, about the truths enshrined in these allegories.

They did not eat or drink before sunset for six days since they thought that 'philosophizing is consistent with the light while the necessities of the body are worthy of darkness'. Many of them fasted for the whole of these six days because they were accustomed 'as they say the cicadas are, to feed on the air'. On the seventh day they assembled for communal worship and a sermon on their holy books. On each fiftieth day, garbed in white, they gathered for a banquet – innocent of meat or wine – that was followed by a sacred all-night festival during which hymns were sung in honour of God before members of the sect went out to greet a new dawn: 'They stand up and turn their eyes and their whole body towards the east. And when they see the sun rising they raise their hands towards heaven and pray for a fair day and truth and keenness of understanding . . .'

Discovery of the Essenes' library, *The Dead Sea Scrolls*, in 1947, and the subsequent controversy about its contents and their significance, have served to distract attention from the Gnostic library found at Nag Hammadi in Upper Egypt two years earlier. This library, hidden at some time in the latter half of the 4th century AD, consisted of 13 papyrus books containing 52 texts, among them previously unknown gospels (listed in Appendix 1 at the back of this book). They included the *Gospel of Thomas*, which represents a tradition as early as, if not earlier than, any of the New Testament books and more than 100 sayings attributed to Jesus. Among the other works were the *Gospel of Philip*, the *Gospel of Mary Magdalene*, the *Gospel of the Egyptians* and the *Apocalypse of Paul*.

Much, but not all, of this literature is distinctively Christian. Some texts derive from pagan sources (such as the *Book of the Dead*), others from Jewish traditions. It is clear, however, that the Gnostics looked upon themselves as the true interpreters of Christianity. Their name indicates that they were seekers after knowledge, not rational knowledge but self-knowledge, which was at the same time knowledge of God, for they regarded the self as being part of the Divine nature, with salvation as nothing more than release of man's spirit from imprisonment within his body, with physical death the final release from the evil material world.

The *Gospel of Thomas* is clearly of great academic importance, but as it consists purely of sayings it does not throw any light on the course of historical events in the first century of the Christian era. However, other documents make it clear that, once they became part of 'orthodox' teaching in the course of the 2nd century AD, the Gnostics rejected the orthodox understanding of the Virgin Birth, which they regarded as the emanation of the Saviour from God the Father, as a spirit, not as a physical birth from a human mother; they denied that Jesus was crucified at the time of the Roman Empire; they regarded the Resurrection as having been spiritual, not physical, suggesting that it is to be understood symbolically, not literally; and they claimed that they had their own secret sources of apostolic tradition, separate from those of Jerusalem. Here is one example from the *Apocalypse of Peter*:

> *I saw him (the Saviour) seemingly being seized by them. And I said, 'What do I see, O Lord, that it is you yourself whom they take, and that you are grasping me? Or who is this one glad and laughing on the tree? And is it another one whose feet and hands they are striking?'*
>
> *The Saviour said to me, 'He whom you saw on the tree, glad and laughing, this is the living Jesus. But this one into whose hands and feet they drive nails is his fleshly part, which is the substitute being put to shame, the one who came into being in his likeness. But look at him and me.'*
>
> *But I, when I had looked, said, 'Lord, no one is looking at you. Let us flee this place.'*
>
> *But he said to me, 'I have told you, Leave the blind alone! And you, see how they do not know what they are saying. For the son of their glory instead of my servant they have put to shame.'*
>
> [*Apocalypse of Peter* 81–82]

The Gnostic form of worship was informal, with no division between clergy and laity. All believers were regarded as equals, and salvation was looked upon as a matter of personal experience. Hence there was no hierarchy. At each of their meetings they chose any member of the congregation, man or woman, to play a priestly role – an informal approach that fatally weakened the Gnostic movement when it was later challenged by the Church of Rome. Gnostic communities were widespread. The indications are that they started in the area between Memphis and the Fayyoum, before spreading to Alexandria then all over Egypt, as Philo says, 'in every nome'. Then again overseas to all parts of the Roman Empire.

The *Gospel of Thomas* is a collection of parables and sayings of Jesus. It does not contain a narrative interpreting the life of Jesus and culminating in a description of his death. It claims that these sayings, properly understood, open the path to salvation and life: 'Whoever finds the interpretation of these sayings will not experience death' (Saying 1).

Many of the sayings have parallels in the four canonical gospels of the New Testament as well as the letters of Paul. For example:

> Jesus said, 'No prophet is accepted in his own village.'
> 'A prophet is not without honour, save in his own country and in his own house'
> [Matthew 13:57 and, with minor changes in wording, Mark 6:4, Luke 4:24 and John 4:44]

The Cross is mentioned in the *Gospel of Thomas*, but as a symbol not of death but eternal spiritual life in the same sense that we find in both the canonical gospels and Paul's Letter to the Galatians: 'Whosoever will come after me, let him deny himself, and take up his cross and follow me' (Mark 8:34) . . . 'I am crucified with Christ: nevertheless I live; yet not I, but Christ liveth in me: and the life which I now live in the flesh I live by the faith of the Son of God, who loved me and gave himself for me' (Galatians 2:20).

The basic religious experience, according to the *Gospel of Thomas*, is not only the recognition of one's divine identity but, more specifically, recognition of one's origin (the light) and destiny (the repose). In order to return to one's origin it is necessary to 'strip off' the garment of the flesh. Then one can experience the new world – a kingdom of light, peace and life.

In the Gnostic myth implied in the *Gospel of Thomas*, individual spirits dwelt originally in 'the All', the spiritual universe of divine beings. Through some primeval cata-strophe – the Fall – some human spirits became imprisoned in the fleshly bodies of the material world and are blind to their true origin. Jesus saves them simply by revealing to them the truth about who they really are – divine beings belonging to another world. This realization frees them immediately from the 'garments' of their material bodies.

Here we find echoes of Therapeutae teaching: the material world and the physical body are rejected as evil; so, too, is sex; by asceticism, the spirits triumph in principle over the body; and physical death is the final release from the evil material world. 'If you do not abstain from the world you will not find the kingdom' (Saying 27).

The source of the *Gospel of Thomas* has been the subject of a great deal of scholarly debate. The basic argument is whether it is another version of the sayings found in the four canonical gospels or is drawn independently from the same imprecise source – 'Q' (from the German *Quelle*, source) – as the sayings of Jesus recorded in the four gospels.

Professor Helmut Koester, who translated the gospel into English, believes that it was possibly written in the second half of the 1st century AD and represents a tradition as early as, if not earlier than, the four canonical gospels because its sayings and parables are generally shorter and pithier, and they lack the allegory, narrative framework and other redactional fingerprints of Matthew, Mark, Luke and John.

As for the sayings and parables themselves, scholars who accept the New Testament account of the life, suffering and death of Jesus as historically accurate clearly have no alternative but to date them to the 1st century AD. However, the *Gospel of Thomas* is close in form to other collections of sayings in the ancient world, that is, they belong to an exceedingly old tradition of *wisdom* literature in Egypt and the Middle East. The Wisdom Texts, which go back as far as the time of the pyramid builders in the 27th century BC, were the most highly regarded old types of literature in Egypt. Imhotep, the architect of the Step Pyramid of Sakkara, was regarded as the first composer of this type of writings. The texts are regularly presented in the form of advice given by a father to his son, and the teaching is based upon experience and the passing of tradition. Wisdom – *Sophia* in Greek – is personified as a feminine character who emanates from God and speaks in proverbs, riddles and other forms of wise sayings.

All of these sects – the Essenes, Gnostics and Therapeutae – were already established in the civilized world (the Roman Empire) at the start of the Christian era, and even in Rome in the first half of the 1st century AD. Precisely how they came to settle in Rome is obscure. One source of converts to a religion that the authorities looked upon as just another mystic sect may have been their own soldiers. Strabo, the Greek geographer and historian, who visited Egypt in 25 BC and accompanied its governor, Aliu Gallus, the following year in his attempt to subdue southern Arabia, recorded that there were three Roman legions stationed in the ancient city of Babylon (modern Cairo), on the other side of the Nile from Memphis. Memphis contained a temple of Serapis, the Egyptian god whose worship was the most popular Egyptian cult of the time. It had spread throughout the civilized world and was to survive alongside – and be looked upon by many worshippers, as we shall see later, as a separate branch of –

emergent Christianity for more than two centuries.

Another source may have been the Jews, both orthodox and the Essenes (Judaeo-Christians). The first Jewish community had been brought to Rome as prisoners of war and slaves after the Roman invasion of Judaea in 63 BC. This would not, of course, explain the presence of Gentile Christians in the city as the Essenes did not accept uncircumcised Gentiles into their movement. However, riots between the Christians, who believed the Messiah had already come, and orthodox Jews, who denied it, led ultimately to their expulsion from Rome by the emperor Caligula in AD 49.

We find a reference to this expulsion in the Book of Acts: 'After these things Paul departed from Athens, and came to Corinth; And found a certain Jew named Aquila . . . lately come from Italy, with his wife Priscilla; (because that Claudius had commanded all Jews to depart from Rome:) And because he was of the same craft' – Paul had been initially a tentmaker – 'he abode with them, and wrought: for by their occupation they were tentmakers' (18:1–3).

However, there had been an earlier expulsion of the Jews, many of whom may well have been Judaeo-Christians (although evidence on this point is lacking), from Rome in AD 19 during the reign of Tiberius, the uncle of Claudius. Jews of military age were expelled, as also were devotees of the Egyptian cult of Serapis. Tacitus, the Roman historian (c. AD 55–115), recalls in the second book of his Annals that

> there was a debate . . . about expelling the Egyptian and Jewish worship, and a resolution of the Senate was passed that four thousand of the freedman class who were infected with those superstitions and were of military age should be transported to the island of Sardinia to quell the brigandage of the place, a cheap sacrifice should they die from the pestilential climate. The rest were to quit Italy unless before a certain day they repudiated their impious rites.

It is possible to date this event to around AD 19, 30 years earlier than the date most scholars accept for the expulsion of the Jews from Rome – because all events chronicled in Tacitus's second volume of *Annals* come to an end around that time.

The early appearance of Christianity in Rome is also suggested by the tradition that Claudius's wife Protonica, who was married to him before he was appointed emperor in AD 37, became a Christian convert during the reign of his uncle, Tiberius (AD 14–37). The accompanying tradition – that Protonica had at this period discovered the 'true' Cross, for whose existence there is no historical evidence – raises the possibility that the story of her conversion may be equally apocryphal. However, in a passage from Paul's Letter to the Philippians members of 'Caesar's household' are the only Roman Christians singled out specifically as sending greetings to their Philippian brethren: '. . . The brethren which are with me greet you. All the saints salute you, chiefly they that are of Caesar's household' (Philippians 4:21–22).

The climate changed when Nero, who had been adopted by Claudius, succeeded to the throne in AD 54 and, before his suicide 14 years later, had achieved enduring notoriety for murder, cruelty and debauchery. By the time of his reign (AD 54–68) the Christian community in Rome had expanded to a considerable size. The historian Tacitus relates in his *Annals* how Nero, accused of setting Rome on fire in AD 64 and in need of scapegoats, 'fastened the guilt and inflicted the most exquisite tortures on a class hated for their abominations, called Christians by the populace'.

By the first half of the 1st century AD, the Therapeutae had also spread far and wide. Philo, whose brother was head of the Jewish community in Alexandria, visited Rome during the brief reign of Caligula (AD 37–41) to protest at the emperor's order that the Jews should place his image in their temple and worship it. It was at this early date, on his return from Rome, that – according to Eusebius (*c.* AD 260–342), one of the early Church Fathers, who wrote an ecclesiastical history down to his own time – Philo set down his most important work, *The Contemplative Life*, in which he described the Therapeutae as 'citizens of heaven and of the universe, and truly acceptable to the father and creator of the world'. He also recorded that the Therapeutae were 'to be found in many parts of the civilized world', but were 'numerous in Egypt throughout each of the districts called nomes, and particularly around Alexandria'. Eusebius identified the Therapeutae as the earliest Christian church in Egypt. At this time there were 42 nomes – geographical districts – in Egypt, often separated by vast distances. For example, it was the better part of 300 miles from Alexandria, the capital, to Mount Sinai at the southern end of the Sinai peninsula. It is hardly to be believed, if the two dates indicated by the gospels for the Crucifixion (AD 30 and 33) are correct, that Christian communities could have spread throughout Egypt – let alone to Rome – in less than two decades when the only means of travel were by donkey, camel or boat.

The existence of Christianity in Egypt so soon after the supposed date of the Crucifixion is also attested in an account by Josephus, the 1st century AD historian, in his book *Antiquities of the Jews*. He records that in the AD 50s a missionary from Egypt appeared in Jerusalem itself where he is said to have had greater success than John the Baptist, gathering 30,000 Jews under his leadership. The newcomer 'said he was a prophet, and advised the multitude of the common people to go along with him to the Mount of Olives . . . He said further that he would show them from thence how, at his command, the walls of Jerusalem would fall down . . . Now when Felix (the Roman procurator) was informed of these things he ordered his soldiers to take their weapons and came against them with a great number of horsemen and footmen from Jerusalem, and attacked the Egyptian and the people that were with him. He also slew four hundred of them and took two hundred alive. But the Egyptian himself escaped out of the fight . . .'

This account by Josephus suggests that the Egyptian must have been a *Messianic* teacher, for the Jews would not have followed him had he been a *pagan* prophet. Later, when Paul made his last visit to Jerusalem in AD 57 and had to be rescued by Roman soldiers from the wrath of the Jews, the Roman captain mistook him for the Egyptian rebel prophet and asked him: 'Art thou that Egyptian, which before these days made an uproar, and leddest out into the wilderness four thousand men who were murderers?' (Acts 21:28).

The question at issue is simple. If the historical Jesus (Joshua) lived, suffered and died in the 14th century BC, what motives lay behind the 'orthodox' Christian Church's identification of the *spiritual appearances of Christ* to some of his disciples and to St Paul – reported to have taken place during the 1st century AD – as representing the *historical Jesus*? Those motives were nothing less than the Church of Rome's need to place the incarnate Jesus – the Jesus of flesh and blood – in AD 1, and to ratify these spiritual appearances as manifestations of the historical Jesus, in order to legitimize its authority and power.

Chapter Nineteen

Paul and Peter

The course of ecclesiastical history in the first 50 years of the Christian era has been the subject of considerable confusion, resulting from a number of misapprehensions. Principal among these are that no Christians existed for Paul to persecute before AD 30 or 33, the two dates given in the gospels for the Crucifixion; that the gospels are historical works whereas their real purpose is theological; that Paul was converted on the road to Damascus and learned his teaching from the Jerusalem apostles; and that Simon (later named in the gospels as 'Simon called Peter',* the first Pope), leader of the Jerusalem apostles, made his way to Rome in the middle of the century and was martyred there during Nero's persecution of the Christians. It is only when these myths are exposed that it becomes possible to reconcile conflicting chronologies and make logical sense of the events of these first 50 years and of those that followed.

The early years of the Christian era were a time of great spiritual expectation. The Essenes were awaiting the return of their Teacher on the Day of Judgement at the end of the world. John the Baptist, later described in the gospel as 'the man sent from God' (John 1:6), was the first Essene to come out into the open and try to initiate all Jews into a baptism of repentance, a confession of the sin of having

---

* As I shall show, the name Peter (Greek, the Rock) did not exist at this time but was a subsequent interpretation of gospel authors. Until we reach that point it will cause less chronological confusion to refer to him generally as Simon.

rejected their Messiah and the need for moral cleansing. In the words of Josephus, who confirmed John as a historical figure as well as a biblical one, John commanded the Jews 'to come to baptism; for the washing (with water) would be acceptable to him (God), if they made use of it . . .'

The evangelist Matthew confirms that John the Baptist was not preparing the way for Jesus to be born, but for his Second Coming: 'In those days came John the Baptist, preaching in the wilderness of Judaea, And saying, Repent ye: for the kingdom of heaven is at hand. For this is he that was spoken of by the prophet Esaias, saying, Prepare ye the way of the Lord, make his paths straight' (Matthew 3:1–3). John's baptist movement aroused such enthusiasm, and such a large following, that Herod Antipas, the governor of Galilee from 4 BC to AD 39, fearing that John might become a rallying point for Jewish dissidence, had him arrested, imprisoned and later executed. The date of John's execution is usually given as AD 28. He was succeeded by Simon (Peter) (Plate 28), another Essene (since his teaching was of a Jewish Christian nature, similar to Essene teaching), who from the time of his accession was looked upon as undisputed leader of the Jerusalem apostles.

They, for their part, not only continued with John's teaching, but claimed that his prophecy had been fulfilled and that they had seen Christ. Because nobody else had seen him, their story was not believed (this is communicated by the account of the episode), and it was generally thought that the person who had risen from the dead was actually John. We find two references to this belief in the Gospel of Mark after the disciples had been sent out two by two to preach repentance: 'And king Herod heard of him; (for his name was spread abroad:) and he said, That John the Baptist was risen from the dead . . .' (6:14), and: 'But when Herod heard thereof, he said, It is John, whom I beheaded: he is risen from the dead' (6:16).

The teaching of Simon (Peter) and the Jerusalem apostles was a mixture of the Old (Mosaic) Covenant, made with

Abraham, and the New Covenant, promised by John the Baptist. The Old Covenant, whose essence was 'keep my commandments', is to be found in Genesis 17:7,10: 'And I will establish my covenant between me and thee and thy seed after thee in their generations for an everlasting covenant, to be a God unto thee, and to thy seed after thee . . . This is my covenant, which ye shall keep, between me and you and thy seed after thee; Every man child among you shall be circumcised.' Although circumcision was an ancient Egyptian custom, this covenant had been applicable only to Jews who observed the custom of circumcision. It brought with it no promise of an eternal life.

Simon (Peter) and the Jerusalem apostles adopted, in addition, the New Covenant of John the Baptist, which also contained no specific promise of resurrection, and they, too, restricted its application to circumcised Jews. The limitations of the teaching of Simon (Peter), compared with the redemption teaching of Paul, can be seen in two verses of the Book of Acts, as it was finally written in the second half of the 2nd century AD: 'Then Peter said unto them, Repent, and be baptized every one of you in the name of Jesus Christ the Messiah* for the remission of sins' (2:38), and 'Repent ye therefore, and be converted, that your sins may be blotted out, when the time of refreshing shall come from the presence of the Lord' (3:19).

It was at this time, in the middle of the second half of the second decade AD, that Paul began to play a crucial role. Paul (Plate 29) was born at Tarsus in Asia Minor during the early years of the Christian era. As a young man he made his way to Jerusalem, some 400 miles to the south of his birthplace, in order to study the Torah – the first five books of the Old Testament, ascribed traditionally to Moses – at the Temple college under a renowned Pharistic rabbi

---

* The origin of the biblical word 'Messiah' (Saviour) is the Hebrew *Mashih*. The English name 'Christ' derives from *Christos*, meaning an anointed one, a king, used in the Greek translation of the Bible in the 3rd century BC.

Gamaliel. In the opening chapter of his later Epistle to the Galatians – Celtic people who lived over a large area of Asia Minor and who had been converted to Christianity by Paul in the course of three epic missionary voyages – he confesses that at this early stage of his life he 'persecuted the church of God, and wasted it . . .'

After his admission about persecuting Christians, which his letters indicate took place in the third decade AD, Paul goes on to give his own account of his conversion that is totally at variance with the account found in the Book of Acts, which claims that, on the road to Damascus, Paul had a vision of Jesus, who asked: 'Saul, Saul (his original name), why persecutest thou me?' (9:4). This encounter is not mentioned by Paul in any of the letters he wrote – more than a century earlier than the appearance of the New Testament gospels – to the communities he had converted to Christianity. Instead, in his Letter to the Galatians, without making it clear where he had his spiritual encounter with Jesus, he goes on to stress that his teaching owed nothing to any man, including the Jerusalem apostles: '. . . it pleased God to reveal his Son to me . . . I conferred not with flesh and blood . . . Neither went I up to Jerusalem to them that were apostles before me; but I went into Arabia . . .' (1:15–17).

The reason for the contradictions between Paul's account of his life and the version we find in the Book of Acts is examined in more detail later, but in the meantime it seems reasonable to approach such discrepancies on the lines suggested by Martin Debelius, Professor of Theology at Heidelberg, in the early pages of his book *Paul*, published in 1953: 'The information about Paul as it is presented in The Acts Of The Apostles is not reliable since it is not autobiographical; and if it contradicts plain statements in the letters [of Paul] it has to take second place.'

Paul makes it clear in another passage from this letter that the precise spot where he underwent his period of initiation in 'Arabia' was Mount Sinai which he compares with

242

Jerusalem, (4:24,25), the Mountain of God* where Moses is said to have received the Ten Commandments during his period of exile some 14 centuries earlier and where the Lord also appeared to him with the instruction to return to Egypt, accompanied by Aaron, to lead the Israelite Exodus.† In another of his letters Paul discloses in addition that it was during the time he spent at Mount Sinai that God revealed to him that 'Gentiles should be fellow-heirs, and of the same body, and partakers of his promise in Christ by the gospel' (Ephesians, 3:3–6).

Mount Sinai has been a place of pilgrimage since the time of Moses. The mountain, nearly 7,500 feet high, is one of many peaks in the arid southern Sinai peninsula that forms the wilderness through which Moses tried to lead the Israelites on their protracted journey to the Promised Land. Even today this wilderness has little water and a few cramped valleys where the marginal soil yields limited supplies of vegetables and dates, sparse sustenance for wandering bedouin families and their flocks.

In the earliest years the area around the foot of the mountain, where the monastery of St Catherine remains a

---

* The Israelite God appeared to Moses at this mountain. The Koran also states that God spoke to Moses at the mountain which had been holy to the local Shasu (biblical Midianites) even before the time of Moses, and it remains holy till now where the St Catherine monastery is a focus for pilgrims.

† As we saw earlier, the strong surviving tradition of St Catherine's monastery at the foot of Mount Sinai identifies the mountain as the setting of the Transfiguration. Mount Tabor, to the east of Nazareth, has been put forward as a rival setting, with a Franciscan church built there for pilgrims. This resolves geographical difficulty if, as the New Testament indicates, the Transfiguration occurred shortly before the Crucifixion. Travelling from Mount Sinai to Jerusalem would have involved an arduous overland journey of some three hundred miles.

‡ Sinai was a haunt of hermits for two reasons. It was the place where Moses spent many years in meditation, and it was the spot where Joshua/Jesus/Tutankhamun died.

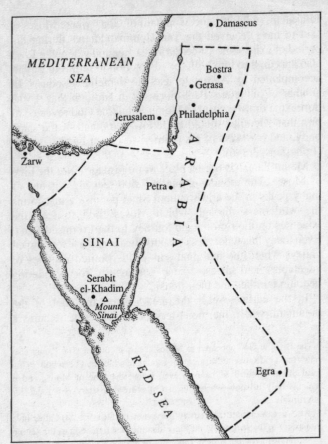

The Roman province of Arabia

place of pilgrimage today, was a haunt of hermits.‡ At the time Paul emerged on the scene, in the first half of the 1st century AD, the Syrian city of Damascus and the area of east Jordan and Sinai were under the control of Nabatean Arabs and their king, Aritas III. To the Nabateans, who had replaced the biblical Midianites (the Shasu, allies of Moses in his wilderness years), Mount Sinai was a holy place to which they travelled in pilgrimage. The long tradition of the mountain as a place of such pilgrimage is clear from inscriptions – in Nabatean, Greek, Latin and Arabic – on the rocks of Wadi Haggag, the Ravine of the Pilgrims, a narrow valley on the major road that led from Eilat (biblical Elath) at the head of the Gulf of Aqaba to the Mount Sinai area.

It is a reasonable assumption that, if the Therapeutae were established in all the nomes of Egypt at this time, one of their settlements would be found around Mount Sinai with its long tradition as a sacred place of holiness and pilgrimage. Certainly, it is possible to detect the ascetic influence of the Therapeutae in Paul's later life. He lived according to the rule of the Therapeutae, never lived with his own family, never married, and never possessed wealth – he spent his life trying to know Christ and spread this knowledge to others. The Therapeutae's concept of wealth held in common is also reflected in the fact that, despite their doctrinal differences, the Church founded by Paul at the Greek city of Corinth used to send financial help to Jerusalem.

Paul gives a precise chronology of the years that followed his conversion, which must have taken place in the fourth decade AD: '. . . after three years I went up to Jerusalem to see Simon (Peter), and abode with him fifteen days. But other of the apostles saw I none, save James the Lord's brother' (Galatians 1:18–19). Despite some scholarly debate, it is generally accepted that the 'three years' indicates the period of Paul's initiation in Arabia.

Before going on, it is perhaps useful to examine the notion of initiation. All knowledge, including the knowledge of writing, was regarded by Egyptians as part of a holy practice. Knowledge is power, so it should not be given to anyone before he has proved himself capable of using it wisely. Not everybody would be able to acquire all kinds of knowledge, for the explanations given by the priests to ordinary people would be different from those they give to a king or to another priest. In acquiring knowledge, no one could move to a higher degree before being tested and found trustworthy for more revelations. Those who reach the highest degree are those chosen by the spiritual powers themselves, through revelation. Irrespective of age or length of training time, those who receive a vision with the spirit are regarded as having reached the highest degree.

We have a good example of this situation in Tuthmose III. As he was neither the son of the queen nor the husband of the royal heiress, he should not have been able to succeed his father on the throne. Nevertheless, during a celebration at the Karnak temple Amun, carried on a boat by priests, approached the spot where the young prince was standing and led him to the holy of holies in the temple, where only a king could enter. This was followed by a vision the prince had (and later recorded in his *Annales*) of a flight to heaven where he saw the god Ra, who placed the royal serpent on his forehead. This meant that Tuthmose was chosen by the god himself; this is the spiritual importance of this king (i.e. David).

St Paul remained in Arabia for three years, the course of someone who was fully initiated into the whole mystery of the sect. We do have some indication of this in his writing. The word 'mystery' appears 17 times in Paul's letters, yet is found only five times in the entire Bible outside Paul's letters; once in Mark and four times in Revelation. Here are some examples:

'For I would not, brethren, that ye should be ignorant of this mystery, lest ye should be wise in your own conceits' (Romans 11:25).

'Now to him that is of power to stablish you according to my gospel, and the preaching of Jesus Christ, according to the revelation of the mystery, which was kept secret since the world began' Romans 16:25).

'But we speak the wisdom of God in a mystery, even the hidden wisdom' (I Corinthians 2:7).

'How that by revelation he made known unto me the

mystery . . . Whereby, when ye read, ye may understand my knowledge in the mystery of Christ' (Ephesians 3:3).

'And to make all men see what is the fellowship of the mystery, which from the beginning of the world hath been hid in God' (Ephesians 3:9).

This mystery is the proof of Paul's initiation into the 3rd degree. Moreover, the accounts of Galatians regarding Paul's encounter with the *spirit of Christ* meant that he became one of the few, which can explain why the Nag Hammadi gospels have high regard for Paul.

The reference to 'James the Lord's brother' (Galatians 1:18–19) is not to be interpreted in the sense of a blood brother, but of a brother in belief. Although the words 'brother', 'brethren' and 'sister' are usually used in the Bible to signify a blood relation, this is not always the case. They are sometimes employed to signify a religious bond. Matthew, for example, quotes Jesus as saying, 'whosoever shall do the will of my Father which is in heaven, the same is my brother, and sister, and mother' (12:50). There are many indications in the early Christian communities that it was through faith that one became a 'brother' or 'sister' of the Lord. Again, Matthew quotes the risen Christ describing his disciples as brothers in the sense of followers when he sends them a message: '. . . go tell my brothers that they go into Galilee, and there shall they see me' (28:10). Paul also uses 'brothers' to indicate a religious bond in his various letters.

In his *Antiquities of the Jews*, Josephus gives an account of a trial that took place in AD 64, which suggests a possible alternative explanation of the appearance of 'James the Lord's brother' in Paul's narrative. It appears that while awaiting the arrival of Albinus, the new governor of Palestine, the Jewish high priest, Ananus, had ordered some opponents to be stoned to death for breaking the law. As a result of protests about the matter from just citizens, Albinus sacked Ananus and replaced him with another high priest named Jesus, whose brother James had been one of the victims of death by stoning.

Paul's own narrative goes on to explain that, after this first visit to Jerusalem, he went to Syria and Cilicia, the part of Asia Minor where he had been born. There his face was unknown and people 'had heard only, That he who perse-cuted us in times past now preached the faith which once he destroyed. And they glorified God in me.' At this time a flourishing Gentile-Christian community already existed at Antioch, then the capital of Syria. Paul became associated with its leader, Barnabas. Ultimately, the community com-missioned Barnabas and Paul to preach the Gentile gospel beyond the confines of Syria. This resulted in the first of Paul's three missionary journeys, beginning with a visit to Cyprus, the homeland of Barnabas.

The conflict between the Christian Churches of Jerusalem Simon (Peter) and Antioch Paul came to a head on the return of Paul and Barnabas from this first missionary voyage. Apostles of the Judaeo-Christian Church demanded that Gentile Christians should be circumcised and made to observe the Mosaic Law (that is, convert to Judaism). Paul eventually resolved the dispute at what is commonly known as the Council of Jerusalem, at which it was agreed that Simon (Peter) would be the apostle of the Jews and Paul the apostle of the Gentiles: '. . . fourteen years after[wards] I went up again to Jerusalem . . . and communicated to them that gospel which I preach among the Gentiles . . . when they saw that the gospel of the uncircumcision was committed unto me, as the gospel of the circumcision was unto Peter (Simon) . . . James, Cephas and John, who seemed to be pillars, perceived the grace that was given unto me, they gave to me and Barnabas the right hands of fellowship; that we should go unto the heathen, and they unto the circumcision' (Galatians 2:1–2,7,9).

Use of the name 'Peter' in Paul's two accounts of his visits to Jerusalem is curious because we have no mention anywhere before the final version of the Books of Acts in the 2nd century AD of anybody named Peter as the leader of the Jerusalem apostles. The Greek originals of the text of Paul's letters (as found in *Novum Testamentum Graece*), show that he never used the name 'Peter' but referred to the leader of the Jerusalem apostles as Kepha or Cephas, the Aramaic word meaning 'dome'. The name 'Cephas' was also used as a synonym for Simon in John's gospel account of how Simon was renamed: 'And he [Andrew] brought him [his brother Simon] to Jesus. And when Jesus beheld him, he said: Thou art Simon, the son of Jona: thou shalt be called Cephas, which is by interpretation, A stone' (1:42). The more liberal use of 'Peter' in the Book of Acts is clearly the work of a later copyist, seeking to support the false view that Peter rather than Paul should be looked upon as the founder of modern Christianity, and also trying to make sense of chronologies that did not match.

The same problem has arisen over the actual date of the Council of Jerusalem. Many modern scholars place it during or just before AD 44, the date of the death of Herod Agrippa I, a grandson of Herod the Great. They base this belief on an account in the Book of Acts of how, shortly before his own death, Agrippa I arrested and imprisoned Simon (Peter): 'Now about that time Herod the king stretched forth his hands to vex certain of the church. And he killed James, the brother of John, with the sword. And because he saw it pleased the Jews he proceeded further to take Peter also . . . he put him in prison . . . intending after Easter to bring him forth to the people' (12:1–5).

We are then told that on the last night of the Passover – the night before he was to be brought 'forth to the people', presumably to be executed like James – Simon (Peter) found himself released miraculously from prison through the intervention of an angel who freed him from his chains and led him, in an understandable daze, past guards and through locked gates to freedom. It is then said that he 'departed . . . and went into another place' (12:17). Scholars who favour

AD 44 interpret the phrase 'went into another place' as biblical shorthand for 'went to his death'.

This dating creates problems, however, for scholars who look upon the gospels as a literal account of the life, suffering and death of Jesus. Deducting 17 years – three for Paul's initiation in Sinai, 14 between his two visits to Jerusalem – means that Paul was persecuting Christians as early as AD 27, three years before the earliest date given in the gospels for the Crucifixion and Resurrection. They have therefore interpreted 'went into another place' as meaning that Simon (Peter) went to Rome and, by implication, returned to Jerusalem for a later conference with Paul. This sequence of events, for which we have no evidence or explanation, is further complicated by the fact that the Book of Acts suggests that Paul had three, not two, meetings with Simon (Peter) in Jerusalem. Here again, as in other contradictions between Paul's letters and the account of events in the suspect Book of Acts, common sense suggests that Paul's personal version of the story is to be preferred – allied to the fact that not a scrap of evidence exists to support this later dating or the view, which is merely a self-serving tradition, that 'Simon called Peter' ever saw Rome.

For a bishop of the branch of the Church in Rome, the political capital of the civilized world, the view from the Vatican in the last decades of the 1st century AD would not have been encouraging if he shared the authoritarian views of the Jerusalem apostles.

Peter was dead (he died in AD 44). Our bishop could no longer look to Jerusalem, the seat of the Judaeo-Christian Church of the Essenes, for support because the Romans had wiped it out. After four years of trying to quell a Jewish uprising against them, they eventually captured the city in AD 70, destroyed most of it and set fire to the Temple. Inhabitants who had not died from hunger during the prolonged siege were either killed or taken captive and sold into slavery – and the Judaeo-Christian Church vanished from Jerusalem.

This was only part of our bishop's problem. The branches of the Christian Church founded around the Mediterranean by Paul were created on the informal lines favoured by the Gnostics, as we saw earlier, rather than the rigid demarcation into an authoritarian priesthood and obedient laity favoured by the Jerusalem apostles. The Gnostics believed that all Christians were equal, having received through their initiation the charismatic gift of direct inspiration through the Holy Spirit. When they met, all members, men and women, took part initially in drawing lots to decide who should serve as the priest to supervise such rituals as baptism of new initiates and the Messianic Banquet. We find this individuality reflected in one of Paul's letters: '. . . when ye come together, every one of you hath a psalm, hath doctrine, hath a tongue, hath a revelation, hath an interpretation . . .' (I Corinthians 14:26).

The beliefs of members of these branches of the Church about the essential nature of Christianity varied. Their gospels – in the sense of 'glad tidings', not of the four canonical gospels we are familiar with today – were rudimentary, usually consisting of little more than snatches of the Old Testament teachings of the prophets and some sayings attributed to Jesus. In addition, many saw emergent Christianity as simply an alternative version of the ancient Egyptian cult of Serapis (discussed in Chapter 22), based upon a 'holy' family made up, as we saw in the Prologue, of Osiris, the Egyptian god of the underworld and judge of the dead, his bride Isis and their hawk-headed son Horus.

Any ecclesiastic of authoritarian views would have seen the branches of Paul's Mediterranean Church as a chaotic free-for-all, upon which order should be restored. This challenge was met in various ways. Principal among these were to establish Jesus as a 1st century AD contemporary of Peter and the person who had appointed Peter head of the Church and was therefore the source of its apostolic tradition; to 'resurrect' Peter and transport him to Rome, where he is said to have been martyred; to identify Joshua, son of Nun, as a pre-existent Christ; to diminish the importance of Paul; to give a historical dimension to the theological account of the gospel by placing the suffering and death of Christ during the time of Pontius Pilate; to include these interpretations in a Creed that Christians were required to believe in order to be accepted as Christians; and to condemn as heretics any Christian who did not accept the Church's teaching.

These aims had been established by the end of the 2nd century AD. They reached their peak after the conversion of Constantine the Great (*c*. AD 274–337). From that time the Church was increasingly looked upon as a unifying force within the declining Roman Empire, an arm of the state that could rely on political and military support against its ideological enemies – those who disagreed with the Church's teaching and refused to accept it.

Chapter Twenty

Keepers of the Keys

The latter years of the 1st century AD saw the emergence of a number of 'bishops' who set about establishing their authority to rule over these rival communities and the task of bringing some order into conflicting beliefs. One of the first bishops to fire a warning shot across the bows of Christians was Clement, Bishop of Rome (*c*. AD 90–95), who was supposed to have been the fourth successor of Peter.

Clement argued that the leaders of the Church had been delegated by God as 'rulers on earth' and that people should submit to the authority of bishops and priests, who were, so to speak, authorized to keep the keys of the kingdom, with the power of discipline and judgement over what he called 'the laity'.

In his first epistle to the Corinthians, he wrote: 'The apostles received the gospel for us from the Lord Jesus Christ . . . they appointed their first-fruits . . . to be bishops and deacons unto them that should believe.' The bishops, in turn, could appoint their successors: 'Our apostles knew through our Lord Jesus Christ that there would be strife over the name of the bishop's office. For this cause therefore, having received complete foreknowledge, they appointed the aforesaid persons (the bishops), and afterwards they provided a continuance, that if these would fall asleep other approved men would succeed to their ministration' (I Clement: 44). (Here no apostle's name – neither Paul's nor Peter's – is given.) The Church in Rome was the first to be organized in this way, an example followed by other branches in the next century.

The 'bishops' needed justification to establish their own authority. They were unable to turn to Paul because he stated clearly that his encounter with Christ was not physical but spiritual, and because he never established a priesthood in the churches he founded.

Paul's letters make it clear that he differed from the Jerusalem apostles not simply in preaching to the Gentiles as well as the Jews, but in his introduction of the concept of a Redeemer born into a wicked world: '. . . our Lord Jesus Christ, who gave himself for our sins, that he might deliver us from this evil world' (Galatians 1:3–4). The belief that a divinely appointed Saviour (the Suffering Servant) had already lived and been sacrificed had first been voiced, as we have seen, by the Israelite prophet Isaiah, writing in the 6th century BC. However, Isaiah's interpretation of resurrection was confined to the Suffering Servant and neither the Essenes nor Simon (Peter) represented the resurrection of Jesus as an act of redemption for mankind. It is the Gnostic gospels and the letters of Paul that first speak of the resurrection of those who believe in Christ.

In addition, Paul had elaborated a 'theology of the Cross'. His Cross was not the Roman cross of punishment, but the *ankh*, the Egyptian cross, which is a symbol of life, not of death. Early Christian communities of the first three centuries used mainly the *ankh* or, as their symbol, a fish (Plate 33), which indicated resurrection in the tombs of Abydos in Upper Egypt from 4000 BC. The *ankh* is also to be seen in relief on the temple walls and tombs of ancient Egypt from the time of Akhenaten (Moses) where the rays of the sun, symbolizing Aten (the Lord), are directed at the king and queen and end in hands distributing to them the *ankh*, the key of life. It was the positive significance of the *ankh* as the symbol of eternal life that persuaded early Christians to adopt it as the sign of Christ's victory over death.

Neither Simon (Peter) nor any of the Jerusalem apostles, James and the Twelve, is ever quoted as speaking of the Cross as a symbol of Christ or of their own community. It was not, in fact, until the 5th century AD that the Roman-Latin cross in which the upright beam projects above the shorter crossbeam became established – through the New Testament story – as the general symbol of the Christian faith, and not until the following century that the body of Christ on the Cross was represented.

The positive significance of the Egyptian *ankh* is reflected in the fact that Paul's theology of the Cross did not focus on the suffering and death of Jesus, but on his resurrection and the promise of eternal life. The *ankh* represents the living Jesus: 'I am crucified' – in the broader sense of 'have died' – 'with Christ: nevertheless I live: yet not I but Christ liveth in me . . .' (Galatians 2:20), which reinforces the Gnostic concept of 'God within'.

As an alternative to Paul, the 'bishops' therefore turned to 'Simon called Peter', whose Jerusalem Church had been organized on the authoritarian lines they themselves wished to foster, and, in order to establish their apostolic line of succession, created the myth that Peter, having made a miraculous escape from prison, had spent the latter years of his life in Rome, where he had been ultimately martyred, and that he had been a contemporary of Jesus, who had appointed him head of the Christian Church.

One of the earliest ecclesiastical references to Peter is said to have been made by Clement, Bishop of Rome. As early as AD 95 he wrote a letter to the Corinthians of which the text is given conventionally as: 'By reason of jealousy and envy the greatest and most righteous pillars of the Church were persecuted and contended even unto death. Let us set before our eyes the good apostles. Peter, who, by reason of unrighteous jealousy, endured not one, not two, but many labours, and thus having borne his testimony went to his appointed place of glory. By the reason of jealousy and strife, Paul by his example pointed out the prize of patient endurance. After he had been seven times in bonds, he had been driven into exile, had been stoned, had preached in the east and in the west, he won the noble renown which was the whole of his faith, having taught righteousness to the whole world and having reached the farthest bounds of the west . . .'

Although the death of someone identified as Peter is mentioned, there is no indication that he ever visited Rome or that he was martyred there. Moreover, the name 'Peter' is not mentioned clearly: it has been supplied by conjecture as the last two letters 'ER' are missing from the text. In such circumstances, the meaning of the word is unclear. It was not until AD 160 that the story developed further. Dionysus, Bishop of Corinth, is quoted by Eusebius in his later history of the Church as saying that both 'Peter and Paul taught in our Corinth and were our founders, and taught together in Italy in the same place and were martyred at the same time'.

By the early years of the 3rd century AD the tradition of Peter's sojourn in Rome and martyrdom was firmly established and remains so to this day, despite the lack of any supporting evidence. Some apparent consolation was provided by the first epistle of St Peter, which Christian scholars date to having been written in Rome shortly before Peter's martyrdom. However, more recent study has indicated that the epistle was written by somebody else during the 2nd century AD. Doubts have also been cast on its authenticity by examination of certain words in the penultimate paragraph: 'The Church that is at Babylon . . . saluteth you . . .' (5:13). Here 'Babylon' has been taken to be a codeword for Rome, but we know of no case in the New Testament or any other source of that period where the name Babylon – referring to cities in Mesopotamia and Egypt (ancient Cairo) – was substituted for Rome by the bishops of Rome. An early Jewish work adduced as evidence that Babylon was a codename for Rome is the *Sibylline Oracles*, a classical pagan prophecy dating from the last quarter of the 2nd century AD. Particular importance attaches to Book 8, which is full of fierce invective against Rome and foretells the punishment that will befall the city. Here again nothing in the text suggests that Babylon is being used as a synonym for Rome.

The campaign in the Church's early years to establish Jesus as a contemporary of Peter, who had appointed him head of the Christian Church, was accompanied by a campaign to diminish the importance of Paul. This second campaign was given literary form in the last quarter of the 2nd century AD with the appearance of the Book of Acts. Authorship of the original version was, by a tradition dating from the 2nd century AD, assigned to Luke, the author of the third canonical gospel, and divided into two sections – the history of the early Church in Palestine, based on documents or oral information, and an account of Paul's later missionary voyages, on which it was said that Luke accompanied him.

The Book of Acts is mentioned for the first time, however, by Irenaeus (AD 130–202), Bishop of Lyon and one of the early Church Fathers, writing between AD 170 and 180. This gap of a century between the events and the book, plus the many contradictions between Paul's letters and the story presented in Acts, led scholars in the last century to the conclusion that, while Luke may have contributed some details of Paul's voyages, the book draws on other sources and was edited substantially in the 2nd century in order to enhance the importance of 'Simon called Peter' and his Judaeo-Christian Church. A. T. Hanson, Professor of Christian Theology at Nottingham University, made the point in his book *The Acts in the Revised Version* that 'we cannot be absolutely certain that Acts was recognized and used widely by Christians before AD 170'.

Comparison between the Alexandrian text, the earliest copy, of the Book of Acts and a later Greek text, known as the Western text, shows clearly the degree of editing that took place, designed particularly to place Paul in a position of lesser importance. The process is particularly striking in the two versions of Paul's conversion. The Book of Acts makes no mention of Paul's visit to 'Arabia'. Instead it presents his conversion in a form that links him with the Jerusalem Church as the source of his faith. It is here that we find details of his encounter with Jesus as he made his way from Jerusalem to Damascus with orders to arrest any Christians he found there and bring them back to Jerusalem for trial. After his vision he is said to have been baptized by Ananias (9:18), a Judaeo-Christian, and, after spending some days with other Judaeo-Christian disciples in Damascus 'straightway he preached Christ in the synagogues, that he is the Son of God' (9:20) – that is, he is said to have preached what the Judaeo-Christian disciples had taught him.

Chapter 9 goes on to relate how, in the face of a Jewish plot to kill him, Paul made his way to Jerusalem where he was at first shunned by Christians until Barnabas introduced him to the apostles, who now received him into their society. He supported them actively in proclaiming the gospel until another Jewish threat to his life caused him to flee, not to Syria and Cilicia, as his own account states, but specifically to Tarsus, his birthplace.

The contradictions between the two accounts of Paul's conversion, and the motive that explains them, were analysed by the German scholar Edward Zeller in his authoritative book *The Acts of the Apostles*:

> *The account is impossible to reconcile in parts with the apostle's own statements in the Epistle to the Galatians . . . On [his] journey to Arabia the Acts is not only completely silent, but leaves no space vacant for it. How could the apostle say he went to Arabia immediately after his call, without previous conference with others, if he had first sojourned for some time with Christians at Damascus and had there begun to preach the gospel . . .?*
>
> *In Jerusalem [according to the Acts] Paul was brought to the apostles, with whom he now associated for some time. In Galatians the Apostle himself asseverates with solemn protestations that he went to Jerusalem to see Cephas (Peter), but of the other apostles he saw none, save James, the Lord's brother . . . The account of the Epistle to the Galatians has the*

*avowed purpose of proving Paul's independence of all
human authority, and especially of all influence of the
primitive (Jerusalem) apostles. But this is just what the
author of the Acts does not want. His narrative is
therefore reversely planned, so as to bring Paul right
from the start into the closest connection with the
Twelve, and with the Jewish people.*

*Hence the silence respecting the journey to Arabia;
hence the curtailment of the three years which elapsed
between the apostle's conversion and his first visit to
Jerusalem; hence the prolongation of his sojourn in this
city; hence the extension of the two apostles whom Paul
really saw into the apostles; hence the fabulous
intercourse with the apostles, which is unknown to the
Epistle to the Galatians; hence the preaching of the
gospel in Jerusalem, which is improbable in itself . . .*

*When all the undeniably unhistorical features in
which a later account deviates are so simply explained
by one and the same motive, it is certainly in the highest
degree probable that the cause of these deviations is to
be sought in the very motive.*

It is possible to cite other examples of the same process. For
instance, although Barnabas was a leader of a rival branch of
the Church, the Book of Acts claims (11:25–26) that it was
the Jerusalem apostles who sent him to Antioch to establish
the Church there. In its account of the Council of Jerusalem
it also suggests that it was the Jerusalem apostles who gave
Paul authority to preach to the Gentiles, although his own
account makes it quite clear that they were not granting the
authority, merely recognizing that he already had it from
another source, a message we find repeated in another of his
letters: '. . . I have written more boldly unto you . . . because
of the grace that is given to me of God, That I should be the
minister of Jesus Christ to the Gentiles, ministering the
gospel of God . . .' (Romans 15:15–16).

Edward Zeller also made the point that, apart from

conflicting with Paul's own account, the Book of Acts' account of his conversion contained such a large number of internal inconsistencies as to expose itself to 'mistrust':

> *Of Paul's companions [at the time of his supposed conversion on the road to Damascus] it is said that they all fell to the ground (26:14); in 9:7, on the contrary, that they all remained standing in amazement while Paul fell down in terror. The two cannot be harmonized . . .*
>
> *Of the same persons it is said (9:7) that they indeed heard the voice that spoke to Paul, but saw no one; (in 22:9), on the contrary, that they saw the light which appeared to him, but did not hear the voice . . . still more important is it that some of the words attributed to Jesus appearing in the vision (26:16–18) are quoted (9:15) as a speech of Jesus to Ananias, in 22:15,21, partly as a speech of Ananias, partly as a speech of Jesus in a second appearance to Paul.*

The sensible approach to contradictions between Paul's own account of events and the Book of Acts version was summarized, as we saw earlier, by Martin Debelius, Professor of Theology at Heidelberg, in his book *Paul.** After the account in Chapter 12 of Simon's (Peter's) arrest and imprisonment, which has been construed as an account of his actual death *c*. AD 44, we find James – who had supposedly been executed before the arrest and imprisonment of Simon (Peter) – presented as the leader of the Jerusalem apostles at the subsequent Council of Jerusalem. This would be a reasonable course of events if Simon (Peter) was dead. However, a few verses before James makes his appearance as the person in charge of proceedings, we are told that Simon (Peter) was still alive – with words put into his mouth that serve only to

---

* 'The information about Paul as it is presented in The Acts Of The Apostles is not reliable since it is not autobiographical; and if it contradicts plain statements in the letters [of Paul] it has to take second place.'

make a liar of him. He is quoted as saying to the apostles and elders: 'Men and brethren, ye know how that a good while ago God made choice among us, that the Gentiles by my mouth should hear the word of the gospel, and believe' (15:7). This could not be true about Simon (Peter). He taught that the New Covenant – 'Be baptized, keep my commandments' – was applicable only to circumcised Jews who kept the law of Moses. All the evidence points to 'Simon called Peter's' name having been inserted at this point as part of the myth that he was still alive.

After the Jerusalem meeting, the name of Simon (Peter) disappears entirely from the narrative, while Paul embarked on his second and third missionary journeys. The Book of Acts describes how, on his final return, he made his way again to Jerusalem where he was accused of polluting the Temple and was about to be killed by a riotous mob when Roman soldiers arrested him. He was remanded to the custody of Felix, the Roman procurator at Caesarea. When Paul insisted on his right as a Roman citizen to be tried before an imperial court, it was decided that he should be sent to Rome, a journey that lasted several months because the ship taking him foundered on the way.

The last verses of the book describe how, instead of actually facing trial in Rome, Paul 'dwelt two whole years in his own hired house, and received all that came in unto him, preaching the kingdom of God, and teaching those things which concern the Lord Jesus Christ, with all confidence, no man forbidding him'. Yet, despite the later tradition that Peter resided in Rome and was eventually martyred there, we find no evidence in the New Testament to support this belief. The Book of Acts narrative of Paul's years in Rome never suggests that 'Simon called Peter' was there, or had ever been there, and Paul's letter to the Roman Church gives no hint that this Church had any connection with 'Simon called Peter'. Nor do we have any precise details of Paul's eventual death, but a 2nd-century tradition existed that it took place at the hands of Nero, the colourful and vicious imperial persecutor of Christians, in AD 64 or AD 67, shortly after completion of the various letters from Paul to scattered branches of the Church that are the first written evidence we have of events in the first century of the Christian era.

Chapter Twenty-one

The Gospels

The four canonical gospels were written, as we saw, as part of the process by which the Church of Rome sought to legitimize its authority through placing the life, suffering and death of Jesus in the 1st century AD. This process, in its turn, provided the basis for a Creed – what it was necessary to believe in order to be an orthodox Christian. Although these four gospels bear the names of Matthew, Mark, Luke and John, the evidence makes it clear that considerable editing took place between the time they were first written and the time they received final acceptance by the Church.

Mark, who is named in the Book of Acts and II Timothy as a companion of Barnabas and Paul, is thought by biblical scholars to have been the author of the earliest of these four canonical gospels. The exact date is not known, but scholars place it generally in the last quarter of the 1st century AD. As there is evidence that both Matthew and Luke relied on Mark, plus other sources, it has come to be accepted that they should be dated after him. Matthew has been dated to the first half of the 2nd century AD. Lucan references, especially those relating to the birth of Jesus, did not feature in the writings of the Church Fathers until the second half of that century, followed in the same period by John, the least historically minded of the four evangelists.

Enoch Powell, the British politician and Greek scholar, who translated the Greek text of Matthew's gospel, noted that it had been subjected to substantial 'doctoring' even before the end of the 1st century AD. He comments in his book *The Evolution of the Gospel*, published in 1994 by Yale

University Press: 'Matthew discloses that an underlying text was severely re-edited, with theological and polemical intent, and that the resulting edition was afterwards recombined with the underlying text to produce the gospel as it exists . . . The trial before Pilate is a second-rate duplicate, re-using material from the trial before the high priest, out of which it was manufactured.'

The *New Catholic Encyclopaedia*, produced by the Catholic University of America at Washington in 1967, concedes that most 'of the biblical writings underwent considerable re-editing and interpolation before final publication. Thus the authorship was much more of a group activity than was once thought.' It will make matters simpler to concentrate on the versions that emerged at the end of the 2nd century AD, and would be accepted a century later as 'orthodox', than trying to establish which bits of them were written by whom.

Ironically, the first known New Testament canon (list of biblical works normally looked upon as 'orthodox' and acceptable) was actually compiled by one of the principal opponents of the Roman Church, a Gnostic named Marcion – and nothing gives a clearer picture of the clash between Gnostic beliefs and the teaching of the emergent, authoritarian 'orthodox' Church than the contents of Marcion's canon and the personal consequences for him.

Marcion was the most active and influential Christian teacher in the first half of the 2nd century AD. Our main – almost only – source of information about him comes from the writings of his enemies, among them Justin Martyr, Irenaeus, Tertullian and Epiphaneus, 'orthodox' churchmen of his time or later. They are also the source of what we know about Marcion's canon, the first version of a New Testament to be put down in writing.

It appears that Marcion, who came originally from Pontus in Asia Minor, arrived in Rome, as a Christian, in the late 130s AD. Within a matter of a few years – about AD 140 – his views had so outraged the Roman Church that he was excommunicated. This was hardly surprising. He did not accept the Old Testament, which formed an important element of the scriptures of the early Roman Church, as part of Christian belief. He recognized Paul, not Peter, as the only true apostle, to whom Christ committed his gospel, and dismissed the Jerusalem apostles as false apostles. In addition, he considered that the 'orthodox' Church had falsified and corrupted the true gospel, which the Gnostics alone preserved in its pure form.

The canon of Marcion consisted of two parts: a gospel of Christ, identical in many respects to Luke's gospel; and a gospel of the Apostle, 10 of the 14 letters of Paul that are to be found in today's New Testament. Four letters of Paul are excluded that deal with a pastor's work, Timothy I and II, Titus and Hebrews, and the last two chapters of Romans. He also rearranged the order of those letters he used, with Galatians, including the account of Paul's conversion, initiation in Sinai and two visits to Jerusalem, placed first. As a result he was not only excommunicated but was later accused of having 'doctored' Luke's gospel by excising from it any details that did not accord with his Gnostic beliefs.

We do not find in Marcion's gospel any reference to Jesus having lived, suffered and died at the time of Pontius Pilate. Some of the principal details missing include: the Annunciation; Mary and Joseph's journey to Bethlehem; the date and place of the birth of Jesus; the family visiting Jerusalem on their way to Nazareth; the return to Jerusalem when Jesus was 12 and preached in the Temple; the mission of John the Baptist and his baptism of Jesus; Satan's temptation of Jesus in the wilderness; Jesus's mother and brothers coming to see him while he was preaching; the importance of Peter as the 'rock' on which the Church would be built; the warning by one of the Pharisees that Herod wished to kill Jesus; Jesus telling the twelve apostles that they were going to Jerusalem; the journey to Jerusalem via the Mount of Olives; the Last Supper; Jesus praying alone on the Mount of Olives; the arrest of Jesus; Peter's threefold denial of him; the Jews insisting on his condemnation when Pilate wished to free him; the Crucifixion; *and* the physical resurrection of Jesus. All of these, and other details, are also absent from Paul's writings as well as absent from the Gnostic gospels found at Nag Hammadi.

Despite excommunication, Marcion continued his evangelical work. Justin Martyr, the early Church Father, was the first to mention him. Writing *c*. AD 150 he conceded that Marcion had made disciples among men of many nations and was still teaching. More than 1,700 years, however, were to elapse before Marcion was cleared of the charge of having falsified Luke's gospel to conform with his own beliefs. At the end of the 18th century scholars challenged this theory, on the grounds that Marcion's work was not only substantially shorter, but had appeared before any example of Luke's gospel. They therefore came to the conclusion that it was the Lucan authors who had *added* to Marcion's canon in order to make it conform to what had become the 'orthodox' view of the life of Jesus in the 1st century AD.

The second element in Marcion's canon – the Pauline letters, and his teaching that Paul was the only true apostle – proved a more difficult problem. Paul, still remembered as an early Christian leader, was a popular figure with many branches of the Church, and his epistles enjoyed wide circulation, even in Rome itself. In the circumstances it was not possible to repudiate Paul simply because of his Gnostic views. His epistles were therefore included in the 'orthodox' New Testament canon of the Church, established by degrees in the second half of the 2nd century AD. However, at the same time, the Book of Acts appeared, dedicated in part, as we saw in a previous chapter, to stressing that the role of Paul in the life of the early Church was minor compared with that of Peter.

The first 'orthodox' list, which introduced non-Pauline material, was produced in the second half of the 2nd century AD. Irenaeus, Bishop of Lyon, writing about AD 180 in his book *Against Heresies*, lists 22 writings that were looked upon as canonical in Rome from that date. They included the four gospels, the Book of Acts and 13 of Paul's letters (not including the one to the Hebrews). Irenaeus also cites a book called Shepherd of Hermas with the formula 'scripture says', indicating that Christian writings absent from today's canon were accepted as scripture at that time.

Origen, the brilliant 3rd-century theologian briefly discussed earlier in this book, made a slightly different list. This was followed by yet another list, compiled by Eusebius (*c*. AD 260–340), the great Church historian, which had minor differences from Origen's. Eusebius divided the books into three categories: acknowledged (the four gospels, Book of Acts, the 13 Pauline letters excluding Hebrews, I Peter, I John, Revelation); disputed (II Peter, II and III John, Hebrews, James and Jude); and false (a number of books, including Shepherd of Hermas, that were still in circulation).

The present 'orthodox' canon, to which nothing may be added and from which nothing may be taken away, is made up of the 27 books in the acknowledged and disputed lists compiled by Eusebius and, as we saw, was given formal recognition by the third Council of Carthage in North Africa, held in AD 397. In more recent times even the *Gospel of Thomas*, discovered in the hidden Gnostic library at Nag Hammadi in 1945, has been rejected by the Vatican as heretical.

The four gospels need to be examined on two levels, as pseudo-historical works and as evangelical works, designed to preach the basic Christian message – Christ has died, Christ has risen, Christ will come again.

It is in the gospel of Mark that we find the first account of Simon's change of name by Jesus: 'And Simon he surnamed Peter' (Mark 3:16). Peter (Greek *petros*) is derived from *petra* meaning 'rock'. This reported change of name is used by Matthew in his account of the founding of the Roman Church: '. . . thou art Peter, and upon this rock I will build my church; and the gates of hell shall not prevail against it. And I will give unto thee the keys of the kingdom of heaven: and whatsoever thou shalt bind on earth shall be bound in heaven: and whatsoever thou shalt loose on earth shall be loosed in heaven . . .' (16:18,19). In passing it is worth making the point that nobody has been able to explain why, if Jesus lived in Palestine and spoke Aramaic, he should have given his principal disciple a Greek name.

Some of the historical inaccuracies we examined in the second section of this book – the era of King Herod and the priest Caiaphas, and the claim that Jesus 'suffered under Pontius Pilate' – are consequences of establishing Jesus and Peter as contemporaries. The curious account of the betrayal of Jesus by Judas Iscariot also appears to have its roots in political events in Galilee in the early years of the Christian era. The narrative tells us that Christ had been in Jerusalem for days prior to his arrest, teaching in the Temple. The Jewish authorities could therefore have laid hands upon him whenever they wanted to. It is not possible to justify their failure to do so by arguing that they feared the anger of the people: only a day later, after Jesus had been arrested and imprisoned, these same people are said to have refused to have him set free, demanding instead that he be crucified. No mention of Judas as the betrayer is to be found in any of the Epistles, indicating that the attribution of this act to him was a later interpretation of events.

On the evidence available it would seem that Judas, who is never mentioned by Paul in his epistles, is based upon the character of a Jewish leader, a Galilean named Judas who led a political rebellion over taxation against the Romans and the Jerusalem authorities in AD 6, the year in which, according to the Gospel of Luke, Mary and Joseph made their way to register in Bethlehem where Jesus was born. From the time of Judas's rebellion Galilee had remained notorious for its opposition to both Roman and Jerusalem authorities. It is thought that Mark placed the mission of Jesus in Galilee – he does not appear in Judaea until he went there to meet his end

– because it would make it easier to accept the conflict between him and the authorities as a political reality of the time. However, Mark does not appear to have been acquainted with the geographical scene: no mention is found of the main towns of Galilee, there is no convincing topographical background, and the scholar G. A. Wells has made the point in his book *Did Jesus Exist?* that 'the link with Galilee, because it is invention, remained thin; just as the conflict with the Jerusalem authorities remained implausible'.

Furthermore, Iscariot has been taken as indicating the location to which Judas belonged. This is not the correct meaning. As the corresponding Greek verb means 'to deliver up', the word can only have been used in the betrayal story as an epithet, 'Judas the Deliverer'. This meaning is reinforced by the fact that the Syrian *skariot* is an epithet equivalent to the Hebrew *sikkarti*, 'I shall deliver up'.

As to the evangelical aspects of their gospels, it is evident that all of the authors involved, who cannot have been eye witnesses of the events they were describing, relied on an earlier common source and a variety of traditions for their accounts: Israelite and Egyptian traditions; references to the Messiah in the prophetic books of the Old Testament; the practices of the Essenes and their beliefs; Paul's references to a Judaeo-Christian community at Jerusalem; the life and death of John the Baptist (never mentioned, incidentally, in any of the New Testament epistles), who preached that the end of days was near; Q (as we saw earlier, from *Quelle*, the German for 'source'), a collection of sources attributed to Jesus; the claim by John the Baptist's followers that they had seen the risen Christ; the Judas rebellion; an account of a prophet who came out of Egypt, gathered his disciples at the Mount of Olives, threatened to destroy Jerusalem and rebelled against the Temple priests; and an established Gnostic theology, preached by Paul, regarding salvation through the death and resurrection of Jesus Christ, represented by the Egyptian cross, the *ankh*, the symbol of life (this will be discussed in greater detail later).

The naming of Bethlehem as the birthplace of Jesus was simply the result of a desire to demonstrate fulfillment of one of the Old Testament prophecies. There was a strong Jewish tradition that the Christ would be born as a descendant of King David, who was believed by the Jews to have been born at Bethlehem in Judaea. Therefore, both Matthew and Luke, who provide accounts of the nativity of Jesus, give his place of birth as Bethlehem; and Matthew (2:5) cites the account in Micah (5:2) in support of his statement.

In his book *The Enigma of Jesus* the French scholar P. L. Couchoud traced the Old Testament roots of many of the chief events found in gospel accounts of the life and death of Jesus, with the tense changed when it suited the author's purpose:

The Virgin Birth. '. . . Behold a virgin shall conceive, and bear a son, and shall call his name Immanuel' (Isaiah 7:14).

The Birth of Jesus at Bethlehem. 'But thou, Bethlehem Ephratah, though thou be little among the thousands of Judah, yet out of thee shall he come forth unto me that is to be ruler in Israel . . .' (Micah 5:2).

The Star in the East. '. . . there shall come a Star out of Jacob, and a sceptre shall rise out of Israel . . .' (Numbers 24:17).

The Magi. '. . . all they from Sheba shall come: they shall bring gold and incense; and they shall shew forth the praises of the Lord' (Isaiah 60:6).

The Flight into Egypt. 'When Israel was a child, then I loved him, and called my son out of Egypt' (Hosea 11:1).

The Passion. 'But he was wounded for our transgressions, he was bruised for our iniquities . . .' (Isaiah 53:5).

The Crucifixion between Two Thieves. '. . . he was numbered with the transgressors; and he bare the sin of many, and made intercession for the transgressors' (Isaiah 53:12).

The Scourging. 'I gave my back to the smiters, and my

cheeks to them that plucked off the hair: I hid not my face from shame and spitting' (Isaiah 50:6).

Jesus's Last Cry. 'My God, my God, why has thou forsaken me . . .?' (Psalms 22:1).

The Crucifixion. '. . . they pierced my hands and my feet' (Psalms 22:16).

The Casting of Lots for His Garments. 'They part my garments among them, and cast lots upon my vesture' (Psalms 22:18).

The Scene at the Cross. 'All they that see me laugh me to scorn: they shoot out the lip, they shake the head, saying, He trusted in the Lord that he would deliver him: let him deliver him, seeing he delighted in him' (Psalms 22:7–8).

Even in the story of the birth of Jesus we find another example of the extent to which the gospels rely on the Old Testament for their content. The Old Testament does not provide any details of the birth of Jesus; Matthew therefore adapted the Old Testament account of events surrounding the birth of Moses, with Herod instead of Pharaoh ordering the death 'of all children from two years old and under', and Jesus laid in a manger where Moses was found among the bullrushes at the edge of the Nile.

The nature of Jesus's mission is also reflected in the Songs of Isaiah, which the Qumran Essenes interpreted as referring to their Teacher of Righteousness. In the *Hymn Scroll*, one of the Dead Sea manuscripts containing Psalms in the first person, 'the Psalmist (the Teacher) repeatedly applies Isaiah's Servant Songs to himself, as Christian writers were to apply them to Jesus a century later'. For instance, both the Psalmist and Jesus declare themselves to be the person whom Isaiah says (61:1–2) was 'sent to bring good tidings to the humble . . . to proclaim the year of the Lord's favour . . . to console the afflicted' (repeated in Luke 4:16,22). In the *Hymn Scroll* the Psalmist repeatedly appears as 'the man of sorrows, overwhelmed by blows and sickness, despised and rejected'. The Qumran Essenes, like John the Baptist, were talking of the anointed Christ, a Saviour who would return on the Day of Judgement when the world came to an end.

The extent to which the New Testament draws upon the Old Testament was the subject of a whole chapter of the first volume of *The Expansion of Christianity in the First Three Centuries*, a monumental work by Adolf von Harnack, the German scholar, published in New York as long ago as 1904. He wrote: 'The Old Testament did exert an influence which brought it (Christianity) to the verge of becoming the religion of a book . . . the New Testament as a whole did not generally play the same role as the Old Testament in the mission and practice of the Church . . . From the Old Testament it could be proved that the appearance and the entire history of Jesus had been previously predicted' – I say 'recorded' – 'hundreds and even thousands of years ago, and further, that the founding of the New People, which was to be fashioned out of all nations upon earth, had from the very beginning been prophesied and prepared for.'

It is now becoming accepted that *not one* of the four evangelists who wrote the canonical gospels was himself an actual witness of the events he describes. However, they had access to, and used, a variety of sources, including the Greek translation of the Old Testament, produced in Alexandria in the 3rd century BC. Moreover, many aspects of their gospels were not meant to be taken literally, but rather symbolically or allegorically. Their prime concern was proclamation of the hidden truth about Christ. For this reason the gospel texts, in their original form, did not contain historical data or geographical locations. It was only later that such details were added by Church editors to provide a historical setting. This can be seen clearly from the Gnostic gospels found at Nag Hammadi which contain none of the historical characters or geographical locations found in the canonical gospels.

Today, thousands of copies of the New Testament, including the four gospels, exist – about 5,000 in Greek alone

– and date from the 2nd to the 16th century AD. No two are exactly alike in all particulars. The state of flux in the Christian Church in its earliest years is reflected in the fact that most of the variations date from the 2nd or 3rd centuries AD. Scribes sometimes changed their manuscripts to accord with what was becoming looked upon increasingly as 'orthodox' belief, either by inserting their Christology into a text that lacked it or modifying a text that could be taken to support contrary views. The present 'orthodox' canon, consisting of 27 books of the Old and New Testament, to which nothing may be added and nothing taken away, did not receive formal recognition until the third Council of Carthage in North Africa, held in AD 397.

Chapter Twenty-two

The Roots of Messianic Belief

One of the important influences in shaping modern Christianity was the fusion of two theologies, Israelite and Egyptian. It is essential that we understand what earlier peoples believed in order to appreciate the contribution made by their beliefs to the emergence of 'orthodox' Christianity. At the heart of the teaching of Moses, as of Akhenaten, was the existence of only one God. The Egyptians worshipped a plethora of gods, but Messianic beliefs, the promise of eternal life and the importance to salvation of the rite of baptism were age-old Egyptian concepts.

The basis of Egyptian salvation beliefs was the divine nature that Egyptians attributed to their kings. From the 4th Dynasty (the 27th century BC), the king was looked upon as the human Son of Ra, the cosmic god. The king's actions were seen as being the fulfilment of his father's commands. This special relationship between the god Ra and the king was manifested in the three principal events in the ruler's life – his holy birth, his anointing at the time of his coronation and his resurrection after his death.

The holy birth of the king is documented not only in texts but in scenes found on the north wall of the central colonnade of Queen Hatshepsut's mortuary temple at Deir el-Bahari and in the hall built by Amenhotep III in his temple at Luxor. Siegfried Morenz, the German Egyptologist, makes the point in his book *Egyptian Religion* that

in both cases the procreation and birth of the king concerned are depicted as proceeding from the union

between the national god (Amun-Ra) and the consort of
the ruling Pharaoh: God, in the guise of the Pharaoh, is
shown approaching the woman thus blessed. The
images and text depict the scene with a fine delicacy, yet
dwell frankly upon the act of sexual union. There is
nothing here of that ascetic spiritual treatment so
characteristic of the late Hellenistic age, which led to
the Christian idea of the miraculous birth of Jesus.

At the time of his coronation the ruler became the bearer of
the divine kingly office. The coronation ceremony included
purification by water, anointing, putting on royal attire,
holding the sceptre of office, having the crowns of the Two
Lands (black and red) placed on his head and declaration of
his fixed royal names and titles. The king was anointed, not
with oil, but with the fat of the holy crocodile. Here we find
the original source of the word Messiah. *MeSeH* was the
word for crocodile in Ancient Egypt, and the image of two
crocodiles was used for the title of sovereign, bestowed on
the king at the time of his coronation.

The final decisive event in the ruler's life was his death
and resurrection. Having entered the world of the divine at
his coronation, a king ceased to belong to the human world
at the time of his death. He was said to have 'become Osiris',
the Egyptian god of the underworld. From the moment of
death the Osiris-king was believed to share eternal spiritual
existence with the gods.

As I have already pointed out, it was an essential part of
Egyptian belief that, while the spiritual element left the body
at death, it would return at some point in the future if the
body could be kept safe and protected by magic formulas.
That is why Egyptians devoted such care to mummification
and to securing their tombs. Veneration of Osiris has been
traced to as early as the 27th century BC, the time of the
builders of the pyramids. He was looked upon as an ancient
king, slain on a Friday (like the Jesus of the New Testament)
by his brother Seth, who dismembered his body in order to

deny him a second life. However, his wife Isis was able to collect his remains and, using a magic ritual, assemble his body again and restore him to life after three days (again like Jesus) – not on earth but in the underworld, where, physically resurrected, he became the god and judge of the dead.

The *Pyramid Texts*, carved on the walls of some pyramid burial chambers, contain the recitation by the priests to Osiris: 'This, Osiris, is thy son. Thou hast caused him to flourish and live. He lives, this king lives . . . he has not perished . . . he endures, this king endures.' The scholar J. Gwyn Griffiths comments in his book *The Origins of Osiris and his Cult*: 'These words, and others like them, are of some significance in human history, for they are the earliest expressions in literature of a belief in life after death.'

Initially the promise of eternal life was confined to kings and nobles because only they could afford the expensive burial rite. From the time following Tutankhamun's death in the latter years of the 18th Dynasty, however, a long process of change in the Osiris theology resulted in the emergence of the cult of Serapis, whose followers could partake of the promise of eternal life *without* the need for mummification, if they confessed belief in the deity and went through an initiation ritual. As a result, the Serapis cult, open to the poor as well as the rich, became the most popular religion in Egypt and eventually replaced other cults as the official religion of the state.

The cult of Serapis was based initially on two Egyptian gods – Osiris and Apis, the sacred bull of Memphis – from whom its name is derived. Apis, originally associated with the ancient god Ptah of Memphis, later became linked with Osiris. From that time the death of the Apis bull became an important event. He was given an official funeral in the presence of a congregation of worshippers who brought him gifts from every part of the country. The Apis bull was believed to enjoy eternal life in the sense that he was reborn as soon as he died. Priests searched the fields for the replacement Apis, which could be identified by a black spot on the forehead, neck and back. Once he was found, rejoicing replaced mourning and the divine calf was installed in his sacred stall at Memphis with his mother, surrounded with a lowing harem.

When they died, Apis bulls were buried in the sub-terranean galleries of the Serapeum at Memphis. It was served by voluntary monks and included a 'sanatorium', visited by the sick in the hope of receiving miraculous cures.

The Serapis cult dated from the Ptolemy dynasty in pre-Christian Egypt. The city of Alexandria had been founded, three centuries before the start of the Christian era, by Alexander the Great, King of Macedonia (an ancient country in south-east Europe), after his conquest of Egypt. It was ruled over subsequently by the Ptolemies until 30 BC when Cleopatra (who had earlier put her brother, Ptolemy XIII, to death) ended her own life by thrusting an asp into her bosom, after her rebellion against Rome with her lover Mark Antony had ended in defeat at the naval battle of Actium. Egypt then came under Roman rule.

In the intervening centuries, Alexandria, the Ptolemies' capital, had become a cosmopolitan city and the cultural centre of the civilized world, a distinction it continued to hold even after the political supremacy of Rome had been established. Large numbers of immigrants had arrived in Egypt – Graeco-Macedonian military veterans, rewarded for their service with rich farmland, Asians, Jews, Syrians and Libyans. These communities intermarried with Egyptians and with each other, creating a society whose traditions and religious beliefs led to a mixed culture. Early in this process of integration, Ptolemy I Soter (*c.* 304–284 BC) introduced, as an official religion and unifying belief for his multi-racial subjects, the Egyptian cult of Serapis (sometimes spelt Sarapis), with the help of Manetho, the Egyptian priest of Heliopolis.

Ptolemy I Soter was a tireless worker in the cause of spreading Egyptian culture throughout the Graeco-Roman

Alexandria in early Christian times

world. As a result the cult of the god Serapis spread swiftly from Alexandria to Greece and Italy and, with the passage of time, found its expression as a 'holy' family made up of Osiris, his wife Isis and their hawk-headed son Horus. In the first half-century of the Christian era the cult was far and away the most popular Egyptian religion in Rome, which had had a Serapis temple as early as 105 BC. The appeal of Serapis, who had inherited many of the attributes of Osiris, including mastery over the underworld, and the mystic rites of Isis, to which women as well as men were admitted after an initiation ceremony, rested mainly upon the explicit promise of immortality that they offered to adherents. Isis herself was seen as a tragic Madonna-like figure who had endured the tribulations of all women.

The authorities took a more jaundiced view. All things Egyptian had been particularly unpopular in Roman corridors of power since the rebellion of Mark Antony and Cleopatra. In AD 19, when Tiberius banished 4,000 freedmen of military age to Sardinia, they included worshippers of Serapis as well as Jews, and the emperor destroyed a temple of Isis and had a statue of her thrown into the Tiber. However, her cult and that of Serapis survived to become important elements in the development of early Christianity.

The cults of Serapis and Isis did not merely survive the emergence of Christianity, but in the 2nd century AD actually increased in popularity. A large number of new sanctuaries are known to have been constructed, accompanied by a massive increase in votive inscriptions compared with those in the previous two centuries. Christianity and the pagan cults existed comfortably side by side at this early stage in the Christian era and were frequently seen as interchangeable. Christians made no distinction between Christ and Serapis and frequently worshipped both. In AD 134, after a visit to Alexandria, the Emperor Hadrian wrote a letter to his elderly brother-in-law, Servianus, in which he commented: 'So you praise Egypt, my very dear Servianus! I know the land from top to bottom, a fickle, tricky land, blown about by every wind of rumour. In it the worshippers of Serapis are Christians, and those who call themselves Bishops of Christ pay their vows to Serapis . . . Whenever the patriarch himself comes to Egypt he is made to worship Serapis by some and Christ by others.'*

---

* New archaeological findings show that the ascetics of Serapis were healers like the Therapeutae. References have been found in fragments of papyri (*Acad. Des Inscript. Et belles-letters, mem. present. Pardivers savants*, 1st series, ii 1852, pp. 552 ff.; *Bibliotheque Imperiale, notices et extraits des mss., t. 18. 1858*, pp. 261 ff.) to some ascetics who were consecrated to the cult of Serapis at Memphis (*c.* 165 BC). These recluses, known by the name

It is easy to understand this dual perception once the account of the life, suffering and death of Jesus in the 1st century AD began to spread. His story and that of Osiris are very similar (it should be noted that Serapis assimilated the qualities of both Osiris and Horus, and replaced them in relation to Isis). Both were presented as saviours to whom men and women could turn for assurance of immortality. In *The Origins of Osiris and his Cult*, the scholar J. Gwyn Griffiths makes the point that, in the case of Osiris and the kings and nobles whose bodies had been preserved by mummification, death was looked upon as a form of sleep, the expectation being that the preserved body would rise again.†

'possessed of Serapis', lived in the temple or a dependent building. They came to obtain a cure, or an oracle by the rite of incubation, for Serapis was a god of healing. It is clear, therefore, that asceticism entered into Egyptian life long before the rise of monasticism. Some scholars have even claimed that Pachomius, the founder of Egyptian cenobitism in the mid-3rd century AD, was himself a monk of Serapis (E. Revillout, *Revue Egyptol.*, 1880, p. 160; G. Grutzmacher, *Pachomius und das Ulteste Klosterleben*, pp. 39 ff.). According to one of the Coptic texts, in the Boharic dialect, St Pachomius, the founder of Christian cenobitism, had been a monk of Serapis, which is also confirmed in an Arabic text (*Annales du Musee Guimet*, xvii. 6 ff., 342 ff.). Following the destruction of the Serapeum in 391, the priests of Serapis declared that the god had ascended to heaven, and joined the Christian Church (Plate 32) (*The Cambridge Ancient History*, v. 13, 1998, p. 635).

† Mummification was introduced by the Egyptians, as they believed that human beings consist of two elements, one physical and one spiritual. If they could preserve the physical body, one day in the future the *Ka* spirit would return to it. That is why they mummified their dead and built secured tombs, placing protective magical spells within them. Only the kings and the rich could hope for the afterlife, since they alone could afford the expensive burial costs. Christianity became so popular because, by contrast, it offered the promise of afterlife to *everyone* baptized in the belief of the risen Christ. However, this belief in the afterlife was mainly Egyptian; none of the other ancient nations had it. The Hebrews believed that death was the end of life, and neither Moses nor Akhenaten had anything to say about spiritual life after death. This explains why neither the Hebrews nor any other ancient peoples practised mummification.

He goes on to say: 'At the same time we are familiar in Christian teaching with resurrection applied to the body, either in the sense that the present body will rise again after death or that a new ethereal body will be given to the believer. The former of these senses is closer to the Osirian belief. To this extent the use of the term resurrection is not entirely misleading. Indeed, the comparison of sleep to death is also found occasionally in Christian thought, as in Ephesians 5:14: ". . . Awake thou that sleepest, and arise from the dead, and Christ shall give thee light"'.

Survival of the ancient Egyptian cult of Serapis alongside Christianity is also made particularly clear in the fanciful novel *The Golden Ass* by Lucius Apuleius, a Platonist, educated in Carthage, Athens and Rome. In his introduction to the 1956 edition of the book, the late Anglo-Irish poet Louis MacNeice recalls that Apuleius, who was born about 120 AD, had 'a foot in both worlds, as was natural when rival mystery religions were fighting for man's allegiance while traditional paganism and the rationalistic philosophies were alike out of the running', and that the early Church Fathers 'detested him'.

His novel recounts the various adventures and mis-adventures of Apuleius after he is by magic transformed into a donkey, which is restored to human form at the end of the book through the merciful intervention of Isis and Serapis. The goddess appears to Apuleius, explains that she is known by many names – Minerva, Venus, Diana, Proserpina, Ceres, Juno, Bellona, Hecate – 'and the Egyptians, which are excellent in all kinds of ancient doctrine, and by their proper ceremonies accustomed to worship me, do call me Queen Isis'.

After daybreak, Apuleius made his way to take part in a religious ceremony where the congregation included 'blowers of trumpets, which were dedicated unto Serapis' and various priests, one of whom accompanied 'a vessel wrought with a round bottom, having on one side pictures figured like unto the manner of the Egyptians'. Once the great priest had restored

Apuleius to human form, he told him: 'Behold, Lucius, thou art delivered from so great miseries by the providence of the goddess Isis . . . make thyself one of this holy order . . . take upon thee a voluntary yoke of ministry.'

Apuleius goes on to describe how he travelled to Rome where his greatest desire was 'daily to make my prayers to the sovereign goddess Isis . . . continually adored by the people of Rome' and increased his religious involvement by becoming a minister to Osiris, 'the sovereign father of all the goddesses', as well as Isis: 'I frequented the sacrifices of Serapis, which were done in the night, which thing gave me great comfort.' Finally, 'the great god Osiris appeared to me in the night, not disguised in any other form, but in his own essence, commanding me that I should be an advocate in the court, and not fear the slander and envy of ill persons, which bear me . . . grudge by reason of my doctrine'.

Apuleius also confirms that the promise of resurrection was contained in the rites of Isis. They assured the *mystae* (followers) that they would see and venerate the goddess in their after-lives. This is an obvious parallel with Christians' expectations that they will see God in the next world: 'Blessed are the pure in heart: for they shall see God' (Matthew 5:8).

As 'orthodox' Christianity spread, the temple of Serapis, built by Ptolemy I in Alexandria, which contained a huge statue of the god in the same style as was used later for representations of Christ in Coptic churches, became the centre for Serapis worship. Paintings of Isis with her son Horus became identified by Christians as portraits of Mary with her son Jesus (Plates 24 and 25). The rite of baptism, part of the initiation ceremony of the Serapis cult, was also adopted by the Church as part of the Christian initiation ceremony, and still survives today.

In an article in the *Journal of Egyptian Archaeology* of 1950, Sir Alan Gardiner, the British Egyptologist, argued that Egyptian baptism should be seen as analogous to later Christian baptism. He cited 36 scenes, one of which is in the

Vatican Museum, that showed different Pharaohs being baptized ritually with water. Similar representations are found in the funerary cult in the tombs of dead nobles or Osirianized kings (meaning they had become one with Osiris). Of the similarity between the two forms of baptism Sir Alan commented: 'In both cases a symbolic cleansing by means of water serves as initiation into a properly legitimated religious life.'

In Hatshepsut's temple at Deir el-Bahri and Amenhotep III's at Luxor their holy birth scenes show the infants being baptized. The accompanying text reads: 'Be pure together with thy ka (soul) . . . thou living [eternally].' In all of these scenes the water being poured from the pitcher on to the head of the person being baptized is depicted as a stream of *ankhs*, the Egyptian symbol of life.

In baptismal practice it was the custom to use, whenever possible, the annual summer flood water of the Nile, looked upon as a sacred life-giving element that also ensured prosperity, fertility and family well-being. With increasing sophistication in engineering matters it became the custom to create a symbolic Nile flood by arranging a system of pipes through which such 'living' water – that is, flowing water – flowed into the basin to be used in the ceremony.

Even as late as the 6th century AD, Christians regarded – as the followers of Serapis had – the summer flood waters of the Nile as having special properties. Those who lived close enough used to gather on the river bank to bless and collect the water when the Nile began its annual rise. Those who lived too far away would bless a basin of water as a substitute for the actual river. The importance of using 'living' water was retained by early Christians. The most suitable water was considered to be water found at springs, in rivers or by the sea. With the spread of Christianity, however, it became less common to conduct baptisms out of doors. Yet care was taken to preserve the old Egyptian practice of using 'living' water by arranging a system of pipes through which the baptismal water could flow.

In later centuries Christians forgot the ancient tradition of the significance of 'living' Nile water for the baptismal rite. Even so, the water used is contained in a 'font' – symbolic of a spring of flowing water or a fount – and the symbol of 'living' water is maintained by pouring it over the head of the person being baptized.

Obelisks – originally solar symbols connected with the cult of the sun – provide a further indication of the affinity between ancient Egyptian beliefs, and what may be described as the second variant of the Christian Church, during these early centuries. Thirteen obelisks, transported from Egypt, are to be found in Rome compared with only eight elsewhere in the world. The largest of the Roman collection – more than 100 feet tall and weighing over 400 tons – stands in the piazza of San Giovanni, a cathedral in the Laterano area of Rome (Plate 35). Stone for the giant obelisk had been quarried 18 centuries earlier by Tuthmosis III (David) at Aswan. At a period of growing fusion between worship of Ra and Amun, the state god whose capital was at Thebes in Upper Egypt, the obelisk was erected in the great temple at neighbouring Karnak, where it was a major cult object.

The Laterano obelisk (see Plate 35) was a gift to Rome by Constantine the Great, initiated in AD 326, 14 years after his conversion to Christianity. Constantine did not see any contradiction between presenting this pagan symbol to Rome and his Christian beliefs. The *New Catholic Encyclopaedia* explains that until he died, he '. . . continued [using] the Sol Invictus (the sun-god unsubdued) . . . legends on his coinage and monuments . . . Besides, the *Sol Invictus* had been adopted by the Christians in a Christian sense, as demonstrated in the Christ as Apollo-Helios' – an image of Christ in the form of Apollo – 'in a mausoleum discovered (*c.* AD 250) beneath St Peter's in the Vatican.'

In view of its enormous size it is not surprising that, when Constantine died in AD 337, the Laterano obelisk had travelled no further than the port of Alexandria. It remained there for another 20 years before Constantius II, the son of Constantine the Great, finally presented his gift to Rome in AD 357. An account of the final delivery, written by the contemporary historian Ammianus Marcellinus indicates clearly that by his action the emperor was moving the religious centre of the world from Egypt to Rome: 'Constantine . . . [had torn] the huge mass from its foundations, and rightly thought that he was committing no sacrilege if he took this marvel from one temple and consecrated it at Rome – that is to say, in the temple of the whole world.'

Chapter Twenty-three

The Creed

One of the principal concerns of the early Church Fathers, having sought to establish their apostolic succession through Peter, had been to lay down a Creed. Such a Creed was needed to unify widely scattered communities whose competing groups were advocating rival theologies and supporting different understandings of Christianity. It was also required to combat the teaching of their principal opponents, the Gnostics, who, as we have seen, did not accept the distinction between priests and laity; looked upon the Virgin Birth as the emanation of the Saviour from God the Father as a spirit, not as a physical birth from a human mother; denied that Jesus was crucified at the time of the Roman Empire,* claiming instead that he had lived many centuries earlier; regarded the Resurrection as having been spiritual, not physical, suggesting that it is to be understood symbolically, not literally; and claimed that they had their own secret sources of apostolic tradition, separate from those of Jerusalem.

The Nag Hammadi documents do not provide details of this apostolic tradition. However, the writings of Paul make

---

* No mention is found in any of the Nag Hammadi texts of Jesus Christ being crucified by Pontius Pilate. As emphasis, it is worth repeating a passage (already given in Chapter 18) from the *Apocalypse of Peter* 81–82, which denies the New Testament account in this regard: 'The Saviour said to me, "He whom you saw on the tree, glad and laughing, this is the living Jesus. But this one into whose hands and feet they drive nails is his fleshly part, which is the substitute being put to shame, the one who came into being in his likeness. But look at him and me." '

it evident that he, too, recognized apostles who, like himself, had had visions of Jesus but had no link with those of Jerusalem. The New Testament itself offers evidence that teachers emerged from Egypt during the apostolic age to spread Paul's Gentile-Christian gospel in different parts of the Roman Empire. One was Apollos, who is mentioned several times in Paul's letters (I Corinthians 1:12 and 16:12, and Titus (3:13) as well as the Book of Acts (18:24)). According to Acts he was 'a native of Alexandria . . . [who] spoke and taught accurately the things concerning Jesus . . .' A variant of the Acts text mentions that Apollos had been instructed in Christianity in his homeland (that is, Egypt). Apollos arrived in Ephesus, the ancient Greek city in Asia Minor that became the centre of Christianity there, even before Paul, who found the Church already in existence when he arrived. Another passage in his letters shows that he and Apollos had both made Christian converts in Corinth, the ancient Greek city: '. . . one saith I am of Paul; and another, I am of Apollos . . . Who then is Paul, and who is Apollos, but ministers by whom ye believed . . .' (I Corinthians 3:4–5).

Although the early Church Fathers had looked to Peter as the source of their authority, they, like Paul, taught in the 1st century AD that the only confession of faith required of Christian converts was baptism combined with the confession that Jesus Christ rose from the dead. As Paul put it in his letter to the Romans: '. . . if thou shalt confess with thy mouth the Lord Jesus, and shalt believe in thine heart that God hath raised him from the dead, thou shalt be saved' (10:9).

The earliest attempt to lay down the basis of a Creed – and reinforce the story of the life, suffering and death of Jesus in the 1st century AD – was made by Ignatius of Antioch, an early Church Father, shortly before he was arrested during persecution of the Christians by the Emperor Trajan (*c.* AD 52–117), transported to Rome and thrown to the lions in AD 107. His quasi-creedal statements read in part: '. . . our Lord

. . . was truly of David's stock after the flesh, Son of God by the Divine power and will, begotten truly of the Virgin . . . truly nailed in the flesh on our behalf under Pontius Pilate, and Herod the tetrarch . . . through His resurrection He might set up an ensign . . . in the body of His Church'. This is the first time that Pontius Pilate is mentioned in connection with the death of Jesus, and also the first time that we have a statement that he was 'nailed'. The chief purpose of this quasi-creedal statement was to affirm a time and place for the death of Jesus, the way he died and his physical resurrection.

It was Irenaeus, among a number of 2nd century AD ecclesiastical writers, who argued that there could be only one Church, which must be 'orthodox' (that is, right-thinking), catholic (universal) and apostolic (Petrine), and that outside that Church 'there is no salvation'. He declared in his book *Against Heresies* that those of 'orthodox' belief would accept and follow the teaching of 'those who possess the succession from the apostles': 'Suppose a dispute concerning some important question arises among us; should we not have recourse to the most ancient churches, with which the apostles held continual intercourse, and learn from them what is clear and certain in regard to the present question?' He also argued that because of its apostolic tradition and the faith 'which comes down to our own time by means of the succession of the bishops . . . it is necessary that every church should agree with this church (the Church of Rome) on account of its pre-eminent authority'. Tertullian (*c*. AD 155–222), another of the early Church Fathers, condemned as heretics all who did not accept the bodily Resurrection of Jesus, including the Gnostics.

By the 3rd century AD the Church had become organized to the point where instructions were being given by the Church of Rome to all local branches, however small, that they were to be organized in a hierarchy consisting of one bishop and at least two elders (priests or officials) and three deacons. But what was 'orthodox' belief? Several variations of the earlier Creed had developed over the years. The first attempt to assemble a body of bishops representing the whole Christian Church resulted in the attendance of more than 300, who were urged by Constantine, presiding over the assembly at Nicaea, to decide on a common Creed. While the Nicene Creed that emerged preserved the basic structure of the earlier Creed, it elaborated its articles to exclude heretical interpretation – in particular the Arian heresy, which denied that Christ had been both true God and true man – and condemned anyone who refused to accept the literal truth of the Nicene Creed. The divinity of Christ was stressed by the insertion of such phrases as 'begotten of the Father' and 'true God of true God', and the Creed ended with the threat that 'the Catholic Church anathemizes' anyone who did not accept its contents.

Some minor modifications were made by an assembly of 150 bishops at the Council of Constantinople in AD 381. The phrase in the earliest Creed 'born from the Holy Spirit and the Virgin Mary', which had been omitted from the Nicene Creed, was restored with slightly different wording – 'was incarnate from the Holy Spirit and the Virgin Mary' – to protect the doctrine of the Third Person of the Trinity. The threat of being declared anathema was also excised. The result was basically the Creed that is still in use today, with some modernization of the language:

I believe in one God, the Father almighty, maker of heaven and earth, of all things visible and invisible; and in one Lord Jesus Christ, the only begotten Son of God, begotten of the Father before all ages; God of God, light of light, true God from true God; begotten not made; of one substance with the Father; through whom all things came into existence; Who because of our salvation came down from heaven, and was incarnate from the Holy Spirit and the Virgin Mary and became man, and was crucified for us under Pontius Pilate, and suffered and was buried, and rose again on the third day according to the Scriptures, and ascended to heaven, and sits on the right hand of the Father, and will come again with glory to judge the living and the dead, of Whose kingdom there will be no end; and I believe in the Holy Ghost, the Lord and life-giver, who proceeds from the Father, who with the Father and Son is together worshipped and together glorified, Who spoke through the prophets; in one holy Catholic and apostolic Church. I confess one baptism to the remission of sins; I look forward to the resurrection of the dead, and the life of the world to come.

By a happy coincidence, the myth that Jesus had been crucified at the time when Pontius Pilate was procurator of Judaea received fresh impetus when Helena, the mother of the Emperor Constantine, claimed to have discovered the 'true' Cross in Jerusalem in AD 325, the same year that her son summoned the bishops to Nicaea to discuss the matter of the Creed. This would have been a remarkable achievement. Historically, the 'true' Cross never existed. Furthermore, according to another tradition it had already been discovered three centuries earlier. Eusebius, Bishop of Caesarea, recorded the tradition in his 3rd-century history of the Church. As outlined earlier, the woman who found the 'true' Cross was said to have been Protonica, the wife of Claudius. The discovery was made, it was said, during the reign of Claudius's uncle, Tiberius, who ruled from AD 14 to 37. Protonica, a Christian convert, travelled from Rome to Jerusalem where St James showed her Golgotha, the hill on which, according to the New Testament, Jesus had been crucified. She found the 'true' Cross after forcing the Jews to hand the hill over to Christians. Subsequently, her daughter, who had accompanied Protonica to Jerusalem, died suddenly, but was restored miraculously to life when her corpse was put on the Cross. This apocryphal story is by tradition attributed to St James, who set it down in writing and sent it to the apostles.

At the time of Protonica's supposed discovery, the

Roman-Latin cross, as we have seen, had not yet been established as the symbol of Christ, and Christians – not yet known then as Christians, but as 'the way', the same term used by the Essenes – employed the *ankh*, the Egyptian cross, or a fish as their symbol. The Gnostics also used the *ankh*: it can be seen on the leather covers of some of the volumes in their Nag Hammadi library.

The tradition of Protonica's supposed finding of the 'true' Cross was not only mentioned by Eusebius but published later in *Doctrina Addai* (the teaching of Addai). According to Christian legend in Syria, Addai was one of 72 disciples of Jesus, who was sent by him to establish the Syrian branch of the Church. *Doctrina Addai*, which is considered apocryphal, came to light in the 4th century AD, which is perhaps significant as the story of Helena's discovery of the 'true' Cross in AD 325, although widely accepted as true, is clearly a replica of the Protonica legend. Helena is said to have gone at the age of 79 to Jerusalem where she, too, found the 'true' Cross as a result of an excavation at Golgotha. In *her* case, the genuineness of her discovery was demonstrated by the miraculous recovery of a crippled woman when she was stretched upon the Cross.

Helena deposited the main part of her find in a church erected over the spot at Golgotha. Of what remained, one portion was sent to Byzantium, the ancient Greek city on the Bosphorus that, as Constantinople, became the new capital of the Emperor Constantine in AD 328, and inserted in the head of a statue of Constantine, and another to Rome where a new church, Santa Croce (Holy Cross), was built to accommodate it. The popular acclaim for Helena's supposed discovery led to small fragments of her Cross – by now established as an essential element of 'orthodox' Christian belief as well as having historic validity – being sold, encrusted with gold and jewels, to rich believers who wished to own so priceless a relic.

Brisk demand resulted eventually in there being, in one form and another, sufficient relics of the 'true' Cross to

amount to several crosses. Today further relics are to be found in Roman Catholic churches throughout the world. An early solution was found to the problem of such a plethora of relics from a finite source: 'The miracle of the "multi-plication of the Cross" was devised so that the relic suffered no diminution (*et quasi intacta maneret* – and, as it were, remained intact)' (*Paulinus Epistula II ad Serverum*),* a form of relic usury.

Here it is instructive to note that at the beginning of the 19th century Edith L. Butcher, who worked with Sir Flinders Petrie, the father of modern archaeology, collected different forms of the Cross she found in Egypt. Petrie himself did the

* *The International Standard Bible Encyclopedia.*

same in Italy, and they published the result together. Mrs Butcher stated that:

> It is generally agreed that the use of a cross by Christians as a symbol of Christ the Redeemer did not come into general use until the time of Constantine. It seems to have been early in use by the Egyptians, who adopted a form of the ankh, the Egyptian hieroglyphic sign which is sometimes called 'the key of life', or 'the life of the world to come', as a link between the old faith and the new.
>
> When the great temple of Serapis was solemnly destroyed by the order of the Emperor Theodosius, there were laid bare certain characters which they called hieroglyphics, having the form of crosses. The Christians claimed these as evidence that the great building had once belonged to their faith. But some of the heathen converts to Christianity who could read the ancient writing, interpreted the inscription. They said that the character resembling the Cross signified in ancient days 'the life to come'.
>
> [*The Cross in Egypt*, by Edith L. Butcher,
> *The Cross in Italy*,
> by W. M. Flinders Petrie, London, 1916, p. 97]

Furthermore:

> The earliest Christian symbol (in Italy) which can be dated is not the Cross, but the XP monogram 'Chi Rho = CHR'. There is no question that this is the military labarum sign found on the Roman coinage as the standard, from Constantine onwards ... We should have expected the ensign to be a vertical cross in a circle; but this form does not appear in use until a century later ... The earliest example (of the XP monogram) as a Christian symbol is said to be of AD 323.
>
> [ibid. p. 102]

And:

. . . it is AD 380 that the (Roman) Cross appears on the coinage of Gratian.

[ibid. p. 104]

Constantine had become emperor in the west of the Roman Empire in AD 312 after defeating Maxentius, his rival and brother-in-law, at the battle of Milvian Bridge outside Rome. A year later, he and Licinius, the Emperor of the East, issued the Edict of Milan, which gave formal recognition to Christianity as one of the religions permitted in the Roman Empire. It appears from his letters and edicts that from then onward Constantine regarded himself as the chosen servant of The Highest Divinity, whom he identified as the God of the Christians. In the course of the next decade his legislation showed many signs of Christian influence. Bishops were given civilian powers. They could settle civil suits in which their decision was final. He made Sunday a public holiday, according to Christian practice.

It was not until AD 324 that Constantine became sole emperor when Licinius provoked a civil war by a renewed campaign of persecution of Christians in the East and was defeated in battle. From this point the increasing piety of Constantine saw him devote more and more of his time to his religious education, reading the scriptures and theological works, listening to sermons and himself delivering homilies to his court, and involving himself in the schisms that raged within the Church at the time. He spent lavishly on building churches at Rome, Constantinople, Antioch (ancient capital of the Macedonian kingdom of Syria) and the holy places in Palestine.

While tolerant of paganism in a half-hearted way, he destroyed a number of famous pagan temples, confiscated the treasures of others and stripped cult statues of their gold. His gifts of gold and land to the Church and his favourites, and his spending on a new capital, Constantinople (formerly

Byzantium and finally dedicated in May, AD 330), were on such a lavish scale that he was forced to introduce new taxes, one on senators as well as levies of gold and silver on tradesmen and craftsmen. He did not exclude himself from this munificence. In his declining years he became a bizarre figure who wore wigs of various colours and flowing robes of embroidered silk, and hung himself about with precious jewels.

Constantine was one of the fortunates. Death came in AD 337, at the age of 64, when he had moved to his Asia Minor palace in the suburbs of Nicomedia, hoping that the bracing air and warm baths would help to restore his failing health. His illness gave him the opportunity to join the body of the faithful formally through baptism, administered by his friend and confidant Bishop Eusebius.

If, as he lay dying, Constantine was familiar with the warning of Chrysostom, he cannot have felt optimistic about the size or brightness of his star. In the course of his life he is said to have been guilty, among other things, of the murder of Crispus, the only child of his marriage to the obscure Minervina. The murder is reputed to have been carried out at the instigation of Constantine's second wife, Fausta, who saw the successful and popular prince as a formidable rival to the ambitions she had for her own three sons by Constantine. It was followed by a bloodbath that earned the emperor comparison to Nero, the legendary persecutor of Christians in the 1st century AD. Constantine had also been responsible for the murder of Licinius after defeating him in the civil war, and later the murder of the son of Licinius, who was also named Licinius and Constantine's nephew; and – although some doubt exists in the matter – the murder of Fausta by having her suffocated by steam in a scalding bath.

All in all, Constantine, the first Christian to wear the imperial purple, has been condemned as a weak and vacillating ruler who had a violent temper, was driven by ambition, who could be both kind and appallingly cruel. In the treatment of his rivals he was both unscrupulous and ruthless. Nevertheless, his action in making Christianity the official religion of the Roman Empire, giving civil power to the Church and supporting it with his generous patronage, had momentous consequences for the future history of the world – even if it would be another 40 years before it began to become clear just how momentous these consequences would be.

Conclusion

As we can see now, the historical core of the Bible accounts, for both the Old and New Testaments, came from Egypt. All the main characters of the Bible are directly related to the Tuthmosside dynasty that ruled Egypt between the 15th and 14th centuries BC. David the King and Abraham the Patriarch were contemporaries, who shared the same wife, Sarah, and became the ancestors of the Israelite tribe, closely related to the Egyptian royal family. It was during this period, too, that the great revolution in our philosophical and religious understanding took place – when King Akhenaten could recognize one power behind all the different deities and heavenly manifestations in the light of Aten, or Adonai, and when his successor Tutankhamun could identify the spirit of man as being part of the eternal spirit of God.

But the world was not yet ready to see these visions. With the fall of the Amarna rule, the memory of both great leaders was officially suppressed in Egypt, and completely forgotten in Israel. While the Egyptians restored their old cults, the Israelites adopted new Canaanite deities such as Ashtaroth and Ba'al. Only during the Babylonian Exile in the 6th century BC, eight centuries after the death of their leader, did the Jewish scribes restore the name of Moses and his teaching, while still denying the violent death of Joshua his successor. The Egyptians, on the other hand, kept the memory of Tutankhamun alive by associating him with Osiris, Hermes and Serapis first, before they used the name 'Jesus' following the translation of the Bible into Greek in Alexandria. For Jesus is the Greek name given to Moses's successor in the Bible that was produced in the mid-3rd century BC.

Two similar, but separate, Messianic groups developed during the last centuries BC: the Jewish-Christian Essenes in Judaea and Jerusalem and the Gentile Gnostics of Egypt and Alexandria. While St Peter belonged to the Jerusalem community, St Paul was initiated into the Egyptian movement. The Jerusalem Church, however, was limited in number, about 4,000 in the 1st century AD, because it only converted members from within the Jewish community, before it disappeared completely in AD 70, following the Roman destruction of Jerusalem. It was the Egyptian Gentile Church, though, that spread all over the different parts of the Roman Empire.

The great success of the new Egyptian religious movement nevertheless represented a threat to the authority of Rome, which never stopped persecuting Egyptian Christians. Alexandria remained the main international religious centre, even when Rome controlled all the countries surrounding the Mediterranean. So when the Fathers of the Church of Rome wanted to establish a hierarchical ecclesiastical system under their authority, they were encouraged by the political power of Rome. In their need for a justification for their authority, the Roman Fathers claimed that Christ did appear physically to his disciples and not just in a spiritual form, and handed them this priestly authority as his representative on earth. As St Paul made it clear in his letter to the Galatians that his encounter with Christ was only spiritual, they chose Peter for this part. A miraculous explanation was given in the Book of Acts to allow Peter to escape from prison where Herod Antipas put him in AD 44, to be executed a few days after the Passover feast. This was followed by assurances given by the Roman Fathers that Peter came to Rome and handed its Church the authority he had obtained from Christ. This was the main reason for choosing Palestine for Jesus to appear in, as this was Peter's country. A time in December was fixed and a place in Bethlehem for his birth, and a crucifixion during the time of Pontius Pilate became part of the Creed.

Ptolemy I had established a new universal cult of Serapis and built the Serapeum in Alexandria to be its centre of worship. The translation of the books of the Old Testament into Greek which followed, where it became available for scholars, led to a philosophical and theological conflict between Egyptians and Jews, which resulted in the definition of a new Christian theology. As this development took place within the Serapeum, Temple and Library, this establishment became the centre for the new Gnostic Christian religion and philosophy. It was from this Alexandrian centre that Christianity reached Rome, as well as many other parts of the Roman Empire.

Nobody knows how the Church of Rome was established. Neither the Book of Acts nor the writings of the early Fathers explain how Christianity did get to Rome. As we saw before, Suetonius, the Roman historian, mentions the expulsion of followers of Chrestus from Rome, during the time of Emperor Claudius *c*. AD 40–50. This indicates that a flourishing Christian community did exist in Rome, even before St Paul went to Corinth or Ephesus in AD 49. By the time of Nero (AD 54–68), the Christian community in Rome was already of a considerable size. How did Christianity reach Rome at that very early date?

Only two routes could have been possible for Christianity to get there: from Judaea with Jewish slaves and immigrants; or from Egypt with the Roman soldiers coming home, or with arriving Egyptian mystery cults. As no evidence exists for Christianity coming to Rome from Jerusalem or Antioch, the only possible route was from Alexandria in the same way as it reached Corinth through Apollos of Alexandria. The Mysteries of Isis and Serapis came to Rome even before 100 BC, and a temple for Isis and Serapis was established on the Campus Martius, not far from the famous Pantheon. It was a vast structure, the central part being 420 feet long, and approached by a long colonnaded court lined with lions and sphinxes. The site of the temple is now occupied by part of the Church of Sant' Ignazio, a section of the Collegio Romano, the apse of the Church of Santa Maria sopra Minerva, and the Via del Pie di Marmo. Serapis was commonly represented as bearded, with a staff like that of Zeus or Asclepius, and wearing the symbolic modius or kalathos also worn by the personification of Hades – a tall cylindrical headdress, wider at the top, sometimes decorated with three upright leafy branches. Like Christ, he healed the sick and had the ability to appear to mortals in their sleep. The priesthood attached to his temples was made up of Egyptians or Graeco-Egyptians, many of whom were of Alexandrian origin, or educated there.

It is a well-known fact that the early worshippers of Christ amongst the Gentiles were also worshippers of Serapis, and it is easy to see how Christianity reached Rome at this early date. This is confirmed by the fact that in AD 19 Tiberius expelled both Jews and devotees of Serapis from Rome. Christianity, like the worship of Serapis, was regarded by the Romans as yet another mystery cult. No doubt the cult of Isis and Serapis was the most popular religion in Rome during the first half of the 1st century AD, when Christianity is first attested to in the capital.

The fact that the new faith came to Rome via Alexandria did not help to bring the two Churches closer; on the contrary, it put them in conflict over the leadership of the Christian movement. From the early days of the 2nd century AD, the newly established bishops of Rome – the centre of political power – showed their intention to establish their authority over all Christian Churches of the empire. The New Testament canon, the Creed, and the institutional structure of the Church emerged in their present forms only in Rome towards the end of the 2nd century. Neither St Paul nor any other of the early apostles of the Gentile Church organized a priestly authority to run the Church. The 1st century Church was not a hierarchical organization and had no priestly rulers, while the elders of the community used to supervise the sacraments of baptism and the Eucharist. During this period numerous gospels circulated among various different and complex Christian groups. By the end of the 1st century, however, the Fathers and elders of some communities established themselves as bishops, ruling their communities. With the appearance of the bishops a new, threefold ministry system emerged during the 2nd century, and the earlier diversified forms of Church leadership gave way to a unified hierarchy of Church office. By AD 200, Christianity had become a hierarchical institution.

When Gnostic Christians refused to accept Roman authority, the Christian movement was split into two groups: Roman orthodox and Egyptian Gnostic. The Gnostic teachers, however, continued to oppose this new development, claiming that those Church officials had no authority, insisting that all believers were equal, and regarded salvation as a result of personal experience. But the Church of Rome, supported by a majority of Churches, took a leading role in rejecting all other viewpoints as heresy. In order to confirm the divine authority of the new order, the bishops hit back at the Gnostics, accusing them of being heretics. Although it was on Paul's gospel that the Gentile Churches had been established, the emerging priestly rulers of the communities looked to St Peter and the Church of Jerusalem to justify their authority. This conflict then developed into a struggle between the newly emerging bishops who wanted to establish their ecclesiastic authority, and the teachers of Gnostic Christianity who opposed them. Thus the early conflict between Peter and Paul – between Judaeo-Christian Jerusalem and Gentile Antioch – had now been replaced by a new conflict within the Gentile Churches themselves, between orthodox Rome and Gnostic Alexandria.

The chance for the bishops of Rome came when Emperor Constantine adopted the Christian faith in the 4th century, and gave them political and legal authority, which they used to enforce their position. The ultimate defeat of Alexandria then followed at the time of Emperor Theodosius I, when Theophilus, his bishop in Alexandria, destroyed the

Serapeum, and the religious centre of the empire hence-forward moved to the Vatican in Rome. It was then that the Alexandrian library was destroyed, all writings which did not agree with the account of the Roman Church were regarded as heretic and burned, and all religious teachers who disagreed with the orthodox doctrines were punished. For ten centuries after this event, only the Bible and the teaching of the Church of Rome were allowed as sources of knowledge and education, in what came to be regarded as the Middle Ages.

That is how the Egyptian origins of Christianity have been hidden for approximately 16 centuries. Thanks only to the archaeologists of modern Europe, copies of the lost knowledge such as the *Dead Sea Scrolls* and the Nag Hammadi Library have been discovered again. Now the real history behind the Bible can be revealed.

Epilogue: The Second Renaissance

Following the assassination of Julius Caesar on the steps of the Senate in 44 BC, his two Roman successors, Octavian and Mark Antony, eventually split and had to fight each other in battle. When the two Roman generals faced each other in 31 BC at the port of Actium on the western shore of Greece, they were representing the two most important cities of the time. While Octavian was defending Rome, Antony was fighting for Alexandria. And although Rome won the war and became the supreme political capital of the entire civilized world, Alexandria remained the religious and cultural centre of the Roman Empire. The temple of Serapeum, which included the Alexandrian Library, became the focus of international worship as well as the centre of world wisdom and knowledge. Only when Rome finally destroyed the Serapeum, four centuries later, did the Roman Vatican replace the temple of Serapis as the religious centre of the world, and the teaching of the Church replaced Egyptian philosophy.

Both the two major Israelite leaders, Moses (Akhenaten) and Joshua (Tutankhamun), had lived and died in Egypt during the 14th century BC. After the end of the Amarna rule, however, their monotheistic religious revolution was suppressed and the old cults of Amun and Re regained their place as the official cults of the state. Nevertheless, from that time onwards, the cult of Osiris and Isis gained more popularity until, by the time of the Ptolemaic dynasty in 300 BC, it became the most powerful religion in Egypt. The king of the dead Osiris became the God of the living, and the religious importance of Isis rose accordingly. Little by little she absorbed and assimilated most of the religious and cultic functions of the other goddesses, and from the last centuries BC her position as the great mother-goddess of Egypt was unchallenged. She was universally revered throughout the country, and the ascent of the Ptolemaic dynasty meant the final acknowledgement of her official position in the new state cult.

From the last days of the 18th Dynasty, a slow evolutionary process took place within the Osiris theology, to explain the significance of the life, death, and resurrection of Tutankhamun, who became identified as the risen Osiris. Any visitor to the tomb of the young king, in the Valley of the Kings, can see for himself the strongest pictorial evidence connecting Tutankhamun and Jesus Christ. The large painting of the Burial Chamber is subdivided into three separate scenes (see plates 17, 18 & 19). The first scene on the right shows Aye (Ephraim/Joseph of Arimathea) already wearing the blue crown with his cartouche above him, as a royal successor of the dead king. Aye, at the same time as being a king, uniquely is also officiating as a priest dressed in leopard skin, to perform the ritual of 'the opening of the mouth', for resuscitation of the dead Tutankhamun, shown facing him as the risen Osiris.

The second scene, in the middle of the wall, shows the risen Tutankhamun entering the heavenly realm of the gods and being welcomed there by the sky goddess Nut. The third scene on the left depicts the king in three different forms. On the left of the scene stands Tutankhamun, in the form of the dead king Osiris, stretching his hands to touch a *second* Tutankhamun facing him, as the ruling king Horus, who is in turn stretching his arms to hold him, while he himself is being followed by a *third* Tutankhamun, representing the spiritual *Ka*, which also stretches its right arm to protect the king.

Undoubtedly, this is the scene which was at the root of the heated theological arguments that lasted for the whole first four centuries of the early Christian Church regarding the nature of Christ and the meaning of his trinity. For here we see Osiris the father, Horus the son and *Ka* the Holy Spirit, all being represented as one person – Tutankhamun – as three different aspects of the same person.

Thus on the north wall of Tutankhamun's burial chamber we find the three important theological points related to the death and resurrection of Jesus Christ. While the first scene represents his *physical resurrection*, the second scene represents his *ascension* and the third scene the *trinity* of his nature. This must have been the reason why King Aye himself officiated as a priest over the arrangements of the king's burial, for no other priest would have been able to understand the new theology that stood behind the reformation introduced by Tutankhamun to the Amarna religious revolution. So the emergence of Christianity in the 1st century AD, *when the apostles declared their witnessing of the risen Christ*, was not an abrupt event, but came as a result of a long process of evolution, out of the ancient cults of Osiris and Hermes Trismegistus.

Although the Egyptian contribution to Western civilization remained unrecognized through the Middle Ages, the new age of the Renaissance came as a result of Egyptian Neo-Platonic and Hermetic philosophy. As the movement of cultural revival spread all over Europe (particularly in Italy where it had its centre in the city of Florence, between the 14th and 16th centuries) ancient Egyptian wisdom was again recognized as the source of Christian philosophy. The general evolution which transformed the Middle Ages into the Renaissance gave rise to an entirely new conception of Ancient Egypt and its relation to Western culture. Florence became the early centre of these efforts and studies, and the new ideas were, to a great extent, given form and shape by the members of its Platonic Academy, founded by Cosimo de' Medici about 1439. A new 'historical' approach to philosophic and scientific problems had to be found, and the rediscovery of continuity in human existence was one of the immediate results of its activities. This movement created increasing interest in Egyptian culture, and people became acquainted again with the fact that many of the most prominent representatives of Greek genius, even Plato himself, had come to Egypt to learn and study, and had returned impressed by its culture and enriched by its learning. Works such as Plutarch's book on Isis and Osiris awoke the interest in Osirianism and Egyptian religion, while Iamblichus's demonological elucidations concerning the mysteries of Egypt, together with the Hermetic literature, fascinated the humanists, and became responsible for their conceptions of what they considered to be Egyptian philosophy.

According to Erik Iversen, the Danish Egyptologist, in his book *The Myth of Egypt and its Hieroglyphs*, Egyptian wisdom, Neo-Platonic philosophy and humanistic studies became in this way consecutive links in an unbroken chain of tradition, joined together and united with Christianity by their common aim: the knowledge and revelation of God. Seen from this point of view, the so-called heathen prophets, including Plato and Hermes, in having been born before the final revelation of this truth at the coming of Christ, were therefore merely 'historical', that is, dependent on time, and therefore inessential. Pre-Christian revelations were regarded as *anticipations* of the final Christian message, and the truth to which the pagan philosophers unwittingly had borne witness was *the cosmic truth of Christianity*.

The general conception of the direct connections between Christianity, the Hermetic literature, and the Neo-Platonic philosophy was already formed by Marcilio Ficino (1433–1499), in his *De Christiana Religione* and his *Theologia Platonica* written 1473–1478. In 1471 he published a Latin translation of Plotinus and in 1497 an edition of Iamblichus, and through his activity in the Platonic Academy he became one of the pioneers of the Neo-Platonic revival. According to Ficino, Hermes Trismegistus was a sage of the Egyptians, a contemporary or maybe even a predecessor of Moses. He had attained a knowledge of things surpassing even that which was revealed to the Hebrew prophets, and comparable only with that of the Evangelists. Pythagoras had become acquainted with his teachings in Egypt, and through his intermission they had been transmitted to Plato, who was a student of Egyptian wisdom himself and had eventually based his own philosophy on the doctrines of Hermes.

This situation, however, was to be completely reversed by the classicists of the Age of Enlightenment, who denied the Egyptian influence on European culture, and regarded Greece as the fount of modern philosophy. The Enlightenment movement appeared in England, France and Germany during the 18th and 19th centuries, and was concerned with the inter-relationship between God, nature and man. The philosophers of this movement thought that it was only through reason, rather than faith, that mankind could find knowledge and happiness. Even the Neo-Platonists and Hermetics became Greek according to this movement, which dominated the academic world and does so to this day. They completely rejected any possible Egyptian influence, either on Christianity or any other branch of knowledge. As the German classicist Rudolf Blum, in his book about *The Alexandrian Library and the Origins of Bibliography*, put it, not only the Alexandrian library was Greek, but in the Egyptian capital itself: 'Greek culture was alive and well, while the old Egyptian culture which had been admired by many educated Greeks had long since been dead' (p. 98).

Thanks to modern archaeologists who began to reveal the remains of the past from the mid-19th century, the Egyptian role in Western civilization can now be re-established. This will be our next step.

Appendix 1:
The Nag Hammadi Library

The Nag Hammadi library, discovered in Upper Egypt in 1945, is a collection of religious texts that vary from each other in their original date and authorship. They are written in Coptic (Egyptian language in Greek) and belonged to an Egyptian Gnostic-Christian community. It was hidden in a cave near the town of Nag Hammadi some time after the burning of the Alexandrian library in AD 391. The collected texts were found in 13 Codices, now in the Coptic Museum in Cairo, as well as another Gnostic Codex kept in Berlin Museum. These Codices include the following texts:

The Prayer of the Apostle Paul
The Apocryphon of James
The Gospel of Truth
The Treatise on Resurrection
The Tripartite Tractate
The Apocryphon of John
The Gospel of Thomas
The Gospel of Philip
The Hypostasis of the Archons
On the Origin of the World
The Exegesis on the Soul
The Book of Thomas the Contender
The Gospel of the Egyptians
Eugnostos the Blessed
The Dialogue of the Saviour

The Apocalypse of Paul
The First Apocalypse of James
The Second Apocalypse of James
The Apocalypse of Adam
The Acts of Peter and the Twelve Apostles
The Thunder, Perfect Mind
Authoritative Teaching
The Concept of our Great Power
Plato, Republic
The Discourse on the Eighth and Ninth
The Prayer of Thanksgiving
Asclepius
The Paraphrase of Shem
The Second Treatise of the Great Seth
Apocalypse of Peter
The Teachings of Silvanus
The Three Steles of Seth
Zostrianos
The Letter of Peter to Philip
Melchizedek
The Thought of Norea
The Testimony of Truth
Marsanes
The Interpretation of Knowledge
A Valentinian Exposition
Allogenes
Hypsiphrone
The Sentences of Sextus
Fragments
Trimorphic Protennoia
The Gospel of Mary
The Act of Peter

The Nag Hammadi Library was first published in 1977. A third edition was published by Harper & Row San Francisco/ E. J. Bill Leiden, in 1988, edited by James M. Robinson and R. Smith.

Appendix 2: Pharaohs of the 18th and Early 19th Dynasties

King	Length of reign	Dates of reign
The 18th Dynasty		
Tuthmosis III	54	1490–1436 BC
Amenhotep II	23	1436–1413 BC
Tuthmosis IV	8	1413–1405 BC
Amenhotep III	38	1405–1367 BC
Akhenaten (alone)	6	1367–1361 BC
Semenkhkare	–	–
Tutankhamun	9	1361–1352 BC
Aye	4	1352–1348 BC
Horemheb	13	1348–1335 BC
The 19th Dynasty		
Ramses I	2	1335–1333 BC
Seti I	29	1333–1304 BC
Ramses II	67	1304–1237 BC

As with so many aspects of Egyptology, scholars disagree about the dates of various reigns, especially from the time of Akhenaten onwards. Why I believe the above dates to be correct is discussed in the text.

Appendix 3: Israelite Chronology

c. **1480 BC** Abraham and his wife, Sarah, make their way from Canaan to Egypt where he introduces her as his sister. Tuthmosis III (DAVID) (*c*. 1490–1436 BC) marries her. On learning that Sarah is another man's wife, he sends her and Abraham back to Canaan, where she gives birth to Isaac, Pharaoh's son.

c. **1413 BC** Joseph the Patriarch (YUYA) – the grandson of Isaac and the son of Jacob – is sold into slavery in Egypt by his jealous half-brothers during the last days of the reign of Amenhotep II (*c*. 1436–1413 BC). He is thought to have been later appointed as a minister to Tuthmosis IV (*c*. 1413–1405 BC) and to his son and successor, Amenhotep III (SOLOMON) (*c*. 1405–1367 BC).

c. **1405 BC** Amenhotep III marries his infant sister, Sitamun, in order to inherit the throne, as was the Egyptian custom, but shortly afterwards marries Tiye, the daughter of Joseph, and makes her rather than Sitamun his Great Royal Wife (queen). Early in the reign of Amenhotep III Joseph is given permission to bring his father, Jacob, his half-brothers and the rest of the tribe of Israel down from Canaan to join him, and they are settled at Goshen in the Kantara area east of the Delta – outside Egypt proper because Asiatic shepherds have been anathema to Egyptians since the earlier invasion and century-long rule by the Hyksos.

c. 1395 BC   Akhenaten (MOSES) is born to Amenhotep III and Tiye at the frontier fortress city of Zarw. As he is not the son of the royal heiress, Sitamun, he poses a threat to the 18th Dynasty. His father therefore gives the midwives orders to kill the child if it is a boy. On learning of this, Tiye sends her son by water to the safe guardianship of her Israelite relations at Goshen.

c. 1378 BC   Akhenaten, aged about 16, makes his first appearance at Thebes, the capital in Upper Egypt.

c. 1378 BC   Akhenaten becomes co-regent with his father. In order further to secure his right to the throne, Queen Tiye arranges for him to marry his half-sister, Nefertiti, the daughter of Sitamun, the royal heiress.

c. 1375 BC   The building of temples to Akhenaten's monotheistic God, Aten, at Karnak and Thebes (modern Luxor) in Upper Egypt arouses such hostility that Akhenaten's mother, Queen Tiye, suggests he should build a new capital for himself at Tell el-Amarna, roughly halfway between Thebes and modern Cairo.

c. 1367 BC   On the death of his father, Akhenaten becomes sole ruler and shuts down the temples of the ancient gods of Egypt. This arouses such increased hostility that, in 1363 BC, he is forced to proclaim his brother, Semenkhkare, as co-regent.

c. 1361 BC   Warned by his uncle, Aye (EPHRAIM and JOSEPH OF ARIMATHAEA), that his life is in danger, Akhenaten abdicates and flees to

Sinai with a handful of followers, among them Panehesy, chief priest of Aten at Amarna, who is also named as PINHAS (Talmud) and PHINEHAS (Old Testament). Semenkhkare survives this abdication by at most a few months, possibly only a few days. Akhenaten is succeeded on the throne by his son, Tutankhamun.

c. 1361 BC   Tutankhamun (JESUS), aged 10, comes to the throne as Tutankhaten. He attempts to create a compromise between Aten and the ancient gods of Egypt, and in his Year 4 changes his name from Tutankhaten to Tutankhamun.

c. 1352 BC   Tutankhamun makes his way to Sinai to try to persuade the Atenists that they can return to Egypt and live there in peace if they accept that different people have different perceptions of God and how he should be worshipped. He is tortured and hanged by the priest Panehesy for what is seen as a betrayal of his father's religious beliefs. Aye, the second son of Joseph, and, as head of the army, the most powerful man in Egypt at the time, claims the body of Tutankhamun and buries his remains in the Valley of the Kings.

c. 1352 BC   Aye rules for four years before disappearing mysteriously.

c. 1348 BC   Aye is succeeded by Horemheb, the biblical Pharaoh of the Oppression, who is an army general and obtains his right to the throne by marrying Queen Nefertiti's sister, Mutnezmet.

c. 1335 BC   The death of Horemheb sees the start of a new dynasty, the 19th, when he is succeeded by his elderly chief minister, Ramses I, the king 'who knew not Joseph'. On hearing the news, Akhenaten returns to Egypt from Sinai to try to reclaim his throne, but fails because of Ramses I's control of the army. He then leaves in the Exodus, accompanied by his followers and his mother's Israelite family. After uniting with bedouin allies, the Shasu (the Midianites of the Bible), they eventually head for Canaan.

c. 1333 BC   On coming to the throne in succession to his father, Seti I sets out in pursuit of Akhenaten (MOSES) and his followers. Akhenaten is among those who die in the heavy slaughter that ensues – and those of his followers who survive begin their years of wandering in the wilderness.

Glossary

Akkadian: Semitic language that appeared in northern Mesopotamia in the 3rd millennium BC, and later became the general official language for all Mesopotamia and the Levant during the 2nd millennium, before being replaced by Aramaic from the 9th century BC.

Aramaic: The language used in the Levant from the 9th century BC, and in Palestine in the early part of the 1st century AD.

Amun: The god of Thebes and one of the most important deities of Egypt, whose temple at Karnak is the best surviving religious complex in Egypt.

Ben-ben stone: Sacred stone at Heliopolis which symbolized the sun-god Ra. It served as the earliest prototype for the pyramid or the obelisk.

Copt: The name the Arabs called Egyptians, following the Greek name 'Egyptos'.

Gnostic: Those Christians who seek to gain spiritual knowledge through mysteries and the attempt to know oneself, and interpret the Scriptures allegorically.

Hathor: A goddess in the form of a cow, the nurse of the King of Egypt as well as the goddess of gold.

Hermes Trismegistus: Thoth, the ancient Egyptian god of writing, became identified with the Greek god Hermes. Hermes Trismegistus means Hermes the Thrice-greatest.

Hermetic: Hermetic literature, a collection of treatises and dialogues dating from the Roman period in Egypt and purporting to be revelations of Hermes Trismegistus. They deal with questions of religious philosophy, astrology, magic and alchemy.

Hittite: Asiatic people who settled in Anatolia in the 3rd millennium BC, and spoke an Indo-European language.

Horus: Falcon-god usually depicted as a hawk. He was a god of the sky as well as being the embodiment of divine kingship, protector of the reigning king.

Another Horus was the son of Isis and Osiris, who was engaged in a long struggle with Set to avenge the killing of his father.

Hyksos: Foreign rulers, who included Semitic and Hurrian elements, who subdued and ruled Egypt for about 108 years between the mid-17th and the mid-16th century BC.

Hypostyle hall: Large temple court filled with columns, forming an essential element in Egyptian religious architecture.

Isis: Goddess who encapsulated the virtues of the archetypal Egyptian wife and mother. She was the sister-wife of Osiris and mother of Horus. She is best known mythologically as the devoted wife of Osiris, whose body she sought after his murder by Set.

Ka: A term used by the Egyptians to describe the creative life-force.

Maat: Goddess personifying truth, justice and the essential harmony of the universe, who was usually portrayed as a seated woman wearing an ostrich feather.

Masoratic: The Masoratic Text of the Old Testament is the Hebrew text supplied with diacritical marks in the 10th century AD to enable correct pronunciation.

Min: God of fertility and ancestor worship; often shown in ithyphallic form.

Muntu: The falcon-headed god of war, who belongs to Thebes.

Mut: The vulture-goddess consort of Amun.

Neo-Platonists: The Alexandrian philosophers who followed the same philosophy as the Athenian Plato, of whom Plotinus of the 3rd century AD is the most celebrated.

Nomen: The name given to the king at his birth.

Nomes: Territorial divisions in Ancient Egypt, which were 36 in total.

Osiris: The Egyptian god of the underworld and judge of the dead. He is associated with death, resurrection and the judgement of the dead.

Ostracon: Term used by archaeologists to refer to shards of pottery or flakes of limestone bearing texts and drawings.

Pranomen: The name which the king receives on his coronation.

Ptah: God of Memphis associated with creation.

Ra: Heliopolitan sun-god whose cult is first attested in the name of the 2nd Dynasty King Reneb (*c.* 2865 BC).

Sea People: A coalition of sea-roving peoples, who came from the Aegean and the Ionian coast of Asia Minor, and attacked western Asia and Egypt during the period *c.* 1220–1190 BC.

Septuagint: The earliest extant Greek translation of the Old Testament from Hebrew. It was made in Alexandria by 70 Jewish scribes in the 3rd century BC during the reign of Ptolemy II.

Set: God of chaos and confusion, who is said to have murdered his brother Osiris and then engaged in a long and violent contest with his nephew Horus, who sought to avenge the death of his father.

Shu: God of atmosphere and air, son of Atum, the creator, and father of Geb, the 'earth', and Nut, the 'sky'.

Talmud: The most important work of religious law in post-biblical Judaism, composed in Babylon and Palestine between the 1st and 5th centuries AD.

Thomas (Gospel of): One of the Coptic gospels found in Nag Hammadi, which includes many previously unknown sayings of Christ.

Thoth: The scribe god, associated with wisdom, learning, writing and the arts.

Uraeus: Type of snake that served as the sacred image of Wa'zet, patron deity of the town of Buto in the Delta, who

represented Lower Egypt, in contrast to the Upper
Egyptian vulture-goddess Nekhbet.

Bibliography

Albright, W. F., 'The Town of Sell (Zarw) in the Amarna Tablets', *Journal of Egyptian Archaeology*, London, 1910.

The Archaeology of Palestine, London, 1963.

Aldred, Cyril, *Akhenaten*, London, 1968.

Akhenaten and Nefertiti, London, 1973.

'Year Twelve at El-Amarna', *Journal of Egyptian Archaeology*, 1957.

'Two Theban Notables during the Later Reign of Amenophis III\, J*ournal of Near Eastern Studies*, Chicago, 1959.

'The Tomb of Akhenaten at Thebes', *Journal of Egyptian Archaeology*, 1961.

Ali, Abdullah Yusuf, trans., *The Meaning of the Glorious Quran*, London, 1976.

Allegro, John Marco, *The Sacred Mushroom and the Cross*, London, 1970.

The Dead Sea Scrolls, London, 1964.

Apuleius, *The Golden Ass*, London, 1956.

Badawy, Alexander, *A History of Egyptian Architecture*, Los Angeles, 1968.

Architecture in Ancient Egypt and the Near East, Cambridge, Massachusetts, and London, 1966.

Baigent, Michael and Leigh, Richard, *The Dead Sea Scrolls Deception*, London, 1991.

Baikie, James, *The Amarna Age*, London, 1926.

Bakir, Abd el-Mohsen, 'Slavery in Pharaonic Egypt', supplement to *Annales du Service des Antiquités de l'Egypte*, vol.18., 1952.

Bennett, John, 'The Restoration Inscription of Tutank-hamun', *Journal of Egyptian Archaeology*, 1939.

Bietak, Manfred, 'Avaris and Piramses Archaeological Exploration in the Eastern Nile Delta', *Proceedings of the British Academy*, London, 1979.

Björkman, Gun, 'Neby, the Mayor of Tjaru (Zarw) in the Reign of Tuthmose IV', *Journal of the American Research Center in Egypt*, 1974.

Black, Matthew, *The Scrolls and Christian Origins*, London, 1961.

Boslooper, Thomas, *The Virgin Birth*, London, 1962.

Brandon, S. G. F., *Myth, Ritual and Kingship*, Oxford, 1958.

Breasted, James Henry, *A History of Egypt*, New York, 1905 and 1909, and London, 1924.
  The Dawn of Conscience, New York, 1933.
  Ancient Records of Egypt, vol. 3, Chicago, 1906.

Bright, John, *A History of Israel*, London, 1960.

Bromiley, Geoffrey W., *The International Standard Bible Encyclopaedia*, Grand Rapids, Michigan, 1982.

Brown, Francis (editor), *Hebrew and English Lexicon of the Old Testament*, Oxford, 1906.

Brownless, William Hugh, *The Meaning of the Qumran Scrolls for the Bible*, New York, 1964.

Bruce, F. F., *Jesus and Christian Origins outside the New Testament*, London, 1974.

Burrows, Millar, *The Dead Sea Scrolls*, London, 1956.

Carter, Howard, *The Tomb of Tutankhamun*, London, Toronto, Melbourne and Sydney, 1933.

Cassuto, U., *A Commentary on the Book of Exodus*, Jerusalem, 1951 and 1961.

Cern'y, Jaroslav, *Hieratic Inscriptions from the Tomb of Tutankhamun*, Oxford, 1965.

(Editor) *The Inscriptions of Sinai*, Egypt Exploration Society, London, 1955.

Clédat, Jean, *Le Site d'Avaris*, Paris, 1922.
  'Notes sur l'Isthme De Suez', *Bulletin de l'Institut*

Français d'Archaeologie Orientale, 1924.

The Tomb of the Vizier Ramose, London, 1941.

Clements, Ronald E., *Studies in Biblical Theology, second series, vol. 5, Abraham and David*, London, 1967.

Conder, C. R., *The Tell Amarna Tablets*, London, 1893.

Couchoud, Paul Louis, *The Enigma of Jesus*, London, 1924.

Davies, N. de G., 'The Tombs of Djehuty and Antef', in *Studies in Honour of F.-Ll Griffith*, London, 1932.

Davis, Theodore, *The Tomb of Iouiya and Touiya*, London, 1907.

Debelius, Martin, *Paul*, London, 1953.

Derry, D. E., 'Note on the Skeleton Hitherto Believed to be that of King Akhenaten', *Annales du Service des Antiquités de l'Egypte*, Cairo, 1931.

Desroches-Noblecourt, Christine, *Tutankhamen*, London, 1963.

Dupont-Sommer, André, *The Jewish Sect of Qumran and the Essenes*, London, 1954.

The Essene Writings from Qumran, translated by G. Vermes, Oxford, 1961.

Edwards, L. E. S., *Tutankhamun*, London, 1979.

Encyclopaedia Judaica, Jerusalem, 1971–2.

Eissfeldt, Otto, *The Cambridge Ancient History*, Cambridge, 1975.

Fairman, H. W., *The City of Akhenaten*, London, 1951.

'Once Again the So-Called Coffin of Akhenaten', *Journal of Egyptian Archaeology*, 1961.

'The Chronology of the Eighteenth Dynasty', *Journal of Near Eastern Studies*, 1966.

'The Supposed Year 21 of Akhenaten', *Journal of Egyptian Archaeology*, 1960.

Fakhry, Ahmed, 'A Note on the Tomb of Kheruef at Thebes', *Annales du Service des Antiquités de l'Egypte*, 1948.

Faulkner, Raymond O., *A Concise Dictionary of Middle Egyptian*, Oxford, 1962.

Finkelstein, Israel, *The Archaeology of the Israelite Settlement*, Jerusalem, 1988.

Freud, Sigmund, *Moses and Monotheism*, London, 1939.

Furumark, Arne, 'The Mycenean IIIC Pottery', *Skrifter Utgivna Av Svenska Institutet I Fom, Opuscula Archaeologica*, vol. 3, Lund, Sweden, 1944.

Gaballa, G. A., *The Memphite Tomb Chapel of Moses*, Warminster, England, 1977.

Gardiner, Alan H., *Egypt of the Pharaohs*, Oxford, 1961.

'A Later Allusion to Akhenaten', *Journal of Egyptian Archaeology*, 1938.

'New Rendering of Egyptian Texts', *Journal of Egyptian Archaeology*, 1918.

'The Delta Residence of the Ramessides', *Journal of Egyptian Archaeology*, 1918.

'The Graffito from the Tomb of Pere', *Journal of Egyptian Exploration*, London, 1928.

'The So-Called Tomb of Queen Tiye', *Journal of Egyptian Archaeology*, 1957.

Egyptian Grammar, London, 1950.

Note on the Story of Sinuhe, Paris, 1916.

The Tomb of Amenemhet, London, 1915.

Gautier, Lucien, *Introduction à l'ancien Testament*, Paris, 1916.

Gibbon, Edward, *The Decline and Fall of the Roman Empire* (abridged), London, 1960.

Gordon, Cyrus H., *The World of the Old Testament*, 1960.

Ugaritic Manual, III, 1955.

Giles, Frederick J., *Ikhnaton*, London, 1970.

Gray, John, *A History of Jerusalem*, London, 1969.

Griffiths, J. Gwyn, *The Origins of Osiris and his Cult*, Berlin, 1966.

Gunn, Battiscombe, *The City of Akhenaten*, London, 1923.

Habachi, Labib, 'Clearance of the Tomb of Kheruef at Thebes', *Annales du Service des Antiquités de l'Egypte*, 1958.

Hamza, Muhammad, 'The Alabaster Canopic Box of Akhenaten', *Annales du Service des Antiquités de l'Egypte*, 1940.

'Preliminary Report on the Kamose Stele', *Annales du Service des Antiquités de l'Egypte*, 1966.

Hanson, Anthony Tyrrell, *Jesus in the Old Testament*, London, 1965.

The Acts in the Revised Version, Oxford, 1967.

Hanson, R. P. C., *Allegory and Event*, London, 1959.

Harris, James E. (and R. Weeks), *X-Raying the Pharaohs*, New York, 1973.

Harris, J. R., 'How Long Was the Reign of Horemheb', *Journal of Egyptian Archaeology*, 1968.

Harrison, R. G., 'An Anatomical Examination of the Pharaonic Remains Purported to be Akhenaten', *Journal of Egyptian Archaeology*, 1966.

Harrison, R. G., and Abdalla, A. B., 'The Remains of Tutankhamen', *Antiquity*, vol. 46, Gloucester, 1972.

Harrison, R. K., *Introduction to the Old Testament*, London, 1970.

Hayes, William C., 'Inscriptions from the Palace of Amenhotep III', *Journal of Near Eastern Studies*, 1951.

The Scepter of Egypt, Cambridge, Massachusetts, 1959.

Helck, Wolfgang, *Untersuchungen zu Manetho und den ägyptischen Königslisten*, Berlin, 1956.

Herford, R. Travers, *Christianity in Talmud and Midrash*, London, 1903.

James, T. G. H., *Corpus of Hieroglyphic Inscriptions in the Brooklyn Museum*, Brooklyn, 1974.

Jewish Encyclopaedia, managing editor Isidore Singer, New York and London, 1904.

Josephus, Flavius, *Contra Apionem*, translated by H. St John Thackeray, London and New York, 1926.

Antiquities of the Jews, London, 1842.

Journal of Egyptian Archaeology, vol. 14, 1928; vol. 25, 1939; vol. 50, 1964; vol. 56, 1970; vol. 76, 1990.

Journal of Jewish Studies II, No. 2, 1951.

Kalisch, M. M., *A Historical and Critical Commentary on the Old Testament*, London, 1858.

Kenyon, Kathleen M., *The Bible and Recent Archaeology*,

rev. ed. by P. R. S. Moorey, London, 1987.

Jerusalem, London, 1967.

Palestine Exploration Quarterly, Jan.–June 1963.

Kitchen, Dr K. A., *Ramesside Inscriptions*, Oxford, 1975.

'Asiatic Wars of Ramses II', *Journal of Egyptian Archaeology*, 1964.

Ancient Orient and the Old Testament, Illinois, 1966.

Koester, Helmut, contribution to *The Future of Early Christianity*, Minneapolis, 1991.

Lambdin, T. O., *Egyptian Loan Words and Transcriptions in the Ancient Semitic Languages*, Baltimore, 1952.

Langdon, S. (with Alan H. Gardiner), 'The Treaty of Alliance between Hattusuli, King of the Hittites, and the Pharaoh Ramses II of Egypt', *Journal of Egyptian Archaeology*, 1920.

Leek, F. Filce, *Tutankhamun's Tomb Series*, vol. 5, Oxford, 1972.

Lucas, A., 'The Canopic Vases from the Tomb of Queen Tiye', *Annales du Service des Antiquités de l'Egypte*, 1931.

Martin, Geoffrey T., *The Royal Tomb at el-Amarna*, London, 1974.

'Excavations at the Memphite Tomb of Horemheb', *Journal of Egyptian Archaeology*, 1979.

Maspero, Gaston, *The Struggle of the Nations*, London, 1896.

(with George Daressy) *The Tombs of Haramhabi and Toutankhamanou*, London, 1912.

Migne, J. P., *Origenis Op. Omn., Selecta in Genesim, PG*, vol. 2, Paris, 1957.

Morenz, Siegfried, *Egyptian Religion*, London, 1973.

Mowry, Lucetta, *The Dead Sea Scrolls and the Early Church*, Chicago, 1962.

Naville, Henri, 'The Geography of the Exodus', *Journal of Egyptian Archaeology*, 1924.

Funerary Papyrus of Iouiya, London, 1908.

Nims, Charles F., *Thebes of the Pharaohs*, London, 1965.

North, Christopher R., *The Suffering Servant in Deutero-Isaiah*, London, 1956.

Noth, Martin, *The Old Testament World*, London, 1966.

Osman, Ahmed, *Stranger in the Valley of the Kings*, London, 1987, San Francisco and Barcelona, 1988.
Moses Pharaoh of Egypt, London, 1990.
The House of the Messiah, London, 1992.

Pages, Elaine, *The Gnostic Gospels*, London, 1982.

Peet, T. E., *The City of Akhenaten*, London, 1923–51.
Egypt and the Old Testament, London, 1922.

Pendlebury, John, *Tell el-Amarna*, London, 1935.

'Report on the Clearance of the Royal Tomb at Amarna', *Annales du Service des Antiquités de l'Egypte*, 1931.

Petrie, W. M. Flinders, *Researches in Sinai*, London, 1906.
Hyksos and Israelite Cities, London, 1906.
A History of Egypt, II, London, 1894.

Polano, H., *Selections from the Talmud*, London, 1894.

Porter, Bertha and Moss, Rosalind, *Topographical Bibliography of Ancient Hieroglyphic Texts, Reliefs and Paintings*, Oxford, 1964.

Posenor, George, (with Serge Sauneron and Jean Yoyotte), *A Dictionary of Egyptian Civilisation*, London, 1962.

Powell, Enoch, *The Evolution of the Gospel*, London, 1994.

Pritchard, James B., *Ancient Near Eastern Texts*, translated by John A. Wilson, Princeton, New Jersey, 1969.

Quibell, James E., *Catalogue général des antiquités égyptiennes du Musée de Caire*, Cairo, 1908.

Ranke, Hermann, *Die Ägyptischen Personannamen*, Münich, 1902.

Redford, Donald B., *History and Chronology of the Eighteenth Dynasty of Egypt*, Toronto, 1967.
Akhenaten the Heretic King, Princeton, 1984.
Studies on the Ancient Palestine World, Toronto, 1972.
Pharaonic King-Lists, Annals and Day-Books, Benben Publications, Mississanga, Ontario, 1986.
'On the Chronology of the Eighteenth Egyptian Dynasty', *Journal of Near Eastern Studies*, 1966.

Reisner, George A., 'The Viceroys of Ethiopia', *Journal of Egyptian Archaeology*, 1920.
 A Study of the Biblical Story of Joseph, Leiden, 1970.
Robertson, J. M., *Jesus and Judas*, London, 1927.
Romer, John, *Testament*, London, 1988.
Rot, Cecil and Wigoder, Geoffrey, *The New Standard Jewish Encyclopedia*, London, 1970.
Rowley, Harold Henry, 'Zadok and Nebushtan', *Journal of Biblical Literature*, vol. 59, Philadelphia, 1939.
 From Joseph to Joshua, British Academy, London, 1950.
Samson, Julia, *Amarna, City of Akhenaten and Nefertiti*, Warminster, England, 1976.
Scharf, Alexander, *Archiv für Orientforschung*, Vienna, 1935.
Schmidt, John D., *Ramses II*, Baltimore and London, 1973.
Schulman, Alan R., 'Military Background of the Amarna Period', *Journal of the American Research Center in Egypt*, 1964.
Scott, R. B. Y., *Solomon and the Beginnings of Wisdom in Israel: Wisdom in Israel and in the Ancient Near East*, Leiden, Netherlands, 1955.
Seele, Keith C., 'King Aye and the Close of the Amarna Age', *Journal of Near Eastern Studies*, 1955.
Simons, J., *Handbook for the Study of Egyptian Topographical Lists Relating to Western Asia*, Leiden, Netherlands, 1937.
Simpson, William Kelly, *The Literature of Ancient Egypt*, Yale, 1972.
Smith, A. D. Howell, *Jesus not a Myth*, London, 1942.
Smith, E. G., *The Royal Mummies*, Cairo, 1912.
Smith, Harry S., *Amarna, City of Akhenaten and Nefertiti*, Warminster, England, 1978.
Smith, Ray, W., *The Akhenaten Temple Project*, Pennsylvania, 1976.
Stern, Avi-Yonah and Ephraim, *Encyclopaedia of Archaeological Excavations in the Holy Lands*, Oxford, 1977.

Thomas, D. Winton, *Documents from Old Testament Times*, London, 1958.

Vermes, Geza, *The Dead Sea Scrolls in English*, London, 1987.

Waddell, W. G., *Manetho*, London, 1940.

Wagner, N. E., *Abraham and David*, Toronto, 1972.
Studies on the Ancient Palestinian World, Toronto, 1972.

Weigall, Arthur, *The Life and Times of Akhenaten*, London, 1910 and 1923.
'The Mummy of Akhenaten', *Journal of Egyptian Archaeology*, 1957/58.

Wells, G. A., *Did Jesus Exist?*, London, 1975.
The Early Christians, London, 1971.

Whiston, William, trans., *The Works of Flavius Josephus*, London, 1842.

Yadin, Yigael, *Hazor*, London, 1975.
Hazor, The Schweich Lectures of the British Academy, Oxford, 1972.

Yahuda, A. S., *The Language of the Pentateuch in its Relation to Egyptian*, Oxford, 1933.

Zeller, Edward, *The Acts of the Apostles*, London, 1875.

A Brief Description of the Principal Monuments of the Egyptian Museums, Cairo, 1964.

Second Quarterly Report on the Excavation of the Eastern Hill of Jerusalem, Palestine Exploration Fund, London, 1924.

The Times Atlas of the Bible, 1987.

The Illustrated Bible Dictionary, Sydney and Auckland, 1980.

New Catholic Encyclopaedia, University of America, New York, 1967.

Index

329

Also available in Arrow

The Sirius Mystery
New Scientific Evidence for Alien Contact 5,000 years ago

Robert Temple

Is the existence of civilisation on earth a result of contact from inhabitants of a planet in the system of the star Sirius prior to 3000 BC? There are tribal cultures in present-day Africa whose most sacred and secret traditions are based on this theory. Central to their cosmology is a body of knowledge concerning the system of the star Sirius that is astounding in its accuracy of detail, including specific information only recently accessible to modern science. Robert Temple traces the traditions of the Dogon and three related tribes back 5,000 years to the ancient Mediterranean cultures of Sumer and Egypt. He shows a knowledge dependent on physics and astrophysics, which they claimed was imported to them by visitors from Sirius.

'. . . he does tell of very extraordinary strange things – so strange that our entire world view could be shaken if the data be correct.'

Dr Peter Nilsson, astronomer, Uppsala University

'I would say of the book that it is the most exciting and scholarly exposition of the theory of extraterrestrial intervention that has been yet written.'

John Michell, author

The new No. 1 bestseller from the author of of *The Sign* and *The Seal* and *The Keeper of Genesis*

Fingerprints of the Gods
Graham Hancock

A drastic re-evaluation of man's past, which uses the high-tech tools of modern archaeology, geology and astronomy, this extraordinary book exposes the eerie network of connections between:

- The Great Sphinx and the pyramids of Egypt
- The Andean temples of Tianhuanaco
- The Mexican Pyramids of the Sun and Moon
- The lost continent that lies beneath Antarctica
- Ancient knowledge of spherical geometry and astro-navigation
- The myths and legends of humanity that have remained strangely consistent across geographical and social devides
- New theories about the causes of the ice-ages

Hancock's new evidence reveals not only the clear fingerprints of an unknown civilisation that flourished during the last ice-age, but horrifying conclusions about the type and extent of palanetary catastrophe that would have had to occur in order to obliterate almost all traces of it.

A Test of Time
The Bible – From Myth to History

David Rohl

By employing the same methodologies used to establish the currently accepted chronology, it has been possible for a group of young archaeologists, including David Rohl, to create a New Chronology which resolves many of the problems permeating ancient world studies. In particular, one model has been developed which has major implications for Old Testament research. Through the revision of the master chronology of ancient Egypt they have unlocked the key to biblical history – the epic events of the Bible really did happen as recorded in the Books of Genesis, Exodus, Judges, Samuel, Kings and Chronicles – the problem was that we had previously been looking for them in completely the wrong place in time.

Many of the conundrums of the past are explained, and legendaryfigures such as Joseph, Moses, David and Solomon find their true political setting. Exodus and Conquest will be restored to history and the magic legend will begin to male its great comeback.

'The New Book of Revelations . . . A scholarly theory that has set the academic world on its ear'

Sunday Times

The Hiram Key
Pharaohs, Freemasons and the Discovery of the Secret Scrolls of Jesus

Christopher Knight and Robert Lomas

Are scrolls containing the secret teachings of Jesus buried in Scotland?

The discovery that the most important incantation of Freemasonry is spoken in ancient Egyptian was the turning-point of a six-year quest to find the lost roots of the Order. Chris Knight and Robert Lomas, both Freemasons, soon found themselves unravelling an extraordinary chain of events that started with the solving of a murder in ancient Thebes and concluded with the deciphering of a strange medieval building on a Scottish hilltop. Their astonishing bestseller *The Hiram Key* raises questions that challenge some of Western civilization's most cherished beliefs:

Do the Gospels of the New Testament describe Jesus, the last claimant to the kingship of the Jews, practising the king-making rituals of the ancient Egyptians?

Were scrolls bearing the secret teachings of Jesus buried beneath Herod's Temple shortly before the destruction of Jerusalem by the Romans in 70AD?

Did the Knights Templar, the forerunners of modern Freemasonry, excavate those scrolls in the twelfth century and then adopt the rituals they contained?

And were these scrolls subsequently buried underneath a detailed reconstrucition of Herod's Temple, on a Scottish hilltop – where they are now awaiting re-excavation?

'A breakthrough book. The last four thousand years are never going to look the same again.'

Graham Hancock, author of *Fingerprints of the Gods* and
Keepers of Genesis